JUST WHEN YOU THOUGHT IT WAS SAFE:

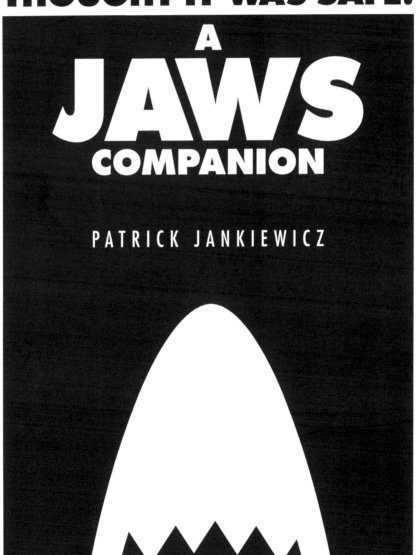

A

JAWS

COMPANION

PATRICK JANKIEWICZ

Just When You Thought It Was Safe: A JAWS Companion
©2009 Patrick Jankiewicz. All Rights Reserved.

All illustrations from *JAWS, JAWS 2, JAWS 3-D* and *JAWS THE REVENGE*
are copyright Universal Pictures, and are reproduced here in the spirit of
publicity.

Published in the USA by:
BearManor Media
P O Box 71426
Albany, Georgia 31708
www.bearmanormedia.com

ISBN 1-59393-334-7

Printed in the United States of America.
Edited by Lon Davis.
Book design by Brian Pearce.

TABLE OF CONTENTS

Dedicated with love and respect to my wife & enabler, Lisa,
my brother Donald — a better sibling, sidekick
and sparring partner I couldn't ask for —
and my Godmother, Casey Slater...
Three people I would never want to see eaten by sharks!

ACKNOWLEDGEMENTS

No book writes itself, so I want to thank everyone who made time to sit down with me, brew coffee and discuss their involvement with the film *JAWS*, the sequels and/or rip-offs.

Kudos also must go to my publisher Ben Ohmart of BearManor Media. BearManor has a hip, eclectic Movies and TV selection and I'm thrilled to be part of it.

Joe Alves and his charming wife Jerri get first props and not because we're going alphabetically — the great Jerri Lauridsen-Alves made sure I had every piece of Joe's *JAWS* production art and design and every question answered by her very busy husband. He was also my first interview for the book (Carl Gottlieb was second). This is only appropriate, as Joe was also the first guy hired for *JAWS!*

Thanks to Roy Arbogast (and his dog, Bear) for showing me the shark prototype (which was later broken and thrown away!) and discussing the pros, cons and logistics of building giant mechanical fish. Thanks also to the gracious and fun Susan Backlinie, Richard Dreyfuss, the easygoing Bill Butler (and his wife, Iris). Ironically, I had the thrill of being filmed by Bill for my bit part in *Beethoven's 2nd* — it was a kick to have the same hand that held a light meter before Bruce held above me.

I am also grateful to Carl Gottlieb and his crazy, likeable cat who were incredibly helpful and quotable (actually, Carl did all the talking — his cat didn't say a damn thing!) It really meant a lot to me to hang with Carl, as he's really the soul of *JAWS* (with his involvement in the original film and two sequels, he also wrote *The JAWS Log* — the best of the modern film books).

Props to Jeannot Szwarc, Ted Grossman, Carl Mazzocone, John Putch (who also provided many of the *JAWS 3-D* shots!), Rob Hall, Linda Harrison, Duncan Kennedy and Andrew Prine — as well as John Hancock & Dorothy Tristan for talking about "an admittedly painful time" in their lives. Joe Dante was a great source of info, on doing *Piranha* and his involvement with "JAWS 3, PEOPLE 0." John Landis, the legendary Richard Matheson, Steve DeJarnatt (whose *Miracle Mile* is my favorite film after *JAWS*, if anyone cares!), Neal Adams, Bryan Singer, Daniel Waters, Adam Simon, Marc Gilpin, Lance Guest, Chris Kiszka and

Greg Nicotero were all generous in sharing anecdotes, Mike Roddy (producer of *The Shark is Still Working* — Thanks for putting me in it!), Tom Jankiewicz and *AICN*'s Quint.

I appreciate Maribeth Priore of Martha's Vineyard for helping me through that amazing event known as JAWSfest (See ya' in 2010, Maribeth!) The town residents who worked on the film were also gracious with their time and stories, including Lee Fierro, Jeffrey Voorhees, Jay Mello and John Searle, Will Pfluger, William E. Marks, Belle McDonald, theater owner Karen Marafhio and Universal Studios Home Video's Michelle Oakes-Slavich. Bostonians Brendan McNeely and Scott Rumrill were kind enough to act as chauffeurs/tour guides/bartenders for Don and me. (Would anyone be surprised to learn a bar in Martha's Vineyard is called SHARKY'S?)

The clambake on Martha's Vineyard, with dozens of people who worked on *JAWS* on both sides of the camera, was a real highlight. (The drunken old gent at the ferry station was also fun.)

Prolific writer Marc Shapiro was my personal Yoda on this project; his wise counsel was appreciated and accepted. Marc just published his 27th book, so I have to do 26 more if I hope to catch up! Dave McDonnell of *Starlog*, and Tony Timpone and Michael Gingold of *Fangoria* were helpful, as were Tara Meisner, Allie & Troy Nelson, Al Callaci, Sister Rita Jeanne Fernandez, Jarrad Arbuckle, Becky Lizama, Mick Garris, photographer Lisa Orris, Jen Orris and Weirton, West Virginia's foremost *JAWS* authority, Celia Wournais.

Special props for my brother, Donald Jankiewicz. Don was my cross-country traveling companion as we took a long road trip to JAWSfest at the last minute. We actually hit New York in a giant cable-TV satellite truck! Don made sure I attended, which made this a better book.

My lovable wife Lisa kept me on task to finish before deadline, and Eric Caidin of Hollywood Book & Poster found hard-to-locate stills. My father, Anthony Jankiewicz, made me write faster every time he mockingly suggested the title "*JAWS* at 50." I also became a proud Godfather and gained a nephew while writing the book, Godson Matthew Calvin Almanzar and my nephew Conan Max Jankiewicz. Welcome to the world, boys.

A moment of silence, please, for the late, lamented Troy Drive-in in Troy, Michigan, where I first saw *JAWS* (On re-release with *Orca*!). A true temple of cinema, but The Philistines went and turned you into a Red Roof Inn! You were too beautiful for this world, Troy Drive-in.

INTRODUCTION

Are you terrified of sharks, even though you live in Sterling Heights, Michigan? Do you constantly feel you "need a bigger boat?" Did you used to hate the water, but can't imagine why? If you answered "Yes" to any of those questions, you're a *JAWS* fanatic!

Admit it, you watch *JAWS* whenever it's on TV. You catch it uncut on Turner Classic Movies and even when it's chopped up for time and content on TBS or TNT. Even when it's sandwiched between wrestling and *Stargate: SG1* reruns on the Sci-Fi Channel. Hell, you even watch it when it runs *en espanol* on Telemundo under the title *TIBURON!* No matter the context, when you hear John Williams' *JAWS* theme music you freeze with anticipation.

You can't explain your love for *JAWS*, or even how you can quote every line of dialogue, no matter how inconsequential ("What's wrong with my printing?" "That's some bad hat, Harry" "Come on, Albert, you goof!"). You've seen the movie so many times, the characters have become like old friends. Your wife groans when you try to make her watch it for the 200th time, or when you mumble in your sleep about "closing the beaches."

You even have a soft spot for the sequels, including *JAWS 3-D* in plain old one-dimension. If you're obsessed with the notion of a giant fish feeding on New England beach communities, you've come to the right literary place! Whether you've seen *Jaws* once or a thousand times, this book is for you.

Hasn't the ultimate "Making of *JAWS*" book already been written? Yes it has, Carl Gottlieb's superb *The JAWS Log* is the best book ever written on the travails of making a movie. He even lived with Steven Spielberg! As a co-writer and co-star of the first film, Gottlieb offers readers a ringside seat to its production.

So, why *another* book, you might ask?

Just When You Thought It Was Safe: A Jaws Companion offers a unique look at the *entire* history of the *Jaws* franchise. *Everything* is covered: Peter Benchley's best-selling novel, Steven Spielberg's blockbuster film, all the infamous sequels, rip-offs and aborted *JAWS* projects. It has never-before-told stories, surprising observations from an array of participants, including Susan Backlinie and all the original shark's victims. There are accounts of the crew, such as production designer Joe Alves, shark-builder Roy Arbogast, and cinematographer Bill

Butler — and all the men and women who went to sea with film cameras and an unreliable mechanical shark. *JAWS Log* author Gottlieb (and the co-writer of two of the movie sequels) is also a major part of this new book.

While many of today's movies are digitally animated and spit out of a computer, JAWS had weight and heft and narrative drive. More than thirty years later, the film and its shark are still as relentless and effective as the day they were released into the collective unconscious. As fearsome as they are, the Terminator, the Aliens and the velociraptors of *Jurassic Park* wouldn't last five minutes in the waters off Amity Island!

"And as you know, tomorrow is the fourth of July and we will be open for business!"

Pat Jankiewicz
Claremont, California,
2008

THE
BOOK

"The great fish moved silently through the night water, propelled by short sweeps of its crescent tail."

Preproduction shark sketch by Joe Alves.

So begins Peter Benchley's terrifying novel about the havoc a killer fish wreaks on a seaside community.

The title character in his book and the film it inspired was Carcharodon carcharias, the Great White Shark, the ocean's most fearsome predator. As a Great White Shark can range anywhere from 17 to 36 feet, has teeth three inches long, skin like sandpaper and is a known man-eater, it made the ideal menace. *JAWS* was the first book and film to highlight the shark, a creature that really had not received its due in either media.

Although they have remained unchanged for millions of years, sharks were usually relegated to bit parts in movies; putting in cameos in pirate films (Where you would usually only see a circling fin) and James Bond pictures, where they were basically treated as just one more obstacle for 007 to quickly overcome.

With *JAWS* the shark came into its own, joining the pantheon of such classic Universal monsters as Frankenstein's monster, Dracula, the Wolf Man and The Creature from the Black Lagoon. The three-ton, twenty-five-foot killer fish seemed to feed on the audiences' collective primal fear of the water. What made it so scary was that it was something that couldn't be reasoned with or dissuaded from its goal. And unlike those other monsters brought to you by Universal, the shark was *real!*

The *JAWS* phenomenon really began on February 1, 1974, when Peter Benchley's novel first hit newsstands. Author Benchley had already been a *Washington Post* reporter by age twenty-three; he had served as a speech-writer for President Lyndon Johnson, and worked as a *Newsweek* reporter and TV news correspondent (a role he reprised in *JAWS*, incidentally).

Benchley had also written for *Time, National Geographic* and *The New Yorker*. As grandson of humorist Robert Benchley and son of author Nathaniel Benchley, he had a lot to live up to. His first book, *Time and a Ticket* (1964), was a nonfiction account of world travel. His second was a children's book, *Jonathan Visits the White House* (also 1964).

For his third book, he told *Publishers Weekly* that it was conceived in a "What if" way: "What if a resort town, dependent financially on summer residents, were to be hit by a natural disaster, say a great white shark?" Benchley had been inspired by the capture of a 17-foot, 4,550-pound Great White Shark off Montauk, Long Island in 1965.

He was also undoubtedly influenced by the shark attacks off the Jersey shore during the summer of 1916, when a large predator attacked five people, killing four and biting off a child's leg. The papers dubbed it "The Jersey Man-eater" and New Jersey tried to cover it up. (The first victim's death was relegated to the very back of the paper, under 'Fish Injures Bather' — a line that Mayor Larry Vaughn paraphrases in the movie.) A great white shark was later caught and killed for the attacks. These shark attacks are mentioned in both the novel and the movie.

"My idea," Benchley said, "was to tell my first novel as a sort of long story, just to see if I could do it. I had been a freelance writer since I was sixteen, and I sold things to various magazines and newspapers whenever I could."

Peter Benchley, filming his cameo in *JAWS*.

Bantam/Doubleday Books paid Benchley $300,000 for the shark story and the book's international publication rights were quickly snapped up by every major country, from Japan to Finland. Doubleday Editor Thomas Congdon assisted Benchley with reshaping his manuscript, adding elements to make it more commercial. This later caused some critics to claim that the book was "written by committee."

After Benchley's death in 2006, Thomas Congdon, told the Associated Press that he sought the author out because he liked some articles Benchley wrote for *National Geographic*. He arranged a lunch with Benchley at a New York restaurant — "a second-class restaurant, not 'first class,' since he was an unknown," the editor remembered. "The lunch didn't go very well. His non-fiction ideas did not seem very promising, but at the end of the meal, I said, 'Have you ever thought of writing a novel?' and he said, 'Well, I have an idea about a great white shark that marauds an Eastern coastal town and provokes a moral crisis in the community.'"

Congdon loved that concept, but felt Benchley was reluctant to start the book because he could not afford to pass up on his magazine articles. To get him focused on writing, Congdon got him a $1,000 payment, for submission of the first 100 pages. "Ninety-five percent of it was jokey stuff, because he thought that was the way you do it. But the first five pages were wonderful. There were no jokes. I wrote heavily in the margin: 'NO JOKES.' He [Benchley] went out and did it again, and it generated whole industries — the movie, amusement park rides. It changed the way people looked at sharks," Congdon said, before dismissing the publishing legend that the book was edited and restructured by Congdon so heavily that it was as much his work as Benchley's.

The stark title "was something of an accident," Benchley told *Empire Magazine*. "I spent months trying to find a title, playing around with all sorts of pretentious things like "Stillness in the Water," "Leviathan Rising," and "The Jaws of Death." Twenty minutes before the book had to go into production, we still didn't have a name. The only thing my editor and I agreed on was the word 'Jaws.' I said, 'Why don't we call it that?' [I] was lucky, it was a great title."

Benchley's book featured a voracious shark, described by a character as being "the size of a station wagon," relentlessly attacking swimmers off Amity Island, a Fire Island style resort. The protagonist is a weary, run-down Police Chief, Martin Brody. Brody is a balding, middle-aged blue-collar local who grew up on blue-blood Amity Island. He only met his wife, society girl Ellen, because he had pulled her rich college boyfriend over for drunk driving. Ellen's wealthy family members look down upon Brody and her wealthy friends shun her. Somewhat weak-willed when the shark starts to chew up the populace, Martin Brody allows the rich mayor (a real estate developer) to keep him from closing the beaches.

As the shark attacks mount, Brody's problems increase. He brings in a rich, sneering ichthyologist named Matt Hooper (whose older brother used to date Ellen) to help him catch the shark or figure out a way to drive it off. Besides looking down on the Chief, Hooper has a smug familiarity with Ellen that makes Brody nervous.

The shark is so vicious in the novel that, almost immediately after he eats a child, he attacks an old man at another Amity beach a half hour later. When the shark eats Ben Gardner — Brody's last hope for catching and

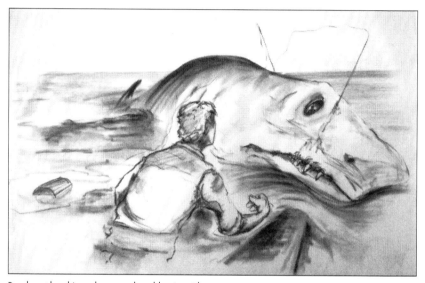

Brody, at book's end, as rendered by Joe Alves.

killing it — Brody realizes he's out of his league and needs help. Meanwhile, Ellen has moved past flirting with Hooper and is now meeting him at clandestine locations.

The local newspaper makes Brody the fall guy for the continued attacks. Brody hires gruff, brutal Shark-hunter Quint, a man so tough he only has one name. (He's even listed simply as "Quint" in the phone book!) Brody also learns that Mayor Vaughn's reasons for wanting the beaches open has to do with the Mafia encroachment on the island, a fact made clear to him when a goon kills the Brody family cat in front of his youngest son, Sean.

Brody finds the only way to stop the shark is to get on a boat (the *Orca*) with Hooper and Quint to catch the fish himself. By this point, he realizes that Hooper is having a full-fledged affair with his wife, and chokes him into unconsciousness. Quint intervenes. The men make several trips out to sea, managing to tag the shark with several barrels. As they pursue the fish, Quint realizes it is also pursuing them. When Hooper is submerged in a shark cage, the shark bites the helpless ichthyologist in half. Brody and Quint pursue it, until the shark slams onto the deck, sinking the *Orca*.

In the process of trying to kill the shark, Quint's leg is tangled in the ropes attached to the barrels on the shark. When the shark descends, it drowns

Quint. Rising up out of the water, the shark charges Brody — he finds himself face to snout with the beast, but the shark is dead. As it sinks, Brody looks down in the water and sees it go, dragging Quint's corpse into the briny deep. He stares until his eyes sting from the salt water.

One of the novel's biggest surprises came at this climax. As the shark is about to attack Brody, the police chief is so defeated by the monster, he can

Universal Studios' announcement of the movie adaptation.

only close his eyes and scream as it charges him. The heretofore indestructible fish dies from cumulative wounds and Brody wins by default.

Benchley felt any other ending would have been "ludicrous," so one can only imagine his feelings on the film's rousing climax.

The novel manages to skewer a number of subjects; the cozy, news-squelching alliances newspapers occasionally form with politicians and local businesses, small-town gossip, the way the media outlets stage events, and the compromises and little sell-outs of which humans are capable.

Critics loved the taut novel, but had trouble with one gratuitous plot element: While Brody is distracted by the shark attacks, his wife is sleeping with Hooper. As the critic for *Rolling Stone* suggested: "The shark was easily my favorite character — and one suspects Benchley's also … Maybe if the sex subplot had paired the police chief's wife with the shark…"

Benchley claimed in 1975 that he hadn't read *JAWS* since it was in proofs. He told Bob Greene of the *Chicago Sun-Times*: "I see people carrying (the book) around with them, but I never say anything to them. It's tempting sometimes, especially when you're in a city where you don't know anyone, but if you said something to them, they'd just want to talk about the book and that's the last thing I want to talk about."

The author managed to squeeze in a tribute to his famous grandfather. At the end of the book, Brody is so nervous the night before the shark hunt, he can't sleep, so he watches an old Ginger Rogers movie on the Late Show. The 1945 movie, *Week-end at the Waldorf*, co-starred Robert Benchley.

The hardback cover of *JAWS* was a simple black and white picture of a stick figure of Chrissie and a shark head that looks like an upside down "U." This is the classic *JAWS* image in its most basic form. When the novel was issued in paperback, an artist under contract to Bantam Books, Roger Kastel, was asked to do the new *JAWS* cover. Kastel, who had done covers for Judy Blume books, fleshed out the spare hardback cover by painting the iconic *JAWS* image of the shark beneath Chrissie.

Snagging the book in galley form, Universal Studios paid the author $175,000 for the movie rights to his book and a first-draft screenplay. When Universal Studios paid Benchley and Bantam for the rights to *JAWS*, they were also given the rights to use the paperback book cover as the film's poster.

Although it was the must-read summer novel of 1974, *JAWS* was going to reach an even bigger audience as a film the following year. Kastel watched his simple paperback book cover become a worldwide movie image.

THE
FILM

"What we are dealing with here is a perfect engine, an eating machine. It's really a miracle of evolution."

HOOPER

JAWS

Release date: June 20, 1975
Tagline: "She was the first."
Produced by Richard D. Zanuck and David Brown
Directed by Steven Spielberg
Written by Peter Benchley and Carl Gottlieb
Based on the novel by Peter Benchley
Photography by Bill Butler
124 minutes

Cast

Police Chief Martin Brody . . . . Roy Scheider
Quint. . . . . .Robert Shaw
Matt Hooper. . . . . Richard Dreyfuss
Ellen Brody . . . . .Lorraine Gary
Mayor Larry Vaughn. . . . . .Murray Hamilton
Meadows. . . . . Carl Gottlieb

Synopsis

Chrissie Watkins, a college girl at a beach party, goes for a midnight skinny dip in the ocean. She is attacked by an unseen predator from the deep. She screams for help, prays to God, even grabs a buoy, but the ruthless undersea attacker pulls her down, as her drunken date sleeps obliviously in the surf.

The next morning, Chief Brody, a New York cop who came with his family to Amity Island to escape the dangers of the big city, is called to the beach. Deputy Hendricks found what is left of Chrissie. Seeing the girl's ravaged remains, Brody talks to the coroner and they realize it's a shark attack. Brody orders the beaches closed. He goes to the hardware store to get paint and boards to make "No Swimming" signs.

On his way to bring in a Boy Scout troop doing laps in the bay, he's pressured by Mayor Larry Vaughn and newspaper editor Harry Meadows to let the beaches remain open. They have already coerced the Medical Examiner to alter his report to "boat accident."

Chrissie (Susan Backlinie) goes swimming.

Poster for a *JAWS* re-release.

Vaughn points out that the Watkins girl has no family powerful enough to cause problems and reminds Brody that "Amity is a summer town. We need summer dollars. Now, if the people can't swim here, they'll be glad to swim at the beaches of Cape Cod, the Hamptons, Long Island…" Brody reluctantly goes along with them.

At the beach with his wife and children, Brody keeps a wary eye out for the fish. As he stakes out the beach, a teen plays fetch with his dog, Tippit. An old man tells Brody the whole town knows of his fear of the water. A little boy gets permission from his reluctant mother to go out for a swim. As the boy makes his way on an inflatable raft, Tippit disappears in the surf. The little boy is eaten in front of everyone. A horrified Brody is powerless to stop the attack.

The boy's mother offers a $3,000 bounty for the shark, bringing in reckless amateur hunters. Brody attempts to close the beaches again, but is thwarted when Mayor Vaughn reminds him that Amity lives or dies as a result of the money spent by summer tourists. A gruff shark hunter who goes by the single name of "Quint," tells Brody, the mayor and the townspeople that *he'll* find the shark

FISH FACTS

▶ *JAWS* author Peter Benchley can be seen in a brief cameo as a TV reporter on the beach. Spielberg's eye for authenticity is demonstrated by having kids on the beach standing behind Benchley waving and making faces, just as kids are prone to do during real on-the-scene TV news stories.

▶ Director Spielberg threw marbles into the water to simulate bullet hits when Brody fires on the shark.

"You all know me…" Quint (Robert Shaw) offers to catch the shark.

"I'll catch this bird for you, but it ain't gonna be easy," Quint says. "Bad fish. Not like going down to the pond and chasing bluegills and tommycots. This shark, swallow you whole. No shakin', no tenderizin', down you go. And we gotta do it quick, that'll bring back your tourists, put all your businesses on a payin' basis. But it's not gonna be pleasant. I value my neck a lot more than three thousand bucks, Chief. I'll find him for three, but I'll catch him and kill him, for ten."

Hunting the wrong shark.

Two local men hunt the shark with a roast and inner-tube, tied to a dockpost. The shark takes the bait and tears the dock loose. The men are lucky to escape with their lives. Amateur hunters catch a tiger shark and the entire town celebrates.

Eccentric ichthyologist Matt Hooper arrives to help Brody with his 'Shark problem'. Hooper is skeptical that the tiger shark ate the boy or Chrissie ("The bite radius is wrong"). Mayor Vaughn prevents him from doing an autopsy on the fish. As Brody, Hooper and Vaughn prepare to leave, Mrs. Kintner, the dead boy's grieving mother, slaps Brody, telling him he knew about Chrissie's death and yet kept the beaches open:

> "You knew — you knew there was a shark out there and still
> my boy is dead."

As she leaves, Vaughn tells Brody, "I'm sorry, Martin — she's wrong."

> "No she's not," Brody replies sadly.

Examining the girl's remains, Hooper realizes "this was not a boat accident! And it wasn't any propeller; and it wasn't any coral reef; and it wasn't Jack the Ripper! It was a shark — a big one." He believes it was a Great White Shark. Brody and Hooper open the dead shark's stomach and realize it's not the killer. Hooper tells Brody, "You've still got a helluva fish out there!"

They go looking for the shark and find the wrecked remains of local fisherman Ben Gardner's boat. Gardner, Brody believes, was the only man capable of killing the shark — and he's nowhere to be found. When Hooper dives underneath Gardner's boat, he finds Gardner's severed head floating in the water.

The town is hurt by the shark attacks. A "WELCOME TO AMITY" billboard is defaced with a shark fin, reflecting local fears. With Mayor Vaughn adamant the beaches remain open for 4th of July Weekend, Brody, Hooper and the Coast Guard all join forces to patrol the beach.

Brody's son Michael wants to take his boat into the water, but Brody asks him to use the pond instead. A dorsal fin surfaces in the swimming area, causing a beach-wide panic. As the men prepare to shoot the fish, they find it's actually just two boys pulling a prank with a cardboard fin.

While Brody and the crowd sigh in relief, the real shark cruises into the pond and attacks the Boy Scout leader, narrowly missing Brody's son. Brody forces Vaughn to hire Quint. Quint takes Brody and Hooper out on his rickety old boat, the *Orca*, to find the shark.

At sea, the men bicker and bond. While chumming the water, Brody sees the shark. Stunned by its size, he realizes, "You're gonna need a bigger boat!"

Quint reveals that he was on the doomed *U.S.S. Indianapolis* and spent several days in shark-infested waters, watching helplessly as the sea creatures devoured his friends. Because of this traumatic incident, Quint vows, "I'll never wear a life jacket again."

After several confrontations and a sea chase, Quint tries to lure the shark into shallow water to drown it. Quint guns the boat's engine until it's flooded and burns out. Hooper goes down in a shark cage, to inject a poison spear of Strychnine Nitrate into the fish's

▲ *JAWS* owes at least some of its success to the classic 1954 Universal horror film, *The Creature from the Black Lagoon*. This influence is most notable in the opening, where Steven Spielberg playfully recreates the scene where Kay (Julie Adams) goes for a swim, unaware that a prehistoric sea creature is stalking her from below.

▲ That's an uncredited Steven Spielberg as the voice of the Amity Point Coast Guard.

▲ The coroner is played by the town's real doctor, Robert Nevin.

▲ Roger Corman claims the best review he ever got was not for one of his films, but for *JAWS*: "One New York paper wrote 'What Is *Jaws*, but a Roger Corman movie with a bigger budget?' I don't know how Steven Spielberg felt about that, but I was thrilled!"

▲ Actor/comedian Harry Shearer (the voice of Mr. Burns on *The Simpsons*) did some of the ADR voices for incidental townspeople in *JAWS*.

▲ June Foray, voice of "Rocky the Flying Squirrel," dubbed the voice of Michael Brody. You can really tell it's her when she delivers the line, "The pond's for old ladies!"

mouth. It slams the cage so hard, Hooper drops his weapon. The shark easily smashes into the cage and Hooper barely escapes.

The shark leaps on the deck of the sinking *Orca* as Brody and Quint try to hold on. An air tank slams into Quint's fingers, causing him to slip towards the shark's maw. Brody grabs Quint's gloved hand, but it's too slippery and Quint plunges to the shark.

JAWS producers Richard Zanuck and David Brown.

After a brief struggle, Quint knifes at the shark before he slides into its jaws and is crushed. He vomits blood and dies, as the shark slips underwater again.

Brody looks for protection in the sinking *Orca*, before the shark crashes in, with Quint's remains all over its teeth. Brody fends it off with the tank that knocked Quint loose (which the shark partially swallows) and hangs onto the mast — the last vestige of the Orca above water. He only has a rifle and a gaffing pole, which he stabs into the shark, to no avail.

As the shark closes in, Brody notices the partially swallowed tank and shoots at it. Missing the tank with his first five bullets, he takes one last shot and mutters "Smile, you son of a —!' and fires, hitting it. The shark explodes. Alone, Brody nervously sees bubbles behind him. Hooper surfaces, and the two men swim for shore.

The screenplay brilliantly compresses Benchley's book. The characters are also more effective in the film than in the novel. Changing Brody into a hardened New York cop coming to Amity to get away from big-city pressure makes him an interesting outsider, not a pathetic loser. This is also a clever way of acknowledging actor Roy Scheider's familiarity from such cop movies as *The French Connection* and *The Seven-Ups*.

▲ The female painter who screams, "Sh-sh-Shark! Shark! He's going into the pond!" was Joe Alves' then-girlfriend, Carla, whom he met on location at Martha's Vineyard.

Steven Spielberg directs Robert Shaw, Roy Scheider and Richard Dreyfuss.

JAWS producer David Brown told *Empire Magazine*: "Steven [Spielberg] added the idea that Brody was afraid of the water. [Brody was] coming from an urban jungle, to find something more terrifying off this placid island in Massachusetts. Steven Spielberg's instinct for hit movies [is] to have someone you care about. In the novel, the wife of [Brody] was cuckolding him with the ichthyologist. Steven said, 'You can't have three people on a boat being pursued by a killer shark, where one of them would like to see the other dead.'"

Upon reading the galleys for Benchley's *JAWS*, producers Richard Zanuck and David Brown knew it would make an exciting film. An incredibly successful producing duo, Zanuck and Brown were behind

▲ Jonathan Filley, who plays Chrissie's date Tom Cassidy, is now a location scout for movies shot in New York.

▲ The clip of the shark about to eat the Kintner boy is now used in public service announcements for the California anti-pollution group, American Oceans Campaign. (Instead of a shark, they have substituted a shot of polluted water.)

The Sting (which won seven Academy Awards), *The Eiger Sanction* and *Patton*. They were intuitive enough to buy the novel before publication.

Of course, the movie would be a massive undertaking. In his book, *Let Me Entertain You*, David Brown confesses that, "When Richard Zanuck and I acquired film rights to Peter Benchley's seminal novel, *JAWS*, we experienced a panic of unpreparedness. If we had read *JAWS* twice, we might never have made the movie. Careful analysis could have convinced us that it was too difficult to make."

STEVEN SPIELBERG

When an earlier director didn't pan out (In a meeting with Benchley, Zanuck and Brown, director Dick Richards kept referring to the shark as "a whale"!), Zanuck and Brown made a creative choice. They hired a young director named Steven Spielberg to do their film, *The Sugarland Express* and he borrowed the *JAWS* galley from their office (In early interviews, he insists he "stole" it) and began lobbying for the directing job.

Zanuck and Brown liked his work so much that they decided to re-team with him for *JAWS*. As Spielberg told the *New York Times*, "They were happy with [*Sugarland*] and said 'Let's do another picture together,' and they really meant it. At the time, they had another director in mind for *JAWS*, but two weeks later, they asked me to do it."

Spielberg with Alves' shark design.

The director liked the book, saying he felt like it "attacked him." "I wanted you to care so much for the characters you wouldn't want to see them get eaten!" Spielberg said. He added that, for realism, he wanted to shoot on the actual ocean.

Adapting and streamlining the novel *JAWS* was a task that started with the book's author. As the first screenwriter, Benchley steered it through three drafts before playwright Howard Sackler (*The Great White Hope*) was brought in.

The third and final writer, Carl Gottlieb, did all of the subsequent work — writing, rewriting and making overnight changes during filming in Martha's Vineyard. He also played a supporting role in the film. Script suggestions came from writers as diverse as Paul Schrader (*Taxi Driver*) and John Milius (*Conan the Barbarian*).

Surprisingly, in an interview with *Variety*, *Columbo* co-creator William Link revealed that Steven Spielberg first offered him the writing job on *JAWS*. Although he passed on it, Link noted "My wife said at the time, 'If Spielberg ever asks you to write anything for him again, *you do it!*'"

Screenwriter Carl Gottlieb was brought onto *JAWS* when "I got a call on a Sunday afternoon from Steve, to meet with him and producers Zanuck and Brown. My whole involvement on *JAWS* came from the fact that it was Sunday and they couldn't find a writer! Where do you get a writer on a Sunday? Two days later, I was on a plane to Boston to rewrite the movie."

While many have likened *JAWS* to Hitchcock's *The Birds*, with its "small seaside town under attack by nature," it's actually much closer to *Psycho*. Like *Psycho*, the film starts with a beautiful blonde woman being unexpectedly killed and has John Williams' Bernard Hermann-like theme. Also like *Psycho*, the film was made with a crew that hailed largely from television.

Hitchcock shot his film with his *Alfred Hitchcock Presents* TV crew, and the *JAWS* crew all had TV roots. In addition to Spielberg, there was Carl Gottlieb, a writer/actor in TV comedies; Bill Butler, who started in Chicago TV; and art director Joe Alves, who first met Spielberg on the *Night Gallery* series.

▲ The screenplay makes it clear that the entire Brody family is present to see Alex Kintner die because they are celebrating Michael's birthday, which Ellen addresses in a previous scene ("Martin, it's his birthday tomorrow"), but the party is never shown.

▲ According to Mrs. Kintner's poster, Alex dies on June 29th, the same day Quint alleges The *U.S.S. Indianapolis* sank.

▲ The shark on the blackboard in Quint's big speech at City Hall is actually the logo on his truck for his shark-hunting business.

▲ In 1979, when *Newsweek* declared it "Hollywood's Scary Summer," with the release of *Alien*, *Prophecy*, *Phantasm*, *Nightwing*, *The Amityville Horror* and *Dawn of the Dead*, Universal hastily re-released *JAWS* in a clever "Back for a Second Bite" campaign.

▲ LVJ Compagno, who is acknowledged in the closing credits, is in fact Dr. Leonard Compagno, shark authority and frequent guest on Discovery Channel's *Shark Week*.

▲ "You're gonna need a bigger boat" was voted #35 on The American Film Institute's Top 100 Movie Quotes.

Like Hitchcock on *Psycho*, Spielberg relied on his imagination instead of spending more money. His determination led him to not only shoot the film on location, but improvise filming in unusual places. Besides having one of the film's biggest "jumps" being shot in his film editor's swimming pool — he even shot a scene in production designer Joe Alves' driveway!

"That's true," Alves laughs. "We actually shot stuff in my driveway. Before I built my house (in a rural Laurel Canyon neighborhood), I built part of their boat, the hull for the *Orca*. Steven came up and directed the shot where the shark is hitting the boat and water comes pouring in." The insert shot, where we see the effect of the shark ramming the boat from the inside, was accomplished by "taking the boat hull and spraying my water hoses through the cracks," Alves reveals. "That's all my driveway!"

Director Steven Spielberg — the man upon whom everything fell — was only twenty-seven years old when he took on *JAWS*. Before coming to Amity Island, Spielberg was raised in Phoenix, Arizona, the oldest child (and only son) of World War II veteran Arnold Spielberg and his wife, Leah.

Spielberg grew up making home movies, usually starring his three sisters. He first put himself on the map with a 24-minute short film called *Amblin'* (after which he later named his production company). *Amblin'* is a story about two hitchhikers who meet in the middle of nowhere and fall in love. The offbeat film contains no dialogue.

"Steven did that great short film as a calling card to the studios," Carl Gottlieb recalls. "It wasn't really a student film because he didn't go to film school! *Amblin'* was shot in 35mm with a very engaging, likable cast of two actors! It was a perfectly professional short film with real humanity from the actors. Anybody seeing it would think 'This film was made by a pro,' but he was only twenty-one. Sid Sheinberg was running television at Universal, saw it and said 'this kid's hot' and gave him a job as a contract TV director."

After helming an impressive pilot segment (starring film legend Joan Crawford) for the Rod Serling anthology show, *Night Gallery*, and directing episodes of *Columbo* and *Marcus Welby, M.D.*, Spielberg turned his attention to *The Sugarland Express*. Goldie Hawn starred in that theatrical film as a fugitive attempting to get her baby back from the authorities. Although ostensibly a fun chase movie, it had a tragic ending.

"When he made his debut feature, *Sugarland Express*, Pauline Kael called it 'The most auspicious debut of a director since Orson Welles did *Citizen Kane*,'" recalls Carl Gottlieb. "Pretty high praise but it was true. *Sugarland* did nothing at the box office, but then he did *Duel* and everything took off. In America, it was a TV-movie starring Dennis Weaver, but it was released as a [theatrical] movie overseas and it was a big success in Europe."

Written by novelist and *Twilight Zone* contributor Richard Matheson (and based on his own short story), *Duel* is a taut, 71-minute film about a hapless motorist (Dennis Weaver) who finds himself the target of a large 18-wheel truck. After *Duel*, Richard Matheson was tapped to write *JAWS*.

"I seem to remember being offered it," Matheson recalls. "But I turned it down, because I thought it was just *Duel* with a shark!" Ironically, he would later write *JAWS 3-D*.

Taking the film on location with an untried mechanical shark, Spielberg's youth and intelligence galvanized the *JAWS* crew. Cinematographer Bill Butler has fond memories of the young auteur: "I think I could best describe him when I worked with him on *JAWS* as being someone who, at one moment, would be very, very young and at another moment, have the wisdom of a seventy-year-old man. He was both, wrapped up in one person. I remember it as a wonderful experience simply because he was so creative."

Fighting the elements, the mechanical shark and studio accountants was stressful. In *Film Comment*, Spielberg compared the exhausting process of directing the film to "working in a textile mill." To calm himself, the stressed, overworked Spielberg would put celery in his pillowcase for the soothing smell. When he finished the shoot and left Martha's Vineyard for the last time, he had an anxiety attack at the Boston Airport, thinking his career was over.

▶ In 2001, *JAWS* was named 'culturally significant' by the Library of Congress and selected for preservation on the National Film Registry.

▶ The main title credits in the original *JAWS*, from the shark's point-of-view going through seaweed, were done off Catalina Island.

▶ The TV show *Mythbusters* did an episode devoted to *JAWS*, and demonstrated that shooting an oxygen tank would not blow up a shark. Peter Benchley also said the tank "would not cause a shark to blow up like an oil refinery!"

Spielberg shooting on the *Orca*.

Carl Gottlieb felt "Steven was a very earnest, serious and dedicated film guy. Nowadays, you take baby moguls and baby filmmakers in stride because there's so many of them, but at that time, you had to work long and hard to become a director. It was quite shocking to see a guy [of] his years with his level of technical expertise."

When he found out that both *JAWS* producer Richard Zanuck and Universal executive (and Spielberg mentor) Sid Sheinberg had both promised the Ellen Brody role to their actress wives (Zanuck was married to *Planet of the Apes* star Linda Harrison; Sheinberg to *Car Wash* actress Lorraine Gary), he reportedly exclaimed "*Oy Vey!*" The problem was solved when Lew Wasserman called Jennings Lang, producer of Universal's profitable *Airport* series, and told him "to add one more passenger"(Harrison) on *Airport '75*. Spielberg claimed he thought of casting Gary as Ellen Brody after seeing her in *The Marcus Nelson Murders* TV-movie, which introduced the world to the fictional detective, Kojak.

"One of the *JAWS* anniversary articles mentioned that, at the time, Steven, Lew or one of the other people said 'Somebody is going to lose a wife over this'," Linda Harrison recalls. "And it was sadly true; Richard and I divorced while Lorraine and Sid are still together."

With the mechanical shark unreliable at best, Spielberg devised a number of scenes to get around it. Ironically, this worked in the film's favor. By not showing the shark and using the camera as the shark's POV, scenes of the camera going around swimmers are quite horrific. By not seeing the shark, you still feel its presence. The director told *Premiere Magazine*: "the film went from a Japanese Saturday matinee horror flick to more of a Hitchcock, the less-you-see-the-more-you-get thriller."

Film critic Roger Ebert praised this approach in his review: "In keeping the Great White [shark] unseen, Spielberg was employing a strategy used by Alfred Hitchcock throughout his career: 'A bomb is under the table and it explodes. This is a surprise,' said Hitchcock. 'The bomb is under the table, but it does not explode. *That* is suspense.' Spielberg leaves the shark under the table for most of the movie. And many of its manifestations later in the film are second-hand. We don't see the shark, but the results of his actions. The payoff is one of the most effective thrillers ever made."

An example of this effectiveness comes when two men try to catch the fish with a roast chained to a rickety old dock. Instead of catching it, the shark tears the dock loose, towing one of the men, Charlie, out to sea and into the water.

We never see the shark, but we see the dock piling turn around and pursue Charlie.

"Swim, Charlie, swim! Take my word for it, don't look back!" his friend screams.

Charlie lived or died in various drafts, before it was decided he could live, just to demonstrate the eerie (off-camera) presence of the shark.

Director John Landis (who would later give Steven Spielberg a memorable cameo in *The Blues Brothers*) was on the set. "I did not really work on *JAWS*, although I did help build the break-away pier for the fishermen," Landis recalls.

"I was flown to Martha's Vineyard by Michael and Julia Phillips to meet Steven Spielberg. They wanted me to do a rewrite on a screenplay by Paul Schrader called *Project Blue Book*. That script eventually became *Close Encounters of the Third Kind*.

"The *JAWS* production was having its legendary problems, so I ended up waiting for over a week to meet with Steve," Landis continues. "I stayed with

Destroying the dock.

Spielberg, Dreyfuss, Rick Fields (Editor Verna Fields' son) and Carl Gottlieb in the house the show had leased for them. Since I was bored, I did help the crew rigging that dock for that scene. Carl Gottlieb wrote a terrific book, *The JAWS Log*, in which he writes about me hanging around, waiting to talk to Steve."

Working around his non-working shark, Steven Spielberg also came up with a number of comical scenes, like Quint harassing a young boy in a music store (He's buying piano wire, which he uses to choke sharks) and a brilliant set-piece involving two boys scaring the beach dwellers with a fake fin.

"There was no pre-planning or scripted sequence for it, it was really kind of a relaxed, improvised scene by Spielberg," remembers Jonathan Searle, who played the younger boy (the older boy was played by his big brother Stephen).

"Steven Spielberg just said to me, 'You're gonna come up and blame your brother … Say, 'He made me do it — he talked me into it!' We did a lot of stuff that hit the cutting room floor, but as far as popping up out of the water, we only did one take of that. I don't know if they only did one take of that because we were freezing or because they were losing the light, but that was only one scene and that's what they ended up using. My second line was unintelligible, because a wave hit me in the mouth!

"Shooting the scene didn't take long at all; they used real divers to tow the shark fin through the beach crowd. Our part was simply to go underwater, hold our breath and hold onto a bag of weights and wait for a diver to roll the fin and signal for us to surface. We popped up and did our thing!"

Searle remembers that "When the fin scares the beach, everybody runs out of the water, the beach is crowded, the sun is bright, but when we shot our scene, you could tell it was later in the day. It's cloudy and we were freezing in that water! We hid on one of the patrol boats so nobody could see us until they needed us. That water chilled us to the bone ... Spitting out water in that scene wasn't planned — that wave just came up and hit me in the face on camera!"

Jonathan Searle, 'the kid with the fake fin.' PHOTO BY PATRICK JANKIEWICZ.

Scenes from *JAWS* — particularly the opening attack — are still picked apart at film schools, which is ironic, as the world's two most famous film schools, USC and UCLA, turned Spielberg down. He eventually graduated with an English degree from Cal State Long Beach.

To really appreciate how impressive *JAWS* is, one need only remember that Spielberg was working on location against the ocean, special effects, kids, dogs and poor weather. He told Mik Cribben, a writer for *American Cinematographer*: "I can't think of any film about the sea that is technically as difficult as this one. Everything is being shot right on and in the sea.

"Morally," Spielberg continued, "I can account for only one-fourth of a day's work done every day. Seventy percent of the problem has been the water. This is the first picture to do half of its shooting on location at sea. Because it's the first, it's bloody expensive. This picture is a mathematician's dream and a filmmaker's horror."

John Milius told *Premiere Magazine* that "*JAWS* is [Spielberg's] second-best movie, after *Schindler's List*. What I love about it is, it's a real primal movie. There's no political correctness, nothing about the attitude of how we should feel about the sea and the sharks. It's about pride of species. This is about a shark that's eating man and man must stop it. You want to get the shark and the shark wants to get man. You kind of like the shark, because he wants to get the man, and you kind of like the men, because they want to get the shark. And it never lets anything get in the way of that."

"You're gonna need a bigger boat..." Roy Scheider as Chief Brody.

BRODY, QUINT AND HOOPER

Character actor Roy Scheider was cast as Chief Brody after meeting Spielberg at a party. Spielberg pitched him the story and Scheider agreed to do it. A longtime movie sidekick, Scheider had his first starring role in *JAWS*, and he made the most of it. His battered good looks helped make Scheider a convincing hero who looks both noble and common. "Roy Scheider looks like a Roman statue with a broken nose," wrote a reporter for *Newsweek*.

Gottlieb fondly refers to Scheider as "'The Lizard Man'! I called him that because he loved the sun. Roy just loved to get suntanned. We'd get memos from the camera department saying, 'Keep him out of the sun, he's changing colors from shot to shot.' If you shot stuff two weeks apart on *JAWS 2*, he just got darker and darker. Roy would be out there sunning himself in his swimsuit, showing off his body and you'd compare material shot a few weeks earlier and he was a completely different color! It posed a problem. Scheider was a journeyman actor, but he did his job and created the character.

"He was one of those guys who was somewhat embarrassed by the success of the movie," Gottlieb reveals. "He felt that way because he thought of himself as a more serious actor. There's not a lot of acting to do in *JAWS*, outside of being sincerely involved with the shark. His co-star was a mechanical creature. Roy was coming off *The Seven-Ups*, which was not an 'A' movie and Gene Hackman got all the good notices on *The French Connection*. Roy was a good New York actor doing his job well."

Englishman Robert Shaw played Quint. A classically trained performer and playwright, Shaw was best known for his larger than life villains in such films as *From Russia with Love* and *The Sting*. He also appeared in such classics as *The Dam Busters*, *The Taking of Pelham One Two Three* (directed by Joe Sargent of *JAWS the Revenge*) and *A Man for All Seasons*.

Interestingly, Robert Shaw was not the first actor considered for the role of Quint. According to Carl Gottlieb, someone who could have done the role even better was Sterling Hayden.

"Hayden, best known as the corrupt police captain in *The Godfather*, was Spielberg's first choice," Gottlieb muses. "He would have been perfect for the part, because he *was* a sailor, a man of the sea, but he had a tax problem and couldn't do it. You truly wonder what the movie would have been like if Sterling had been there."

Robert Shaw nevertheless made the role his own. He has a show-stopping monologue, in which he recounts his experiences in shark-filled waters after a World War II mishap. Shaw is incredibly convincing, even though he told *Time* he thought the book "was a piece of shit, written by a committee." Despite this strong opinion, he played another Peter Benchley-created character in *The Deep*.

Gottlieb recalls that Shaw "was a terrific guy, but he liked to needle people. He was a genius at finding your most tender points and zinging you! He would

Robert Shaw as Quint, a man so tough he only has one name!

lean over to Dreyfuss just before a take, when they were doing a scene together on the boat, and just as the slate was coming out of the shot, Shaw would say 'Mind your mannerisms now,' thereby ruining Dreyfuss's concentration and making Shaw look good — he was full of tricks like that! An old ham, but a terrific guy. We lost a wonderful actor when he died."

Hooper checks the bite radius on the tiger shark.

Richard Dreyfuss landed the role of Matt Hooper. The Brooklyn-born performer had a bit part in *The Graduate* (making *JAWS* the second movie he did with Murray Hamilton) and already had one fish movie under his belt — *Hello, Down There*, directed by Jack Arnold (*The Creature from the Black Lagoon*). In this musical, Dreyfuss actually sings to a fish! When he first met with director Steven Spielberg and screenwriter Carl Gottlieb, he wore the hat and glasses he sports in the film.

Gottlieb liked Dreyfuss. "We were in the same [improv] group, The Committee," Gottlieb says. "There's also a moment that gets a big laugh in the movie, which came when we were trying to talk Richard into doing *JAWS*. We were sitting in a Boston Holiday Inn when room service brought coffee in a white plastic cup. Ricky drinks his coffee and crushes the cup. It goes 'Pop!' Spielberg and I looked at each other and go, 'Wait-a-second, if Quint crushes a beer can and Ricky crushes a cup, we got a moment here!' That was the first joke that we came up with. It's a great confrontation between the intellectual and the animal."

As was the case with Shaw, Dreyfuss was not the producers' first choice.

"The studio wanted Charlton Heston for [Quint] and Jan Michael Vincent for [Hooper]," Gottlieb chuckles. "You can tell how the movie would have turned out — it was total B-movie thinking. The dramatic parts of *JAWS* worked only because we got Ricky and Robert Shaw. They were worthy adversaries; each one had a tremendous quality to them."

Dreyfuss remembers *JAWS* as "a very tough shoot, the shark did not work and filming on location was very rough on all of us … Remember the scene where I talk to Brody and Quint before I go down in the shark cage? Right after we shot that scene, the chain broke holding my shark cage to the boat! The cage went into the water, taking me with it! I couldn't breathe — I was trapped as I

"This was *not* a boat accident!" Richard Dreyfuss as Matt Hooper.

Hooper in the surf.

went straight down in the water! It felt like I was down there for hours, but the crew all jumped into the water and had me out of there fast!"

Dreyfuss had worked for George Lucas in *American Graffiti* and John Milius in *Dillinger*; in the latter he portrayed the sadistic gangster, "Baby Face" Nelson. As hyperkinetic ichthyologist Matt Hooper in *JAWS*, Dreyfuss gets to play off the nervous Brody and bicker with the brutish Quint. Interestingly, Spielberg asked Dreyfuss not to read the novel, as the character was being completely revamped.

Dreyfuss was reportedly unhappy with the delays on *JAWS*. While shooting in Martha's Vineyard, he referred to the film-in-progress as "The turkey of the year." His opinion is best expressed in a 1974 *New York Times* interview, in which he states, "It was a waste of my time as an actor. It was not fulfilling. I had no sense of getting off on it. It was kind of like *The Guns of Navarone* — I'd rather see the movie than act in it."

The actor also told the *Times* that the five-month shooting schedule on Martha's Vineyard "drove me crazy! I'm not a sun person. After a while, I felt like Papillion, I had to escape. Martha's Vineyard is a lovely, lovely place — but I don't ever want to go there again."

Happily, his opinion of *JAWS* changed when he saw the finished film. In his book, *Let Me Entertain You*, *JAWS* producer David Brown remembers Dreyfuss saying, "It's the greatest. If I'd had any idea it would be this good, I'd have had a better time making it."

"You've got to remember [Dreyfuss' career] was very limited at that point," Carl Gottlieb explains. "He was the lead in *Hello Down There* with Tony Randall and only had one-liners in *The Graduate* and *Valley of the Dolls*. He was firmly convinced that *JAWS* was just a potboiler!"

On NBC-TV's *Later with Bob Costas*, Richard Dreyfuss recalled the day a mishap occurred, causing the *Orca* to sink with the actors and crew on board: "While I'm trying to get this seventy-year-old soundman [Fred Zendar] to straddle the side of the boat and make it down," Dreyfuss said, "I hear Steven [Spielberg] saying [through a bullhorn], 'Get the actors off the boat! Get the actors off the boat!'

"I say, 'Steven, he's seventy years old!'

"[Steven says], 'Fuck him! Get the actors off the boat!'"

The crux of the film's story is Martin Brody becoming the leader of his community through decisive action. When we first meet Brody, he's myopic and clumsy (he knocks over a container of paintbrushes in Amity Hardware), and ineffectual (He can't keep the beaches closed or even fix his kids' broken swingset); he's afraid of the water (he gets seasick and he can't swim) and he's easily cowed by Mayor Vaughn and the others. After the shark strikes again and again, Brody relies on others (the hunters and Ben Gardner), in the hope that someone else will solve the problem for him.

When that fails and his children's lives are literally threatened, he finally takes matters into his own hands and goes out to sea with the crazed shark-hunter Quint and the reasonable ichthyologist Matt Hooper. While he allows both colorful men to call the shots at first (he even shamefully realizes he's outclassed when they compare scars), Brody eventually finds it's all up to him when Quint dies and Hooper flees. He sheds his glasses when they are literally knocked off his face and becomes a Man of Action. In the finale, it all comes down to him in primal combat with the shark as the formerly mild-mannered sheriff devises a strategy that rids his community of the menace. Brody comes back a fully realized man.

Martin Brody is a better person than other archetypal Spielberg protagonists in that he stays with his community when given an option of easy escape (Ellen even proposes going back to New York, when the shark almost eats their son Michael). Unlike Roy Neary of *Close Encounters of the Third Kind* and Indiana Jones of *Raiders of the Lost Ark* — both of whom abandon their loved ones for selfish pursuits — Brody chooses the more difficult task of defending his town. By the end of the film, Brody is a free-thinking He-Man in black sweatshirt, equal parts Quint and Hooper.

AMITY ISLAND

Martha's Vineyard, an island south of Cape Cod, was the real-life setting for the fictional town of Amity. Steven Spielberg used a number of locals in the film, including Christopher Rebello for the part of Chief Brody's oldest son Michael and Jay Mello for the part of younger son Sean. Other island residents appeared in smaller roles or as extras. Jonathan Searle, who was "the kid with the fake fin," has vivid memories of being in the blockbuster film:

> "I was eight years old, and had just done my third-grade school play, *Androcles and the Lion*. I assume the production people approached the drama teacher at Edgartown Elementary School, because they rounded us all up and set us up for readings with Steven Spielberg. I remember not caring much either way about Steven Spielberg when I met him because he was an unknown at the time, but I did like him because he was a young guy who was nice and talked to us like a regular human being. My brother and I were trying out for the parts of Brody's sons — every team of brothers on the island was trying out for that.
> "Steven Spielberg and [casting director] Shari Rhodes had us in and said 'Pretend you're fighting, pretend you're happy,' but we didn't get the parts. We were called in to work as extras for the summer. My parents loved it … They looked at *JAWS* as free daycare where we actually made money! We played at the beach all day and they picked us up at the end of each day's filming. As time went on, being extras on the beach every day, we heard the rumor that they were gonna do a big scene with two boys and a fake shark fin.
> "I approached one of the crew guys and I said, 'Hey, my brother and I can do it!' The crew guy said, 'No, we're gonna have divers come do it.' A couple days later, they called both my brother and me over the loudspeaker on the beach. We showed up and they said, 'we want you to do it.'
> "That's my *JAWS* experience in a nutshell!"

Eerie estuary! Martha's Vineyard today. PHOTO BY PATRICK JANKIEWICZ.

Appearing in the film "was one of the most fun experiences in my whole life," says Belle McDonald, who played Mrs. Posner, wife of the town selectman.

> "*JAWS* coming to Martha's Vineyard was like the circus coming to town. It was exciting, with trucks and people — I came down at the end of June to do *JAWS* and we weren't

Belle McDonald, *JAWS* actress. PHOTO BY PATRICK JANKIEWICZ.

going into the water at that point. We were mostly filming on the beach. In the beginning of July, we started endless shots of 'everybody in the water/everybody out of the water!' About the tenth time of being sent back into the water, the crowd started howling because it was so cold. The water doesn't get warm around here until September, so it was very cold, I admit that, but it was wonderful.

"I was picked for the Selectman's wife in *JAWS* because I was the right age and right type. The guy playing my husband, Cyprian 'Phil' Dube, was a real selectman in Edgartown. A wonderful, sweet man — I'm sorry to say that he's since passed. That scene where the Mayor makes us take our family into the water was great. We were pushing the raft around and looking around nervously for the shark, because we knew he was out there. Nobody else follows us in. I remember pulling the children around on the raft and when everyone goes in the water for the scene with the shark fin, the great big fella pushes right through our raft and me and the children go into the water! I came up screaming for the children — it was so fun. I love that scene and the movie. *JAWS* fans have been coming up to me for over thirty years, saying, 'You're the one in the black bathing suit.'

It was great: Steven Spielberg was a wonderful young man — a real nice fella."

Jeffrey Voorhees, who had just moved to Martha's Vineyard when he landed the part of doomed Alex Kintner, remembers:

"Everyone filming it here was really nice, except for one guy, the old drunk, Robert Shaw. He ignored the island kids. They would have baseball games and cookouts for all the extras and kids on the island — all the actors would show up, except Shaw. He wanted nothing to do with 'The Island People,' as he called us. As a little kid, I would go over and talk to him, 'Hi! How are you today?' He would just glare and say, 'Just go away.' He was always drunk, just a mess. I don't know where he drank. I know more about bars now, because I have run them on the Island."

Schoolteacher Cathy Weiss appeared in the film as an extra.

"*JAWS* was sort of a family affair for us," she says. "My daughter Andrea was three, and she and I raced in and out of the surf again and again during the 'panic on the beach' scenes. My then-husband, Woody Schuman, was Rick Dreyfuss' stand-in for the scene in Quint's shack.

"I was excited because the shot of me holding my daughter as the beach runs away in panic was a billboard for *JAWS* in Sweden and you can see us on the back of *The JAWS Log!* You can see us in the film, too, but I was surprised how much attention that shot of my daughter and I running out of the surf got. We shot that at State Beach. Most of the actual shark attacks were shot away from the crowd, but they did a lot of us screaming and running from the water.

"My daughter Andrea was getting scared. I said, 'Don't worry, honey — we're just acting! There's not really a shark …' I'm also one of the people pointing off the jetty after another attack, screaming, 'Oh, my God — the shark! The shark!' It was so confusing for my daughter at the time, because she was only a baby at three. For the shots of the shark coming underneath the crowd, they asked for good swimmers who could work in deeper water. They had an underwater camera and wanted us all to swim really fast and frantically around the camera, so I volunteered. The water was very cold — because we did it before summer — and very deep, too.

"Here's something I never told anyone: Steven Spielberg approached me and offered me one hundred dollars if I would drop my three-year-old daughter in water over her head, and

Panic on the beach!

then freak out saying, 'My baby! My baby!' I was aghast that anybody would ask me that. I didn't know who he was at the time — nobody did until after *JAWS* — but I said to him, 'Are you kidding? You'd have to be crazy!'

"It was bad enough what I was doing to my daughter by screaming, '*Shark! Shark!*' — and scaring her half to death. I see from one of the *JAWS* shots they brought out for JAWSfest that he actually found a mother to do that, but they didn't use it in the finished film. My daughter lived and sailed in the Caribbean for a number of years, but would never swim in deep water because she was so scared of sharks from making *JAWS* as a child. She was too young to understand it was all make-believe when we were running from the shark, and it really traumatized her!"

Of all the "local hires," the most successful crewmember was the future Emmy-winning FX man Kevin Pike.

"I was living in Martha's Vineyard, when *JAWS* came. I worked at a local restaurant as a busboy. I was at The Harborside Restaurant, the main restaurant in Edgartown. A

JAWS crewmember Kevin Pike. PHOTO BY PATRICK JANKIEWICZ.

character in *JAWS* calls it 'The restaurant all the way down the street.' It's the one place in town where everybody went. On April 13th of '74, a large party came in — six guys, animated, energetic — different from the locals — who were politely sipping their lobster bisque.

"I kept them bussed and watered to give me a chance to overhear what they were so excited about. When they left I noticed that one of the gentlemen had forgotten his attaché case. I rushed it to them in the parking lot and it happened to belong to (production designer) Joe Alves. He said, 'Oh, that's great! It's so important, you wouldn't believe it! It's the storyboards for the movie.'

"I said, 'What are storyboards?'

"Joe told me that storyboards are 'Comic-book pictures that we make of what's gonna happen in the movie.'

"I said, 'What's the movie about?'

"Joe said, 'It's about a shark that's gonna eat your entire island!'

"I ended up going to The Kelly House, where the crew was staying, looking for better work than being a busboy on the island and putting my name on a list for a possible hire.

"On the 17th of April, I ran into Jimmy Woods at the post office — he was one of the guys from the dinner party. I told Jimmy, 'I can do anything, if you show me once ...'

"He put me to work the next morning, for $3.50 an hour! We were working on the *Orca* in the Boat House on Fuller Street — a second *Orca* that could sink on cue.

"Jimmy Woods gave all the local hires 'the Hollywood speech.' He said, 'I know you all build homes out here that last 100 years, great New England carpentry. We're not gonna do that. We just need to whip these sets together, paint 'em, shoot 'em and then rip 'em apart and throw them in the dump. Don't build 'em to last forever. I don't want anybody goofing off. I wanna see nothing but assholes and elbows. Any questions?'

"I raised my hand and asked 'Can I be one of the elbows?'

"He said, 'You're with me.'

"I ran time cards, coffee, coffee breaks and information for the production office. I segued into different departments. I worked on it for six months, was involved with the shark and it got me into FX. I didn't even know what 'Special FX' meant before *JAWS* came to town.

"In the boathouse, where we worked on the sharks and special FX, they had a board explaining what all these Hollywood expressions meant for the locals working on the movie. Because of that board, we would know what terms like 'hot set' meant. That was 'Don't touch it, it's a hot set!' I remember, one day on set, I was told to get my breakfast off the truck. I said 'I don't have any money' and he said, 'It's free!'

"I thought that was great!"

On Martha's Vineyard, during a long shoot with nothing to do after filming finished each day, the male crew hooked up with the college girls who worked as waitresses and clerks. "That made filming in Martha's Vineyard interesting," says Susan Backlinie, who plays Chrissie, the first victim. "In Martha's Vineyard, the ratio of guys to girls was incredible, absolutely incredible. The girls were all over the guys! How they got that movie shot, I'll never know. Some of the guys were going with two girls at the same time! I just said 'My God, how do you guys get up in the morning?'"

JAWS was intended to be a 55-day shoot, but stretched on to 159 days. When the production showed up, the money Universal brought was a Godsend, but as filming dragged on, residents were ready for them to leave. In the summer season, when Martha's Vineyard, like Amity, thrived on tourist dollars, residents became tired of the trucks, cables and blocked streets. Vandals slashed tires and put sugar in gas tanks of boats used by the production. Several residents put up "JAWS GO HOME" signs.

Shooting the movie had its share of mishaps. Besides the malfunctioning maneater, the weather and townsfolk, the *Orca* — the non-sinking *Orca* — sank.

"I'll never forget that day," Kevin Pike laughs. "When the *Orca* sank, our job was to crane it up out of the water, dry it out, fix the bottom, put the new wood in, and get it back in service as fast as possible. I did that with Roy Arbogast as quickly as we could!"

Bruce is loose!

BRUCE THE SHARK

The believability of the mechanical shark was the overriding contributor to the movie's ultimate success or failure. Production designer Joe Alves remembers that "The big question on *JAWS* was 'Would it work at all? Would people laugh at the shark or be scared by it?' Happily, it worked and I think it's a timeless movie, it's still really strong.

Alves attributes that strength to three factors: "Spielberg's genius, the three main actors being a great ensemble and bringing something unique to the audience: a huge, Animatronic creature that really had not been done before."

To bring the shark to life, legendary mechanical FX man Robert Mattey was pulled out of retirement. As former head of the Disney mechanical special FX department, Mattey did amazing work on *Mary Poppins*, the VW "Herbie" for *The Love Bug* series and the squid in *20,000 Leagues Under the Sea*. For *JAWS* he would build three sharks, made mostly of plastic, weighing over a ton and costing $150,000 apiece. Each mechanical shark would require fourteen operators. One model was a platform shark, which would be attached to an undersea track by a crane. This allowed the shark to surface whenever the filmmakers wanted it to. The other, a sled shark, was connected to an undersea sled, allowing it to 'swim' through the water. The sharks had tubular-steel skeletons and of the three, two were only 'half-sides' — one side was all shark; the other all hydraulics.

Of these half-sharks, one could turn right to left, the other left to right. All ran on hydraulic pistons and compressed air. Roy Arbogast was a protégé of Mattey's and remembers the FX man as "an incredible guy. When you saw how dedicated and hardworking he was, there was nothing you could do but follow him. He was a role model and I don't think anybody could have had a better mentor."

"I remember the day the [mechanical] sharks came in," marvels Kevin Pike. "They were in the back of the trucks and encased in molds to protect them on the way down from California. The shark was huge and we were thrilled with 'em. The shark's eye would even roll over white when it bit, like a real shark did — Joe and Roy did that to give it authenticity. I was a naive twenty-two-year-old kid, so I asked Roy Arbogast, 'Did you test these in the Pacific Ocean?' Roy said, 'We haven't even had them in the water yet — the third shark, we haven't opened the mold, so we don't even know if the skin is good ...' When he told me that, I knew right then and there, this was gonna be a long haul! We also had the smaller rubber tiger shark built, for Brody and Hooper to cut open and do the autopsy on."

For a movie called *JAWS*, it's ironic that the mechanical shark's biggest problem was its jaws!

"We had a lot of problems with the jaw because of the jowls and how much the jaw could open up," Pike groans. "The jaw had to open so wide, that the elastimer — the material the shark was made out of — had to stretch so far, it put a demand on it. The shark's skin would tear and it got beat up! He'd get hit by one of the boats and just take a real beating on the ocean every day. He would get dried out at the boathouse, then we would sand him down, fix the skin and repaint him. Fix him up for the next day, when the ocean would beat him up all over again!"

The mechanical star was evidently quite popular with crewmembers, as Kevin Pike attests: "Everybody wanted pictures of themselves with the shark. We all did it — I and everyone else would get pictures of our heads in the shark's mouth. One magazine got leaked shots of it and the demand came down that the sharks had to be covered up at all times when they weren't working on camera. They made these giant canvas covers that we had to use when we put the sharks to bed. You would cover this 20-foot shark and see only his tail sticking out. It protected the paint from being bleached on the shark, as we took him to Edgartown and back. More and more visitors came to watch us shoot 'that shark movie.'

"The guy who ran the FX was Gary Wood — he's since passed on, but everybody called him 'Geronimo.' Bob Mattey was in charge of the shark. Bob really was a genius. I was Bob's assistant on *JAWS 2*. He was the greatest guy you'd ever want to be around — his ideas were so big and so beyond. You have to understand, the only reason *JAWS* got made was because Bob said 'Yes' when everybody else said 'No.' He ran the FX shop at Disney and pulled off that amazing squid in *20,000 Leagues Under the Sea*. He was a personal friend of Walt Disney, and his work in animatronics inspired some of Walt's ideas for the park."

Roy Arbogast visited Mattey shortly before his death in 1992, and the conversation turned to the 1974 filming: "We talked about how much work it was — it was one of his proudest achievements," Arbogast recalls. "We talked about a lot of the fun times and hardships around *JAWS*. He built the best creature for its time."

Mattey also did spaceships for the Buster Crabbe *Flash Gordon* serials, a giant alligator for Tobe Hooper's *Eaten Alive* and crocodiles for the Johnny Weissmuller *Tarzan* movies that still work over seventy years later.

Those who worked closely with the shark feel that "When the shark worked, it just looked amazing," says Dick Warlock, who served as Richard Dreyfuss' stunt double in the shark cage scene. "I shot all the shark cage stuff in the tank on the MGM lot and it really looked amazing, with the snapping jaws and thrashing fins … It truly looked fearsome."

Kevin Pike remembers: "When we painted the shark, we used chopped-up walnuts, sand and dust in the paint to give the skin texture on the surface. Ward Welton showed me how to paint the shark and how to paint that grey/white line down the shark. Joe Alves gave the shark a really sleek design — if you look at *National Geographic* documentaries, bigger sharks have more girth — they really look like fat cows!"

Before the shark was used, it had to pass muster with documentary filmmakers Ron and Valerie Taylor (*Blue Water, White Death*) to determine accuracy.

"When Ron and Val came in, they looked at it from top to bottom and they told us what sex the shark was," Pike remembers. "A male shark has claspers on the back, which forms the penis of the shark — you can see his claspers in the movie. Ron and Val explained, 'This means you have made a male shark.'"

Michael Lantieri, Academy Award winning special FX man whose work can be seen in such films as *Jurassic Park*, *Terminator 2: Judgment Day* and *Hulk*, "was around when Steven was making the first *JAWS* and I worked a little bit on it as an assistant at age seventeen. I had just got into the business when they were working on the sharks. I worked a little bit on it in the shop.

"FX movies are never easy in the first place and when you try to work on the water, you compound your problems, and I'm not sure people would be excited about doing that again. I knew Bob Mattey, Roy Arbogast and Kevin Pike. We all worked out of a shop in Universal Studios and we all felt the shark was gonna work — you have to believe it will to get into that sort of work, but I don't think you ever achieve what you really want.

"Steven will tell you that [the *JAWS* shark] was 'the biggest mechanical FX made up to that time.' When you'd see the barrels on the water, that was because the shark wasn't working that day and it wouldn't go as fast as he wanted it to go. That's where Steven's mind comes in and makes all of us look good," Laniteri smiles. "We count on him for stuff like that!"

The shark was infamous for being troublesome during the making of the film. His eyes crossed, his jaws wouldn't close, his skin shriveled in the water, he sank to the bottom of the sea. Because of these difficulties, the crew took to calling the movie "Flaws" and Spielberg dubbed the construct, 'The Great White Turd'.

In his book, David Brown ruefully writes that "Richard Zanuck and I more than once saw our careers going to the bottom of the Atlantic while the sharks sank and frogmen were sent down to rescue them."

Gottlieb recalls that the mechanical shark was difficult for the crew: "We would have been satisfied to get all the shark footage that was in the script shot, but we couldn't, because the shark was always a problem! It was the first time someone had built it, so it was an erratic process," he explains. "It worked some of the time, didn't work the rest of the time. The grand concept of having a shark anchored to a platform to make it manageable died when the platform got mangled in a storm. We wound up shooting the spare shark ninety percent of the time, because that was the only shark that worked. With the shark, you took what you got — otherwise we'd *still* be shooting!"

Linda Harrison, then wife of *JAWS* producer Richard Zanuck, remembers "the dailies were so depressing, because they were full of endless shots of the shark's eyes crossing, or his jaws being stuck open — oh, those poor guys had the hardest time with that shark!"

Len Murphy agrees: "That shark never worked — it just never worked."

Murphy, with his wife Susan, used to tow the sled shark and the *Orca* for the filmmakers during the shoot. "That poor shark took a beating in the water. The frame shark was a lesson — you can't put brass, iron, aluminum and plastic together into salt water because it bubbles up like a jellyfish. Electrolysis ate at him while he lay on the bottom of the ocean for thirty days while waiting to be seen and when they needed to see him on camera, he just didn't work."

Before shooting began, Steven Spielberg took George Lucas, Martin Scorsese and John Milius to see the mechanical shark in the FX shop. Spielberg told *Premiere Magazine* that upon seeing it, Lucas told him, 'If you can get half of this on film, you will have the biggest hit of all time.' When Lucas stuck his head in the shark's mouth, Spielberg used the controls to clamp down the jaws. As a harbinger of things to come, the jaws would not open and Lucas had to pull his head out!

"The mechanical shark was nicknamed 'Bruce' after Bruce Ramer, Steven's lawyer at the time," Carl Gottlieb laughs. "He was a powerful Hollywood entertainment lawyer, who got a big kick out of it. It was like the old joke: Three lawyers go fishing, one falls into the water. A shark appears, circles him and

Rob Hall and his Corman shark. PHOTO BY PATRICK JANKIEWICZ.

swims away. They pull him out of the water, ask why he didn't get eaten and he says, 'Professional courtesy!'"

Robert Hall, of Almost Human FX, says, "The shark in the first *JAWS* looks amazing on film — considering the time they made it in and what they had to deal with. I built a mechanical fish for the movie *Frankenfish* and it's hard work.

"I started out working for Roger Corman on low-budget horror films and everything had to be done yesterday. In the 'nineties, I was doing stuff for Roger all by myself, out of my garage. They called me one day and asked, 'Hey, can you make a shark that eats people?' I had to build it in a weekend and I am pretty sure they didn't make *JAWS* that way!"

DA-DUM-DA-DUM

A movie about a primal force required a primal score. Composer/conductor John Williams' 'da-dum-da-dum' main title score is the most recognizable theme in film history. Scary and memorable, it won a well-deserved Academy Award.

Once known as "Johnny" Williams, the Long Island-born, Julliard-educated composer got his start in the late 1950s, providing the music for such low-budget movies as *Daddy-O* and *Gidget*. Williams' reputation was earned from writing the themes to the blockbusters, *Star Wars* and *Superman*, as well as such science-fiction television shows as *Lost in Space* and *Land of the Giants*.

In an interview with the *New York Times*, Williams explained how he invented his eighty-piece symphony score for *JAWS*: "The idea is 'Okay, we have a two-hour film, how quickly can we condition the audience to get to the point that when they hear this music, their reaction will be programmed?'"

The shark motif consisted of eight basses and five trombones.

Williams was particularly proud of the scene where Ben Gardener's head rolls out of the boat at Hooper. You expect to see the shark, not a head, because Williams' shark motif is played very softly during the scene.

Williams said, "The trick is, one thing is promised, another thing delivered."

In the *Roanoke Times*, Spielberg remembered the day "John Williams just played the [*JAWS* theme] music. I began to laugh and I said, 'You're joking,' and he said, 'No, I think this could be fun. What do you think of this?' and I said 'That's it!'"

Spielberg later told *Premiere Magazine*: "John Williams rediscovered my vision through his *JAWS* theme and gave *JAWS* an identity, a personality, a soul."

John Williams told *The Hollywood Reporter*: "I'd have to say that *JAWS* was the first major film opportunity that I had. It was a film that had, I think, deserved broad success, particularly for the second two-thirds of the film when it was at sea with the shark attacks and so on. They were wonderful pieces of moviemaking and a great opportunity for me to do what I was able to do.

"With Spielberg," Williams continued, "it was the beginning of our relationship, really, and a lot of opportunities came my way, including the *Star Wars* films. Spielberg introduced me to George Lucas, and he was directly responsible for that relationship developing."

CHRISSIE'S FATE

The film's opening of the girl swimming as the shark's point of view racing towards her has become a textbook example of suspense.

"The way that opening goes? With the shark's Point of View as it comes up underneath her," says cinematographer Bill Butler, "That opening was Spielberg's thing — that was all his."

The swimmer's attack was achieved in an offbeat way.

"The girl (Stuntwoman Susan Backlinie) was in a harness that went all around her hips," explains Butler, "With three fasteners on, one in the front and one on each hip. Those ran into lines underwater fastened on pulleys at the bottom of the sea. Then, the lines ran underwater, up to the beach. Groups of people pulled those ropes on cue to throw her back and forth and finally pull her towards camera and down underwater."

"It hurts!" Chrissie gets attacked.

Carl Gottlieb recalls that "Susan Backlinie was a very beautiful stuntwoman. When the dailies came back from the lab of her naked in the water, it was over-exposed, so it got all the detail. You were looking from underneath at a woman naked from the crotch, so we had to print it way down dark. She's truly naked in the shark's Point of View shots."

While rumors of the stuntwoman suffering from a broken rib or hip have been told and exaggerated in various film trivia books and on the internet, in reality, "Nothing happened to me," Susan Backlinie laughs.

"But the *potential* was always there." Carl Gottlieb notes. "She could have been ripped apart by the harness, but everything was fine."

When Chrissie strips on the beach, "she runs along this weathered old snow fence," says Kevin Pike. "Joe Alves put that snow fence on the beach and he was breaking some of the slats in the fence so it would wiggle in the wind, look real and give it character. It was really amazing to watch. He weathered it even more, when Brody and Hendricks find Chrissie's remains on the beach. I was impressed by his attention to detail."

THE BOY ON THE RAFT

When a child — Alex Kintner — takes his inflatable mattress into the water, we see Tippit the dog disappear into the surf and the boy follows, as the shark grabs Kintner and goes into a death roll. Kintner's attack is actually accurate with real-life shark attacks on surfers. The shark mistakes them for seals, with their shape and rhythmic kicking. Reportedly, having a dog in the water also increases your odds of a shark attack, due to the added vibrations.

Because the Kintner boy is attacked in front of Brody (after he let the beaches remain open), Brody's guilt, shame and horror are conveyed by what Bill Butler calls "A reverse 'Hitchcock shot' on Roy Scheider where we're dollying out and zooming in at the same time!" Ironically, this is now called the "*JAWS* shot" in film school.

Joe Alves recalls that, "I directed [the inserts] from that sequence where the shark comes up and takes the little kid on the raft. Steven shot the sequence and there were a few shots he hadn't gotten that he asked me to get. He gave me very specific instructions. One was a shot of the shark coming up under the kid and another of the shark breaking the water's surface back-lit by the sun."

While the scene is perfect, Alves remembers "One shot that we never got, but I wanted to, was [where you could see] the kid on the raft with this huge shark coming up under him." (That idea was later used for the poster of the *JAWS* rip-off, *Great White*.)

"That rollover when the shark grabs the kid worked perfectly," says mechanical FX man Kevin Pike. "Roy Arbogast and I built that shark tail, and it worked fine. Where you see the shark's fins as it rolls over after grabbing the kid? The rest of the shark had all kinds of problems all the time, but that shark gag worked perfectly!"

"He's right," agrees Jeffrey Voorhes, who played the unfortunate Alex Kintner. "Those fins worked great every time. The shark was nowhere near me in my scene, just this machine that blew blood up in the air. When the shark grabs me, they had those fins that would do the rollover. It was the left side of the shark; the other side was all mechanical machine parts that made the shark work."

Spielberg worried he made the scene too intense and bloody. In his book *Easy Riders, Raging Bulls*, Peter Biskind writes that Steven Spielberg stood in the back of the theater, during *JAWS'* first test screening in Dallas, Texas. When Alex Kintner is attacked, "A man in the front row got up to leave and broke into a run. Alarmed, Spielberg thought to himself, 'He must really hate it!' The man reached the lobby and threw up all over the carpet, went to the bathroom and returned to his seat.

'That's when I knew we had a hit.'"

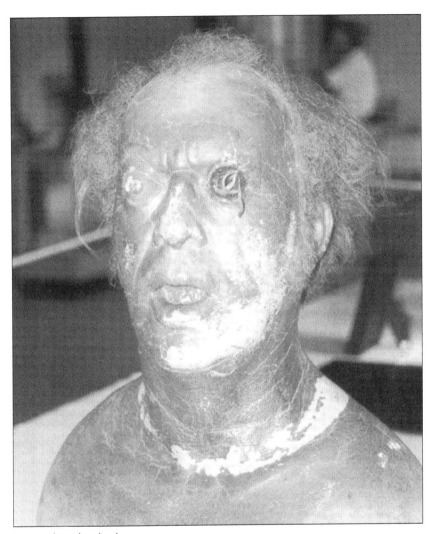

Ben Gardner's head today. PHOTO BY PATRICK JANKIEWICZ.

THE HEAD

In a pivotal scene, Brody and Hooper find fisherman Ben Gardner's abandoned boat while searching for their shark. Hooper dives underneath, only to come face to face with Gardner's severed head. It was a moment that never failed to scare the hell out of audiences.

"Ben Gardner's head bobbing out of the bottom of the boat gets one of the biggest screams of modern movies," Carl Gottlieb says proudly.

"When *JAWS* came out, it was not an A-picture — it was considered a big B-movie," Gottlieb explains. "Here in Hollywood, we were in a theater east of Vine, not in one of the big theaters, but a B-movie theater called The World.

My friend was manager of the World and I knew what the showtimes were, so I would go there just to see the audience jump [at that one particular scene].

"The theater sold out every night. If the show was at 8:00, at 8:42 you knew that the head would appear," Gottlieb grins. "At 8:40, I would get to the theater, stand in the back, and watch 3,000 heads go whoosh when Ben Gardner popped out! The theater physically moved, I'd get my little rush and go home.

"It was great fun to watch a picture physically affect an audience like that. You rarely see a whole audience physically react the same way at the same moment. You know you got 'em when they do that."

To achieve the maximum impact, Steven Spielberg re-shot the scene to perfection.

"The 'head scene' existed, but the original filming of it was not to Steven's satisfaction," Gottlieb said. "He struggled and struggled to improve the scene with editing, and finally, he said 'We gotta re-shoot this.'

"They told him 'You can't do it, the budget's gone, there's no money left, the picture's shot, you're editing now!' He said 'I have to re-shoot it somehow. We have the head, we have the boat — the props are still up at the Universal backlot in storage.'

"The picture was being edited. Verna Fields was cutting it at her house in Van Nuys. She had a little backyard swimming pool about the size of this room (6 x 6 feet), so Steven said, 'We'll re-shoot it in Verna's pool!' He got the boat with the broken hole in it (For the head to come out of), they got the head, and they borrowed the cameras. Steven said 'I'll pay for this myself. We need this shot so badly, I will pay for this myself!' Everybody did it on the cheap.

"Five or six guys and (production designer) Joe Alves turned out, somebody got an underwater camera, they stole a couple lights from Universal, and got black plastic to tarp over the pool. They put the boat and head in, threw a couple quarts of milk in to make the water look milky and textured, so it would catch the light correctly. The scene was shot in Verna Fields' swimming pool, cut into the film — and the biggest shock in *JAWS* was done six months after principal photography!"

JAWS' cinematographer Bill Butler remembers watching the scene in a movie house "and seeing everybody at that moment back up in their seats! That's a pretty impressive feat. Spielberg was able to pull that kind of effect off because of his sense of timing, his sense of holding back." The cinematographer recalls Spielberg constantly re-tooled JAWS so that it would have the maximum impact.

"After the film was finished, scenes were shot over and over to make them work," Butler states. "When the fisherman's head fell out of the bottom of the boat, his timing was just perfect — the right moment. It was someone looking for something, and just when you think he hasn't found it, the head falls out.

"To get that timing just right when the head floated out was very important — we shot it four times. I didn't shoot all of them, someone else shot part of them."

The 'head scene' was originally shot in the tank at MGM, where all of Hooper's scenes in the cage were done.

"The stuff on the surface on the boat at night (With Brody and Hooper) was done on the backlot at Universal, in the Sgt. Bilko Lake," Bill Butler says. "When we shot it originally, it was done in broad daylight and Carl Gottlieb's character, the newspaper editor, came along with them."

Martha's Vineyard resident Craig Kingsbury played the crusty Ben Gardner. Kristen Kingsbury Henshaw, the late Craig's daughter, remembers "Dad always

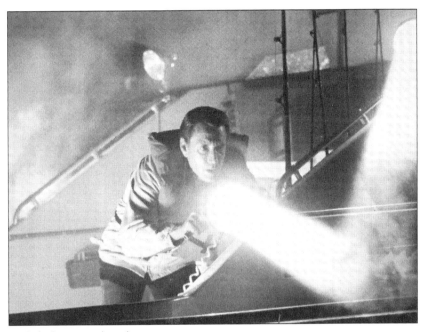

Brody finds Ben Gardner's boat.

got a kick out of people screaming when his head popped out of the boat. He always said, 'That doesn't make sense — if the shark ate me, why would he spit my head back in the boat?!'"

What happened to Ben Gardner's chewed-up head after the film is an adventure in itself.

"The head actually sat in Steven Spielberg's office for the longest time and then he eventually gave it to Universal," explains *JAWS* historian Chris Kiszka. "Universal then put it on display in Florida, in conjunction with the new JAWS ride. Somebody had this great idea that nobody wanted to see it anymore, so they took it off the display and put it back in the archives somewhere.

"Universal Studios would put on a 'haunted house' exhibit every October, as part of their Halloween Horror Nights and some genius got the great idea to take the head and nail it to the wall as a severed head," Kiszka states. "Michael Roddy, who worked for Universal, saw it and said 'Hey, don't you people know what this is? This is Ben Gardner's head from *JAWS!* You aren't gonna nail this to the wall!' They gave it to him and that's how we obtained it."

THE ESTUARY VICTIM

Stuntman Teddy Grossman's death scene in the pond is easily the film's most gruesome. It was so gruesome, in fact, it was shot twice. As several beachgoers and Chief Brody's young son Michael look on in horror, Grossman — in the

Teddy Grossman gets eaten the first time, with Mike Brody (Chris Rebello, left).

role of the Boy Scouts' swimming instructor — is knocked out of his rowboat and eaten by the shark.

Sunbathers watch the massive fish chew him up in the shallow water. His severed leg, still wearing a sneaker, sinks gently to the sandy sea bottom. Ironically, as the shark approaches Grossman in the pond, we see that he's barefoot. When his severed leg appears, it's wearing a sneaker.

In the first take on the scene, the shark is eating Grossman, when it makes a go for Michael Brody. The dying Grossman pushes Michael out of the way as the shark takes him out to sea. Grossman recalls that during his death scene, "When the shark was chewing me up, his teeth were rubber, but they used hard plastic for other shots. I think one of the teeth actually cut me during one take!

"They re-shot the scene where I was eaten. Originally, he [the shark] is chomping on me and there's blood everywhere — in the first version we did, it was really bloody. It would have definitely gotten the film an 'R' rating!" His recollections are confirmed by existing stills that show him clutching young Mike Brody while being eaten (an action not in the finished film) and the shark gnawing him from behind while he vomits up blood (Also not shown). That shot was only seen in Gottlieb's book. In the final version, Grossman is rowing over to help the boys with their sailboat, when the shark attacks him.

Carl Gottlieb feels that "Teddy kind of hammed it up with all his scream-ing — I don't know why they used the version they used! When blood was coming out of his mouth, that's where he was really overacting, thrashing around

Grossman gets devoured again!

and screaming. God bless him, Teddy's a great guy, but he's a stuntman, not an actor!"

The attack on the pond victim is the most explicit gore in the film, particu-larly when his severed leg drops to the bottom.

"I think they had to edit that to get a PG rating," Gottlieb recalls. "There were several different leg drops filmed to get a PG rating. I do know the big argument was over how much blood and gore they could have. There was a lot of debate over that; 'Could you show the leg dropping or could you dwell on it? Could you just have it pass through the frame? Could you see the stumpy part, with the bone and ligament showing?' ... You would negotiate for how many frames of meat, how many frames of the foot we could show, but it was very effective.

"The scene makes Brody's vendetta against the shark personal. That was all Steven's doing. [He said] 'If we're gonna care for this guy, we gotta put his family in jeopardy and give him a personal reason to go after the shark.' Dramatically, it made much more sense to have his family involved. Mike, Brody's oldest kid is in jeopardy and his younger son, Sean, a little kid, is sitting there traumatized by seeing his brother almost eaten.

"There's that great moment where they drag Brody's kid out of the water and you're not sure whose leg you saw drop, and then the kid is pulled out and there's a close-up: you see two feet and think 'Thank God, it's not Brody's kid who was eaten, just some stranger.'"

Gottlieb likes how the scene toys with audience expectations.

"When the beach is reopened, there're a lot of precautions, there's a false moment where you think it's the shark, but it's the two kids with a phony fin. Then the real shark cruises into the pond and you realize there *is* going to be a death. Brody hears the cry 'Shark' and gets there just in time to see his kid in jeopardy as somebody else is killed and eaten. You'll notice he doesn't go into the water and somebody [else] pulls the kid to safety."

QUINT'S DEMISE

When Quint, the only man in the film who truly believes he can kill the shark, is actually eaten, *JAWS* sets up its chilling no-holds-barred climax. Bill Butler reveals shooting the scene also frightened the crew.

246e QUINT SLIDES INTO SHARK—
STABS AT SHARK'S HEAD

"When the shark took what was supposed to be Robert Shaw underwater, it was a stuntman, who also happened to be named Butler, but was no relation. [His full name was Dick Butler.] Dick looked so good as Shaw, we could shoot him rather close. The shark took this guy underwater and he stayed under ... and under ... and under ... He scared us all to death!" Bill Butler laughs. "Stunt guys love to do this! He did it as a joke, but it really scared us. We all thought he drowned!"

246f QUINT IN RAGE

Arbogast explains how they created Quint's horrifying finish.

"When it ate Robert Shaw, that was a lot of work. We had

246g SHARK GRABS QUINT

Alves' storyboards for Quint's big finish.

blood tubes running down the shark's teeth and a rubber section of Quint's chest so you could see the actual biting of the shark into him."

"I was there for when the shark ate Robert Shaw," Pike adds. "It all went well. I remember watching and thinking how exciting it was. I remember the knife

"The thing about a shark, he's got lifeless eyes, like a doll's eyes, until he bites ya — "

being stuck in the side of the boat for him to grab, and Shaw climbing into the shark's mouth before they brought in the stuntman. I cut the glass for the window when the shark crashes through it to go after Brody, and the shark worked perfectly for that and when he ate Quint!"

Brody and Quint.

THE *INDIANAPOLIS* SPEECH

Certainly one of the film's most indelible moments comes during Brody, Hooper and Quint's hunt for the shark. Alone at sea, the three men bond: drink, joke and compare scars, until Quint stuns them into silence by recounting his experience after his ship, the *U.S.S. Indianapolis*, sank during the final year of World War II...

> "Japanese submarine slammed two torpedoes into our side, Chief. We was comin' back from the island of Tinian to Leyte... just delivered the bomb. The Hiroshima bomb. Eleven hundred men went into the water. Vessel went down in twelve minutes. Didn't see the first shark for about a half an hour. Tiger. Thirteen-footer. You know how you know that when you're in the water, Chief? You tell by looking from the dorsal to the tail. What we didn't know, was our bomb mission had been so secret, no distress signal had been sent. They didn't even list us overdue for a week. Very first light,

Chief, sharks come cruisin', so we formed ourselves into tight groups.

"You know, it was kinda like old squares in the battle like you see in the calendar named 'The Battle of Waterloo' and the idea was: shark comes to the nearest man, that man, he starts poundin' and hollerin' and screamin' and sometimes the shark go away... but sometimes he wouldn't go away. Sometimes that shark, he looks right into ya. Right into your eyes. And, you know, the thing about a shark... he's got lifeless eyes. Black eyes. Like a doll's eyes. When he comes at ya, doesn't seem to be living ... until he bites ya, and those black eyes roll over white and then ... ah then, you hear that terrible, high-pitched screamin'. The ocean turns red, and despite all the poundin' and the hollerin', they all come in and they ... rip you to pieces.

"You know by the end of that first dawn, lost a hundred men. I don't know how many sharks, maybe a thousand. I don't know how many men, they averaged six an hour. On Thursday morning, Chief, I bumped into a friend of mine, Herbie Robinson from Cleveland. Baseball player. Boatswain's mate. I thought he was asleep. I reached over to wake him up. Bobbed up, down in the water just like a kinda top. Upended. Well, he'd been bitten in half below the waist.

"Noon, the fifth day, Mr. Hooper, a Lockheed Ventura saw us. He swung in low and he saw us ... He was a young pilot, a lot younger than Mr. Hooper here. Anyway, he saw us and he come in low and three hours later a big fat PBY cruiser comes down and starts to pick us up. You know that was the time I was most frightened ... waitin' for my turn. I'll never put on a lifejacket again. So, eleven hundred men went into the water; 316 men come out and the sharks took the rest, June the 29th, 1945. Anyway, we delivered the bomb."

This moment defines Quint's character. The retelling of this true-life account was so suspenseful that no one seems to have noticed that he got the date wrong: the *U.S.S. Indianapolis* sank on *July* 30th, 1945.

It also ties in with the obsession Steven Spielberg has with World War II (in which his father served), and his early work has constant references to World War II, like JAWS and the returned airmen in *Close Encounters of the Third Kind*. Spielberg noted in several interviews that he called his screenwriter friend and military buff, John Milius, for his expertise on the subject.

Milius, who directed *Conan the Barbarian* and *Farewell to the King*, was also an ace Hollywood scripter, who wrote *Apocalypse Now* and came up with the line "Do you feel lucky, Punk?" for *Dirty Harry*. Milius would also make contributions to his friends' films when they asked him to. It was Milius who reportedly suggested the Normandy graveyard sequences that bookend Spielberg's *Saving*

Private Ryan. And perhaps most significantly (at least to this writer), he is credited with relating with Quint's tragic maritime experience.

"The *Indianapolis* Speech," as the scene came to be known, is also cited as *JAWS*' most chilling scene. With no mechanical shark or visual effect to rely on, it terrifies you simply by showing a man telling a story.

This sets up the climax, and allows us to care for the otherwise terse Quint. The tough sailor's voice rises in horror, as he gets lost in the memory: "I don't know how many sharks, maybe a thousand," he mutters. "I don't know how many men. They averaged six an hour."

It makes the shark even more frightening as we see it in our imagination, and it's far more frightening than any FX-built monster. Quint seems to predict his own demise, with the line that a Great White Shark "doesn't seem to be livin'" until he bites you and those black eyes roll over white." Quint revealing that it "was the time I was most frightened… waitin' for my turn."

You suddenly realize that Quint's turn has finally come — thirty years later.

Carl Gottlieb has strong feelings about the scene. "There's a misrepresentation of the truth that John Milius wrote the *Indianapolis* speech," he states. "The substance of my argument is, I was there and I tell you I did not write that speech — *Robert Shaw* wrote it. Who do you believe, a guy who was there and tells you that somebody else wrote it or a guy who wasn't there and tells you he wrote it?"

"Milius contributed some ideas to that scene and a line of dialogue that was used elsewhere in the movie. Shaw says, "I'll find him for five, but I'll kill him for ten" — that's a Milius line. In anticipation of an arbitration for screen credit, I saved all my notes from that movie and I wrote the book, *The JAWS Log*. I didn't mention the Shaw episode in the book, but I really think I should have."

The story went untold until Milius was quoted in an *American Film* article called, "Great Speeches at the Last Minute," on how he wrote the *Indianapolis* scene. Quint's "*Indianapolis* Speech" went through several different writers: Howard Sackler, Milius and Gottlieb. The rest of the scene was clearly written by Gottlieb, as the tone of uneasy humor is consistent with the rest of his work on the film.

The *U.S.S. Indianapolis*/shark story first surfaced in a draft by Howard Sackler, the writer on *JAWS* between Benchley and Gottlieb. As Sackler was a playwright (*The Great White Hope*), one can see why Quint's speech is such a great theatrical moment.

As Gottlieb notes, "Howard Sackler, now deceased, was a diver and amateur sailor whose research discovered the *U.S.S. Indianapolis* incident and introduced it into a version of the script that preceded my involvement on the project."

Milius' presence can be felt, with his keen sense of military history and terse writing style. Gottlieb says the sequence where the three men compare scars "was also a Milius' suggestion. I don't mind giving him credit for that — he said it was kind of a macho thing to compare scars and Steven said, 'Can you do something with that?'

"I said, 'I think I can' and wrote the scene. I credit Milius with the idea.

"I'm sure he [Milius] honestly thinks he wrote [the entire scene]," Gottlieb says. "I know what happened … Steven called a lot of his friends; Milius and (*Taxi Driver* writer) Paul Schrader, because we were getting into a difficult scene: the scene on the boat where the men talk. It was a scene we always referred to as 'Just before the battle, Mother', because it was like one of those scenes in a war movie, where the guys are writing home before the big battle. It's in every war movie, the scene where the guys are writing home and swinging in their hammocks, talking about the terrible battle they face the next day. It's a classic moment in action movies and that's how the scene was conceptualized.

"There were going to be a lot of problems, so Steven called everyone he knew for suggestions, help or dialogue. John Milius was consulted and Steven conversed with him at length. I took notes, used what I could and discarded the rest. What happened after that was Robert Shaw, a gifted actor, and what most people didn't know about Shaw, was that he was a gifted writer — he wrote many novels. One called *The Hiding Place* became a *Playhouse 90* and he wrote the play, *The Man in the Glass Booth*, which was a successful film.

"Robert took all of this stuff that everyone had done — the research, Howard Sackler's dialogue and all this material — mulled it over to figure what would fit in his mouth as an actor, and came up with that speech. That was a great moment," Gottlieb fondly recalls.

During filming, "Steven and I shared a house in Martha's Vineyard and one night while we were talking about that scene, Shaw came over to the house after dinner. It was me, Steven, Zanuck, Brown, Richard Dreyfuss, Verna Fields and Ric Fields — Verna's son — who was an apprentice on the picture, [and is] now an editor himself.

"Over dessert and brandy, Shaw comes over and says, 'I had a go at that speech.' The housekeeper dimmed the lights, from dinner to conversational, and Shaw read the speech as you hear it in the film — he basically performed it for us. Everybody said, 'That's it, shoot it!'

"When we shot that scene a week or so later, that's what he did."

In an interview with *IGN Filmforce*, John Milius said, "There was no speech (before Milius wrote it for the scene). There was no reason why this guy hated sharks. They needed a reason why he hated sharks. I think they called me about a week earlier. It was Steven's idea, but I think he and Rick Dreyfuss were trying to figure this out. Why does this guy hate sharks? I don't think Rick Dreyfuss wanted me to write a really good speech for the other guy [Shaw], but they called me and said 'Could you do this?'

"At the time," Milius continued, "I thought of two battles during W.W. II. One was sharks, one was his incident during the Guadalcanal campaign, [but] that was too complicated. This one seemed ideal; the ship was torpedoed, it was a wonderful, ideal situation, because these guys were left in the water for days [with] sharks eating them."

Milius told IGN: "You've got to give credit [to] Robert Shaw, because he was given that script — I wrote that thing and they gave it to him [when] he was drunk. Could barely walk, he was really drunk. They had the script, I was writing that script until nine in the morning, I called in, that was their time and I was writing it over the phone. They went out that afternoon and shot it. They gave it to him, 'Read this script'. Steven tells the story really well.

"Robert Shaw had just been caught fucking the nanny, and he's sitting there, he's really drunk, and they're trying to get him on the boat," Milius recalled. "[He] falls half off, and they're really 'How are we going to do this?' He's sleeping … Reading the script and sleeping. They finally get him to start rehearsing it, and he hated Rick Dreyfuss.

"He sort of makes a swat at him … and he starts saying, 'You ever see a shark's eye? It rolls up, it's a dead eye. Like your wife, when she tells you about the nanny.' And he's talking about, 'What happens when you get put in the water all alone, after fucking the nanny.' … He gets them so strung out about his own personal life, and he's convinced that he's never going to do the scene, then, when they turned on the cameras, he was perfect."

Reportedly, Spielberg just let the camera roll during Shaw's incredibly personal monologue, not wanting to intrude on the actor's pain. The next morning, a deeply embarrassed Shaw reportedly apologized to the director and did the scene perfectly.

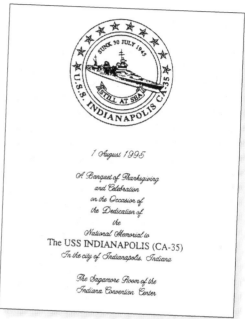

USS Indianapolis' annual get-together, 50th anniversary. August 1, 1995.

In the *JAWS* documentary *The Shark is Still Working*, Peter Benchley revealed that his maid quit after the movie came out, because her father died in the *Indianapolis* incident. Film critic Pauline Kael felt the speech was so effective, she worried it would upset *Indianapolis* survivors and their families. According to Gottlieb, it had the opposite effect.

"In 1975, while I was promoting my book, *The Jaws Log*, I did a radio phone-in talk show in Ohio. One of the callers was a survivor of the *U.S.S. Indianapolis* who told me he enjoyed the movie, as did many of his fellow survivors, who still meet yearly for a dinner and dance."

MOTHER CUTTER

Verna Fields had previously edited such films as *Paper Moon* and *American Graffiti*. She also edited Steven Spielberg's first film, *The Sugarland Express*. When she edited and did second unit direction on *JAWS*, her work helped give the film its incredible pacing and impact. So beloved was she by the crew that Fields was given the nickname "Mother Cutter."

"Verna was a great person," Roy Arbogast recalls. "She would come to the shop and say, 'Roy, come to the editing room and let me show you what we need. Don't worry about the whole shark — if we can just get his tail to do this one little thing, we got it!' She was a good liaison between myself, Bob Mattey and the company.

"Everybody loved 'Mother Cutter,'" he continues. "She was a very bright lady, a kind person, but also very ballsy and sharp — she was the first woman I ever worked for and she was wonderful!"

Verna Fields, like John Williams, won an Academy Award for her contribution to *JAWS*. But incredible as it may seem, Steven Spielberg would not even receive a nomination.

THE OPENING

In the 1970s, summer was not the tentpole launching, billion-dollar gladiatorial match between major studios that it is today. It was instead the dumping ground for low-budget horror and teen sex comedies. Because of its beach setting, the studio decided to release *JAWS* on June 20th and spent $700,000 to advertise the movie on TV.

Three nights before *JAWS* opened, Universal cleverly had thirty-second spots running for the film on all three channels of network television. The ads were scary and effective, with character actor Percy Rodriguez as the narrator of the original trailer, dramatically announcing: "It's as if God created the Devil and gave him ... JAWS! See it before you go swimming."

Initially, *JAWS* could be seen on 409 theater screens. While it was originally slated for a wider opening, Universal CEO Lew Wasserman suggested it start smaller, so people would have to seek it out and build word of mouth. The studio then "went wide" with it on June 25th, to 675 screens. Today, big studio product routinely opens on anywhere from 3,500 to 4,000 screens.

JAWS made an unprecedented $7,061,513 million opening weekend on 409 screens — with an amazing per screen average of $17, 265.00 gross. The next weekend (when it went wide), it made $6,150,000.00. *JAWS* was the first movie to break the $100 million dollar mark, a figure studios had no idea could be attainable with a single film. It had a final gross of $260,000,000.

George Lucas' prophecy had been fulfilled.

JAWS easily swept past previous hits such as *The Godfather* and *The Exorcist* (both of which were also based on best-selling books) and made more money than all of Richard Zanuck's father's films combined (His father was Darryl F. Zanuck, the head of 20th Century-Fox).

"*JAWS* changed the business forever," Peter Biskind writes in *Easy Riders, Raging Bulls*. "As studios discovered the value of wide (releases) and massive TV advertising, costs mounted and the willingness to take risks diminished proportionally … *JAWS* whetted corporate appetites for big profits quickly."

JAWS' reign as the highest-grossing film lasted until *Star Wars* opened two years later. When that occurred, Spielberg took out full-page ads congratulating Lucas. The celebratory ad showed R2D2 fishing for the shark.

JAWS gets the credit (or the blame) for giving birth to the high-concept summer blockbuster, with plots that can be summed up in one line. These 'tentpole movies' — big summer genre films whose profits can hold up the whole studio slate — are the final result of the blockbuster. Many fail to notice that *JAWS* is a much more creative and entertaining film than the mindless movies it allegedly inspired.

THE CRITICS

When *JAWS* opened, many critics failed to see it as the groundbreaking film it is. To show how misguided they were, it was often lumped in with disaster movies like *The Poseidon Adventure* and *The Towering Inferno*. Some critics questioned Spielberg's talent; some resented him for being so young and gifted; others resented *the film* for being so successful; and still others predicted that Spielberg's career had peaked. This last point apparently irritated the young director so much that he began referring to *JAWS* (if he referred to it at all) as "That shark movie."

Of those who didn't care for *JAWS*, Stephen Farber of *Film Comment* was the most vitriolic. Calling Spielberg's "direction of the mechanical shark competent, his direction of the actors cretinous," Farber derided *JAWS* as a "shabby piece of factory-constructed Grand Guignol" and claimed "Making an audience jump on cue is the easiest trick for a schlock director."

Stanley Kauffman of *New Republic* smugly declared that it was dull and apparently concurred with Farber: "There's no great trick to frightening a person."

Vincent Canby of *The New York Times* announced he was too old and his opinions no longer mattered by snidely commenting: "It's a measure of how the film operates that not once do we feel particular sympathy for any of the shark's victims. In the best films, characters are revealed in terms of action. In movies like *JAWS*, characters are simply functions of the action. They're at its service. Characters are like stage hands who move props around and deliver information when it's necessary."

Charles Champlin of *The Los Angeles Times* made himself culturally irrelevant when he complained that "*JAWS* is too gruesome for children and is likely to turn the stomach … It is a coarse grained and exploitive work which depends on the excess for its impact. Ashore it is a bore, awkwardly staged and lumpily written."

Happily, these reviewers were in the minority. Stephen Farber should pay strict attention to the last line of his own review: "Once *JAWS*-mania dies down, the critics are going to be very embarrassed by their reviews."

At least one of them will, eh, Mr. Farber?

Hipper critics recognized it as an instant classic. Judith Crist of *New York* magazine found *JAWS* "an exhilarating adventure." Pauline Kael, who compared Spielberg to Orson Welles in her review of *Sugarland Express*, called it "the most cheerfully perverse scare movie ever made … [with] more zest than an early Woody Allen picture." Arthur Cooper of *Newsweek* correctly felt it was "Destined to become a classic" and Arthur Knight of *The Hollywood Reporter* found it "Gripping and terrifying." Rex Reed compared it favorably to *The Exorcist. Variety* critic A.D. Murphy hailed Spielberg's directing, while noting that Robert Shaw's Quint was "absolutely magnificent." Even the National Council of Churches came out for the film, praising its "Unrelenting pace" while carefully noting that "it is clean horror"! And *Time* declared that the opening attack was the "Hitchcock technique in a context that the master has never explored" and praised Spielberg for the way "he twists our guts with false alarms …

"Spielberg," the perceptive critic went on to say, "is confident not only of his material but also of the virtues of simple, straightforward moviemaking."

SPIELBERG ACOLYTES

JAWS was a great influence on many impressionable young filmgoers. Director Bryan Singer (*The Usual Suspects, Superman Returns* and *X-Men*) named his production company "Bad Hat Harry" after a line Brody says to an old man on the beach ("That's some bad hat, Harry!"). Singer grew up in the same Princeton neighborhood as Peter Benchley, and selected his company title by trying to find the most obscure line from the film.

"I truly love *JAWS*," Singer confesses. Horror producer Peter Block named his company A Bigger Boat, after Brody's famous line. "I wish one of those guys called their company 'What's wrong with my printing,'" jokes Jeffrey Kramer, using his Deputy's most famous quote.

Screenwriter Daniel Waters *(Heathers* and *Batman Returns)* admits, "I wanted to write for the movies after I saw *JAWS*. It's not the most esoteric movie in the world; I wish I could say *La Dolce Vita* made me become a screenwriter, but it was really *JAWS*. I always liked to write, but that made me want to write for film."

JAWS fan/screenwriter Daniel Waters. PHOTO BY PATRICK JANKIEWICZ.

Oscar-winning director Steven Soderbergh (*Erin Brockovich*) calls *JAWS* his favorite film. Another Academy Award-winning director, Peter Jackson (*Lord of the Rings*), also cites *JAWS* as one of his all-time favorites. And Roger Corman protégé Adam Simon (*Carnosaur*) admires the film's directorial technique: "Spielberg was truly a prodigy. I don't think someone like that comes along more than once in a generation, someone who was born to do it. The rest of us still have to struggle to learn how to use this complicated piece of machinery, which is the process of making a movie. It's astonishing when you look at the early Spielberg films, to see that he already knew it."

JAWS-MANIA

When *JAWS* opened, the public went crazy. There were also lines around the block nationwide at movie theatres and shark sightings off oceans, rivers and lakes. *JAWS*, and its scary star, had truly invaded the public consciousness. As *Newsweek* noted, the film "offered an excursion in the ancient and simpler pleasures of being scared witless." In a cover story, *Time* boldly declared 1975 as "The Summer of the Shark."

The competition for *JAWS* looked truly formidable: *The French Connection II*, *Breakout* (a prison break picture with Charles Bronson), *Rollerball* (a futuristic

Spider-Man and Superman battle sharks! SPIDEY SUPER STORIES @1976 MARVEL COMICS. ACTION COMICS @1975 DC COMICS.

gladiator movie with James Caan), *Night Moves* (a romantic thriller with Gene Hackman and Melanie Griffith), Roger Corman's *Death Race 2000* and *The Wind and the Lion* (starring Sean Connery). Despite the star power and high budgets connected to those films, *JAWS* swallowed them all.

In the summer of 1975, swimming in the ocean was done only by the brave. Universal's hit was guaranteed mentions on the news for the long lines outside the theaters and at the beach, if so much as a fin was seen by a swimmer. Richard Zanuck said that was the plan: "There is no way that a bather who has seen or heard of the movie won't think of a Great White Shark when he puts his toe in the ocean."

Merchandising tie-ins flooded the market. There were *JAWS* puzzles, *JAWS* necklaces, *JAWS* toys (The most popular toy gave players a gaffe stick, to remove such items as cameras, lanterns and tires out of a big plastic shark's stomach; the winner would remove the most items before the shark's mouth would snap shut!), rubber *JAWS* sharks, *JAWS* Slurpee cups, *JAWS* T-shirts, *JAWS* records, and, of course, *JAWS* beach towels.

The film was satirized, parodied and spoofed in every way possible. There was a *MAD Magazine* version, while NBC-TV's *Saturday Night Live* introduced "Land Shark" — a great white shark (played by Chevy Chase) that went door to door seeking potential victims. The same sketch had John Belushi doing a perfect parody of Richard Dreyfuss in the film. On *The Carol Burnett Show*, Harvey Korman took his turn as Quint (Instead of strapping himself into a chair, he ties himself onto a toilet seat!)

Ghost Rider fights a shark "in the gripping tradition of *JAWS!*" GHOST RIDER @1975 MARVEL COMICS.

Colt .45 did a commercial spoof with a man casually drinking on a table floating in the middle of the ocean, as a shark keeps attacking. Bob Hope joked he was too scared to bathe because "My rubber duck keeps circling me" and *JAWS* became a punchline on numerous TV comedies. (Example: Rerun, a fat character on the ABC-TV sitcom, *What's Happening?*, claims he was in the movie *JAWS*: "I was the main meal!")

To show the film's impact on pop culture, comic book superheroes were now pitted against sharks, instead of their usual opponents of robots, aliens and human villains. Superman, Batman, Spider-Man and Ghost Rider were all now duking it out with toothy terrors in, the breathless covers promised us, the gripping tradition of *JAWS!*"

Comedian Dickie Goodman released a lame comedy record called "Mr. Jaws." *JAWS* was also mentioned in the classic Queen song "Bicycle race": "You say 'shark' and I say 'Hey, man/ *JAWS* was never my scene and I don't like *Star Wars!*"

Even the death of Tippit the dog (who's chomped off-camera, just before the shark takes the kid on the raft) is referenced in The Surf Punks' song "Shark Attack": "Hey, Mister, where's my pup?/I threw a stick in the water and he didn't come up!"

JAWS attacks the Universal Studios Tour. PHOTO BY PATRICK JANKIEWICZ.

In 1976, due to the film's enormous popularity, Universal opened the *JAWS* ride on their Hollywood backlot, complete with a giant *animatronic* shark. As the tram rounds a corner, passing a "Welcome to Amity" billboard, John Williams' "Promenade (Tourists on the Menu)" score can be heard. The tour guide points out a fisherman in a rowboat ("Wave Hi to Ed, everybody!"), and "Ed" is immediately attacked by the unseen shark in a pool of blood, A dorsal fin zooms through the water as the shark charges the tram to Williams' *JAWS* theme.

It should be noted that while a Spielberg movie becoming a theme park attraction is commonplace today (Disney's *Indiana Jones Adventure,* Universal's *E.T. Adventure, Jurassic Park: The Ride* and *Back to the Future), JAWS* was the first.

The snapping jaws of the mechanical shark are directly facing the tourists, a perfect photo opportunity for anyone seated on the right side of the tram.

Recently, the Universal Hollywood tram ride added the shark knocking over a gas tank to add a bit more *Strum und Drang* to the 32-year-old ride. In the 1990s, Universal Studios Florida opened an elaborate *JAWS* water ride, complete with a boat chase and the New England Fishing Village of Amity surrounding it. This Amity sells a variety of JAWS tchotchkes, like toys, key chains and T-shirts.

While the earliest sharks on the ride bore little resemblance to the fish from the film (The very first shark had big fake teeth that looked like giant carrots), the current models actually do resemble the shark from the film. The Florida *JAWS* shark is three tons, 32-feet long and made of fiberglass and steel, with urethane teeth and latex skin.

JAWS: THE SITCOM

Television writers were quick to cash in on the *JAWS* phenomenon. The first TV movie rip-off was 1976's *Shark Kill*. Written by Sandor Stern, it had two seamen (Richard Yniguez and Phillip Clark) hunting a great white shark. The rubber shark looked more cute than scary. They blow it up with a flare gun and have enough time to win a parking lot brawl before the closing credits.

Even Universal got into the act and ripped itself off, using *JAWS* and sharks on such shows as *The Six Million Dollar Man* and *The Bionic Woman* (with Lindsay Wagner's stuntwoman wrestling a very docile shark), *The Misadventures of Sheriff Lobo* (with poor Claude Akins splashing around like a fool in the *JAWS* pond from the Universal tour) and The Hardy Boys (which had Shaun Cassidy in the same overexposed pond).

Bruce the shark also made cameos in such pathetic outings as *The Nude Bomb* and *The Harlem Globetrotters on Gilligan's Island* (where the once-great shark is thwarted by a mouthful of basketballs!). Saturday Morning cartoons quickly introduced *Jabberjaw,* a singing great white shark who talked like The Three Stooges' Curly Howard and 'Mr. Jaws,' a shark in a top hat voiced by Artie Johnson from TV's *Rowan and Martin's Laugh-In*. Every show, it seems, did ridiculous *JAWS*- related episodes.

The *JAWS* pond can currently be seen on the TV Land reruns every week. It became "Cabot Cove" in the opening credits of the CBS show *Murder, She Wrote*, starring Angela Lansbury as mystery writer Jessica Fletcher. Ironically, next to Ms. Fletcher's happy little home sits a large mechanical shark — just out of camera range. Every indication that it's "Amity Island" on Universal's backlot has been carefully hidden. The boat in the show's opening is a mock-up of the *Orca*, but its name is hidden by a 'Cabot Cove' life preserver.

JAWS AND POLITICS

Perhaps even more significant than commercial and television tie-ins was how *JAWS* impacted the political scene of the 1970s. Politicians and political cartoonists interpreted the film in many unique ways. Pundits saw the omnivorous shark as a symbol for many different causes including Communism, United States' intervention policy, the economy, even the Women's Movement.

One cartoon parodying the *JAWS* poster, showed Gloria Steinem as Chrissie, swimming down to bite the shark! There were so many political cartoons using *JAWS*, Universal ran a full-page newspaper ad of them instead of the usual poster.

Cuban leader Fidel Castro saw the film as an indictment of capitalism and *Washington Post* columnist George Will wondered why, in a land where "Congress is regularly on view, people pay to see this movie about a small-brained beast that is all muscle and appetite." Some feminists complained about how phallic the ad was (The shark's conical head rising underneath a naked woman).

As *JAWS* was made during difficult financial times and set in a financially strapped town, many could relate to the characters' anxiety. The shark could be seen as a symbol of the recession — an angle that appealed to screenwriter Carl Gottlieb: "The town is being consumed from without and consumed from within. When they take a stand and do something, they survive. When they try to surrender to the circumstances and pander to public tastes, they're in trouble, which is not a bad message."

This message was best exemplified by the May 29, 1978 cover of *Newsweek*, a take-off on the *JAWS 2* poster. The large shark head looms over a victim, but instead of a curvaceous water skier, it's about to devour a poor family on a dingy raft. Above the shark's head is one word: INFLATION.

JAWS: THE TV EDITION

When *JAWS* came to television in November, 1979, it was a slightly different version than the one audiences had seen in theaters. Some scenes, such as the attack on the little boy, had been trimmed down to TV standards and Quint's dialogue had also been hilariously re-dubbed to be as inoffensive as possible.

The television version cuts the Kintner boy's close-up as the shark kills him, the shot of the man's leg sinking to the bottom of the pond and Quint vomiting blood as the shark bites into his stomach were also excised. Besides these expected cuts, viewers saw *new* footage. The network premiere utilized scenes that had been cut from the original film to extend the running time, because lengthening the film meant more commercials.

New scenes included an extended visit to the Brody kitchen with such activities as feeding the family dogs (including one played by Spielberg's own pup, Elmer). This is funny because in the cinema version, when Brody gets out of bed, his wife reminds him to feed the dog, but he never does. The kitchen scene is good-naturedly chaotic, with can openers humming, telephones ringing and realistic dogs and children. There's also a nice Hooper moment, where he tells Brody about his $1,200 phone bill when he was involved with a girl who liked phone sex.

Another new scene comes when Brody and Hooper dissect the tiger shark. There's a new scene here where they discuss sharks with an "arty" shot of the two men through the dock, looking down on them.

For the 25th anniversary of the film, Universal released a new version of *JAWS* with added footage. This version is the one that can now be found running on basic cable channels AMC, TBS, Sci-Fi Channel and TNT. This cut of the film has a longer scene where the fortune-crazed fishermen hunt the poor tiger shark, spilling blood, arrows and weapons all over themselves, and crashing into each other's boats.

There is also the hilarious, never-before-seen moment where Quint goes to a music store to buy piano wire to catch the shark and intimidates a nervous saxophone-playing kid (who resembles a young Steven Spielberg) as he tries to play 'Ode to Joy'.

This new version also includes a longer scene with Tom Cassidy (Jonathan Filley), Chrissie's date, and Brody, as they walk up the beach and find Hendricks with her remains. When Brody suggests she ran out on him, he coldly insists "she must have drowned," because he can't imagine a girl running out on him, before casually talking about summering on the Island.

On the downside, this version contained all-new sound FX, despite the fact that *JAWS* won an Academy Award for Best Sound and the art on the DVD box re-draws the iconic poster, with a new narrow-nosed shark substituting for Kastel's classic one.

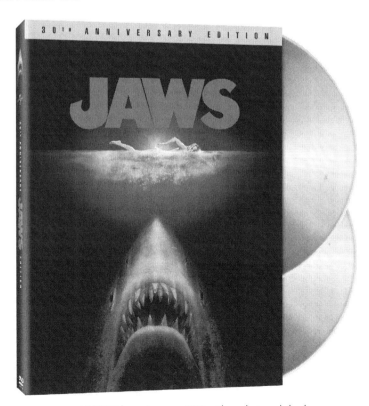

JAWS 30th anniversary DVD with re-designed shark.

.

CONVERSATIONS WITH THE PLAYERS

JEFFREY VOORHEES: THE KINTNER BOY

Visiting Amity Island, a young boy named Alex Kintner pleads with his Mother (Lee Fierro) to let him go out on his rubber raft one last time. Unfortunately for him, it *is* the last time, because he's taken by a 25-foot Great White Shark!

As a general rule, big Hollywood movies don't kill kids — and when they do, they certainly don't kill them in the gory way Alex is dispatched. The shark grabs him and we see the boy scream with geysers of blood as the fish finishes him off. For a PG movie, JAWS clearly got away with murder. Alex's death is always trimmed when the film runs on basic cable TV.

"Believe me, I hear about it when it's on," smiles Jeffrey Voorhees, the Martha's Vineyard resident who portrayed the ill-fated Kintner boy. "When they filmed *JAWS*, I had just moved to the island the year before — and the first thing that happens to me in Martha's Vineyard? I *die*! Eaten by a shark! Over the years, every time I die-by-shark on TV, friends call and I get a royalty check!

"When they came to make the movie, the water was ice-cold, because it was pre-summer and we all went down to be extras. They also needed a few speaking parts. Me and a few friends got those speaking parts and they paid those of us cast $138.00 a day, while friends who were just extras only got $38.00 per day and a sunburn."

Filming Alex' death scene proved problematic. "Every day we shot that scene, I screwed up in the water, so they would yell, 'Cut.' My friends would be freezing cold, while I went to my nice, warm dressing room because I had a speaking part. It would take three hours for all the blood in the water to clear out before they could try it again.

"I would swim out on my little raft, and then Spielberg would yell, 'Cut!' They walked out this strange-looking machine, filled it up with fake blood and put half a raft over that. They said, 'Lie on top of this and when this thing blows up, go underwater!' I was twelve years old, but I said, 'This thing's gonna blow up?

What the hell are you talking about?' I was a nervous kid, when it went BAM! All this blood shot into my face!

"Every time I messed up, they said, 'As soon as this blows up, go underwater and stay under as long as you can.' My arm would surface or leg would show under the water. After five days of this, they said, 'Enough's enough!' and got the guys in wetsuits. After about five tries, they got the guys in the wetsuits to help out. That's why I go up and down during my attack by the shark — these guys in wetsuits were yanking me up and down!"

Director Steven Spielberg "was really nice. He was young then; *JAWS* is what got his ball rolling, but he worked really hard when he came to Martha's Vineyard. I could tell he was trying to get along with everyone. He coached me for the scene by explaining what was gonna happen. They gave me the lines and [he] said, 'Beg your mother to let you go back in the water.' They let me ad lib it a little, Spielberg said to me, 'Really ask her for more time in the water — just *beg!*'"

The shark "was nowhere near me, just the machine that blew the blood up in the air. When the shark grabs me, they had those fins that would do the rollover. It was the left side of the shark, the other side of him was mechanical machine parts. I laughed when they talked about how the shark was guarded under lock and key. Me and the other kids on the island used to break in and screw around with the shark! The shark was in the Edgartown boat dock and, living in Edgartown, we all knew how to break into those things. A bunch of us kids were constantly in there, abusing that poor shark and the people working on it!"

In his bloody close-up with the shark, "That's me doing the scream as the shark eats me. That was just stuntmen yanking me up and down in the water, until they finally yanked me under and gave me air underwater. They had an air tank under the water waiting for me, so they wouldn't have to wait three or four hours for all the blood to clear to try it again. It looks like I'm out pretty deep, but I was only in four feet of water. I could just barely stand up in it and I wasn't that tall."

JAWS "didn't scare me, because I knew how they filmed it," he explains. "If you know the island at all, watching *JAWS* is funny, because when you go around the bend in the road, it's State Beach, you go around the corner, which means you should be in Edgartown, but in the movie, all of the sudden, you're in Menemsha or Chilmark! We shot my scene on State Beach, which I see every day because that's where I run my dogs."

"The Wharf Restaurant in Edgartown, where I work, put an 'Alex Kintner Burger' on the menu. It's a fish sandwich with all the toppings. The owner put it on the menu, just so the waitresses could get even with me if I was being too mean to them," he laughs. "That way, the waitresses could point at me in front of the customer and say, 'See the manager over there? That's Alex Kintner from *JAWS!*' Then I have to go over to talk to them and be nice … Even as an adult, I am used to being recognized.

"I get letters and phone calls all the time from *JAWS* fans," Voorhees continues. "Some of them are pretty odd … One guy said I helped him through his life, because he watched the movie so many times. My brother Ted started answering them, writing 'I was also in the movie!' Ted was an extra, so he mailed them all off. Ted is a kid on the beach during the attack."

"When the movie crew came back to the island to do *JAWS 2*, we all went down to be extras again. They went down the line and when they got to me, they said 'Wait a minute — you can't be in this, you're already dead!' I said, 'That was two years ago, I look different!'

Mother and Child Reunion: Jeffrey Voorhees and Lee Fierro. PHOTO BY PATRICK JANKIEWICZ.

"They said, 'No, you are dead. If anybody notices you, you'll ruin the movie, so go away!' I walked away, depressed. My friends were in the second one, but the year after that, the first film hit TV and I didn't know you got royalties … The first time it was on network TV, I got a check for $14, 500.00! I bought all sorts of things with my *JAWS* money: a bike … the first time I took my family down to Disneyworld in Florida…"

One of Voorhees' most memorable events of recent years was being reunited with the local actress who played his mother in the film.

"Lee Fierro was [in the Wharf Restaurant] with her friends, but it had been a few years and I didn't recognize her. I suddenly heard one of Lee's friends say 'The Alex Kintner Burger? Wasn't that your name in *JAWS*?' and that's when I realized it was Lee! I thought, 'I'm gonna have some fun with this…'

"I walked up to Lee and said, 'Do you believe in reincarnation? If you think that's an odd question, I think I died years ago and you were my mother!'

"She laughed and said, 'My son died twenty-five years ago — he was killed by a shark!'

"I said, *'I* was killed by a shark!'

"Lee finally told her friends why, because they were all looking at us like we were nuts! I gave her a free dinner — after all, she's my mother!"

LEE FIERRO: MRS. KINTNER

As Mrs. Kintner, Alex's Mother, Lee Fierro has an emotional role in *JAWS*. In a pivotal scene, she slaps Chief Brody and tells him, "My boy is dead. I just wanted you to know that." By doing this, she awakens his sense of duty and he resolves to kill the shark.

"I think it's the slap that changes Brody," Lee Fierro theorizes. "He feels so much guilt over this poor woman losing her son, because he kept the beaches open. You can sense this in the film, because after I slap him, the mayor says 'Don't think about it, Martin, she's wrong' and Brody says, 'No, she's not.'"

Fierro also has one of *JAWS'* most unnerving shots — after the panic on the beach, she forlornly calls for her son Alex, as we see his bloodied, chewed-up raft lolling gently in the surf.

"That was a sad scene — she's looking for her son, who is no longer around," Lee Fierro states. "We shot the shark attack scene on the beach in one day, with all the kids in the water, the heavyset lady, the old man in the black swim cap ('That's some bad hat, Harry'), the young couple screaming and the dog chasing the stick — all that was done in one day."

What's amazing is that Steven Spielberg would trust such an important dramatic role to an unknown, untested local actor. But Fierro pulled it off so beautifully. *JAWS* came her way "because I had a friend who had a theater class. My friend was helping casting director Shari Rhodes find island people for parts in *JAWS*. My friend told Shari, 'Do something with Lee Fierro if you can.' She told me to go down and meet Shari, but I wasn't interested. I wasn't interested in theater or movies, but she made me go down. I was busy raising my kids, teaching natural childbirth and building a house."

"I went down reluctantly. Three weeks later, I got a call from Shari, saying, 'Would you please come down and meet Mr. Spielberg?' I had heard of him, because I had been reading the local papers about *JAWS* coming to town. I went down and did a scene for him. The first thing that Steven Spielberg asked me was, 'Could you cry on cue?'

"I said 'On or offstage?'

"Steven had me improvise the scene with Shari, the beach scene where Alex comes out of the water and wants to go back in, but I say 'No'. I was told that I didn't want him to go back in the water — that's what Steve wanted me to express. So I obeyed him and wouldn't let Shari go back in the water. She kept trying, asking me in every way she knew possible to get to go back in the water, however I was stubborn and wouldn't let her! Steve finally stopped and said, 'Lee, you've got to let Alex go back in the water or we don't have a movie!'

Director Spielberg "was just a dear, a sweet, wonderful person. It shows in all of his movies, which are sensitive, real and direct — they're wonderful, just like him. Three weeks after that, they called me down to do it. I had spoken to Shari about the swearing. There was an awful lot of swearing in the book and I said to Shari, 'I won't swear.'"

"When she called and asked me to be in *JAWS*, I said, 'Is there any swearing?' and she said, 'I am not sure.' I went down to get a copy of the script, with what ended up being the slapping scene, I looked at it and there was swearing all over the place!

"As originally written, there was a lot of swearing right before my scene. The next day, I took the script back to Shari and said 'I am sorry, but I can't do this.' She said, '*Can't* or *won't?*' I just turned in the script, went home and forgot all about it. Three days later, they called me and asked 'If you didn't have to swear, would you be in the movie?'

"I said, 'Yes.'"

For the scene where she slaps Brody full in the face, "I really slapped him and we did seventeen takes of it that day," she laughs. "I think the slaps were done at different degrees. I had been taught how to slap, not fake slap, but how to really slap on the stage. I had been taught that in acting classes — you do that with a loose arm and a very loose wrist so it doesn't hurt the person being slapped. It stings, but doesn't really hurt. Unfortunately, it probably does when the poor man has to be slapped that many times. They didn't stop me — Steven Spielberg didn't say a word about that! In one take, I knocked off Roy Scheider's glasses by mistake and came out of character to say, 'Oh, Roy, I'm so sorry —'

Steve said 'Don't be sorry, Lee — it was wonderful!' He was sad that he couldn't use that take, because I broke character."

How did Roy Scheider take being slapped 17 times?

"It must have been hard for him, but he didn't say a word. He didn't talk to me (about it), he didn't do anything — he just stood there. It turns out that he was doing his best to stay in character, and get ready to be slapped, but not be prepared for it. Just to be able to act relaxed and not look like he was anticipating being slapped in the face."

Scheider reportedly saw a chiropractor after filming the scene.

"There was another scene that was included early on, but taken out before the film was released," Fierro continues. "It was a middle scene, of me coming out of the town hall, looking for my car after posting the $3,000 reward for the shark. They took that out. When I offer the bounty, that's when they start looking for the shark and the movie kicks into high gear, but not before the scene where I slap him."

Fierro, who moved to the island in 1969, is stunned "that I still get recognized from *JAWS*! Sometimes people on the street recognize me, or think they know me. It doesn't happen as much now that I'm older, but they know they have seen me from something — that happens every time I go somewhere. It's sweet. I'm just surprised that people are looking for me or want to meet me. I don't know what to say, it amazes me so much."

After *JAWS* wrapped, "They kept my costume, but that Christmas, after the movie opened, I got a package in the mail. I opened it up and I was amazed to see that they sent me my bathing suit from *JAWS*, which I was able to wear for several years!"

CARL GOTTLIEB: ACTOR/SCREENWRITER

Like the many colorful characters he's written, Emmy-winning screenwriter Carl Gottlieb is amiable and intensely likeable.

"I started out as an improvisational actor in a show called The Committee," Gottlieb recalls. "From that, I wrote television comedy for The Smothers Brothers. I wrote a lot of television comedy and then I did *JAWS*."

While he co-wrote Steve Martin's *The Jerk*, directed *Caveman* and sections of *Amazon Women on the Moon*, Carl Gottlieb is best known for his contributions to *JAWS*. He not only co-wrote the screenplay with Peter Benchley, but acted in the film as well, wrote *The JAWS Log*, and co-wrote the film's sequels, *JAWS 2* and *JAWS 3-D*. He appears in the original *JAWS* as newspaper editor Harry Meadows, the corrupt Mayor's sidekick.

JAWS actor/screenwriter Carl Gottlieb. PHOTO BY LISA ORRIS.

"The most painful thing I did as a writer on *JAWS* was to write myself out as an actor," he laughs. "Meadows was much more important in the script that I inherited and started with." In the book, Meadows helps Mayor Vaughn keep the beaches open and blames Brody, but also supplies Brody with crucial information. In the end, he reveals that the town's officials made Brody keep the beaches open while Brody took the rap. The character remained pivotal in Benchley's original screenplay and Howard Sackler's drafts.

Unfortunately, "In the course of writing and reworking the movie, Meadows became less and less important. I actually cut a couple of dialogue scenes with Meadows," he says ruefully. "As an actor, your ego suffers. You think, 'Oh, shit — I'm out of this movie as an actor! I'm just here and there doing a couple of lines,' but it was necessary.

"In most action movies, it helps to narrow the focus on a few principal characters and just let them carry the ball. We had such a terrific ensemble in *JAWS* that you had to let them do that. In *JAWS 2*, most of the action is at sea, so there was no place for Meadows. Murray Hamilton is so wonderful as the villainous mayor anyway, why not let him carry it?

"That's why Meadows wasn't in *JAWS 2* or *JAWS 3-D*. We had enough to do to get the movies made, much less bring in a new character at the last minute."

He became involved with *JAWS* because "Steve [Spielberg] and I were very close friends before we made the movie. Steven was a contract director at Universal and very active in television. The height of that work was *Duel*, which everyone knows. Besides *Duel*, he did *Night Gallery*, a wonderful *Columbo*, some TV pilots and other stuff. He was an active TV director, and his stuff was off-center, not typical TV.

"I acted in a couple of his TV films — ones that aren't in his filmography. *The Savage Report*, a pilot he did with Martin Landau and Barbara Bain playing investigative reporters. I also did his TV movie *Something Evil*, which had the same premise as *The Exorcist* before *The Exorcist* came out. It was about a little girl possessed by the Devil in a suburban tract house who has to be exorcised by a Catholic priest. The special FX weren't as grand as *The Exorcist* because *Something Evil* was a quickie TV movie!"

Much of *JAWS'* terror comes from the fact that the fearsome shark is unseen through most of the film. "It was *The Thing*, an elemental force," he notes. "It was 'the beast'. We called it 'Bruce' just because it was easy to characterize it, but it was not a character, it was a force. The major aesthetic discussion was, 'How long can we hold back the shark?'

"Howard Hawks' [1951 science fiction thriller] *The Thing* was a movie that Steven and I were both very familiar with and loved. The value of [Hawks' film] is that you don't see "The Thing" until the very last reel of the movie and yet, you're terrified of it all through the movie. For *JAWS*, we thought, 'Boy, it would be great if we could hold the shark back until it assumes these mythic proportions — everybody will have this mental picture of what the shark is and it will be much more terrifying than if they know it's a rubber creature 18-feet long.'

"The problem with the shark was, 'how much do you show?' We deliberately withheld the shark as long as we could — you never see the shark fully until the last act of the movie when they're at sea. You see it cruise with just a fin, and then it sinks out of sight."

Gottlieb found *JAWS* an unforgettable experience. "It was fun making a movie. My background is in theater and television, which are really 'hands on' productions. I was stage manager, hung lights and an actor. I really liked being on the floor, getting my hands dirty making a TV show. The best part about [being a writer on] *JAWS* was that we were all making entertainment together — we were all at the same level, nobody but the *story* was the star.

"We were all involved in the nuts and bolts of editing. Every night we would have dinner and talk about the changes with the editor, the director, the writer and the producers. It was a great way to make a movie. To this day, it's the happiest film collaboration in my life. Everything worked the way it was supposed to. I lived with the director," he smiles. "I'd make cocoa in the morning as Steven and I would talk about what needed to be done. It was terrific; like being room-mates in college and making a movie."

Gottlieb re-wrote the script on a daily basis. He was able to restructure the novel into a terrifying film. "One thing you need as an adapter is to be free to do whatever you want," he explains. "When you explore everything, you can start to narrow in your focus. In most adaptations, the problem is not what to

"A very important scene." Brody and Hooper confront Vaughn at the defaced billboard.

include, but what to cut. What do you leave out of the story? In *JAWS*, we cut out the love affair (between Ellen Brody and Hooper), the Mafia, and all that stuff which was totally extraneous to the story."

The film is full of witty lines and snappy dialogue. Gottlieb is especially pleased when Brody and Hooper argue with Mayor Vaughn in front of an Amity bill-board defaced with a shark fin. "That's a very important scene," he said, "because we use it to give you all the information you need about sharks — and Hooper has that funny line about 'I'm just standing here arguing with a guy who can't wait to line up to be a hot lunch!'

"That whole billboard scene was a nice bit of dialogue and beautifully shot, because Spielberg made it look like one long, continuous take. Very skillfully done. That scene serves a wonderful purpose — it gets out a lot of exposition and data about sharks. Because it's done in a 'hot dialogue scene', with a lot of interaction and arguing between the characters, you accept all this information about sharks.

"I love the line, 'You're gonna need a bigger boat,' which was an ad lib from Roy Scheider." Gottlieb remembers how the line came about. "The sound of the shark, undoctored, is compressed air," he reveals. "The real sound the shark makes is [does sound FX] 'Pu-Pish-Pu-Pish-Pu-Pish', because it had pistons and air rams driving it."

In that scene, when the shark surfaces behind Scheider, the actor was not

Brody and the shark, "in full cartoon confrontation."

expecting it. "It came right after a laugh line and the timing was impeccable, it was 'joke-beat-terror!'" he says gleefully. "The audience was coming down off a laugh, so when the shark's head appears, it was a perfect accident of timing. It wasn't the selected take of that scene, but when they put it in the movie, its perfection only became apparent way after the fact, when the film was being edited.

"When you took out the cursing of the technicians at the mistake of the shark coming up too soon and the sound of the air, which was a hissing sound, it was very effective. When that scene was being watched by the guys who were timing the negative, technicians preparing the film for its release print, the first appearance of the shark always made people jump! Hardened film guys were taken by surprise. Nobody expects the shark at that moment because it's right on a laugh.

Since then, we've seen lots of laugh scenes turning into horror, but at the time, it was a device that had not been explored.

"The whole reason I was on *JAWS* in the first place was to 'Yuk it up'. My background was comedy and I was hired to put some laughs in and humanize the characters. I did more than that and added some heavy structural work. The original intent was to take what was basically a humorless story and make it

"He should live" — Hooper's death in the book, by Alves.

much more human … You do that by adding jokes."

Gottlieb has nothing but praise for the film's director. "Steven, at that time, already had a terrific head for business; he knew how the game was played," Gottlieb avers. "He had all those skills, plus he was a terrific filmmaker. He had all the social insights for success, and the rest followed."

On *JAWS*, "Steven was not 'STEVEN SPIELBERG' yet, just a director struggling with his second [theatrical] movie. It was a big action picture, but not the biggest action picture of the year — Universal had bet all their money on *The Hindenburg* and *Airport '75!* As that was where all their attention was, they knew *Hindenburg* would be a hit (It wasn't). Because of that, they let us go off the lot to do our special FX, they just didn't care. *JAWS* had a substantial budget for that time, but it went over budget by about two million, which was extraordinary. What saved the movie is that the work was so good and so clean, everybody accepted it."

In the big climax, Brody and the shark have a running battle on, in and through the boat. Gottlieb thought up Brody's quip 'Smile, you son of a — !' "We had to give the guy a line," he explains, "Because by that time in the movie, you're almost in full cartoon confrontation. Superman always has a smart line when he smacks the bad guy and sends him flying, like 'How's this for a knuckle sandwich?' You have to come up with something and that's what we gave Roy Scheider to say."

The film radically alters the book's finale, with ichthyologist Matt Hooper surviving and Shark Hunter Quint being eaten alive by the fish. "We had to do that — we had to have somebody die," Gottlieb reasons. "We were debating on whether to kill Matt Hooper, right up until the last few days where we had that option.

"I said 'Aw, let him live — he's lovable, he's Ricky, he's a friend, he should live!' Besides, since he didn't have the affair with Brody's wife, there's no need for him to die, we don't have to punish him for having sex! In the old-fashioned movie morality at work here, we let him live.

"Quint was the brute, going *mano e mano* with the shark — he's the elemental man facing the elemental beast, so he could die, preferably as bloodily as possible. Because we kill him, we had to concoct a way to kill the beast as a result of the action of the hero, rather than natural causes! In the book, that didn't make any sense."

"The shark does everything and then dies of old age!" Gottlieb chuckles. "We needed some way to kill the shark. We couldn't do it with a bullet, because we made the shark invincible to all normal shark-killing devices, so we had to find something that would be extraordinary.

"That exploding air-tank seemed to be the most useful trick. I think it was Joe [Alves] who pointed out those tanks were explosive in the first place. We said, 'That's good, but how do we get it in his mouth? Why would a shark swallow an air tank?' We had them struggling in the boat, he uses the tank to fend off the shark; the shark takes it when it leaves, but it gets stuck in his mouth. Sharks do have this enormous biting pressure, so it was conceivable that something could get stuck in there ... The shark has the tank stuck like a cigar, wedged in the corner of his mouth, so Brody can shoot it and kill him."

It's particularly rewarding because earlier in the film, Brody knocks over a tank and Hooper screams that air-tanks are explosive. "That was clever foreshadowing on everybody's part," Gottlieb smiles. "When that stuff works, you never notice it. If you set up successfully, it becomes part of the audiences' consciousness without their studying how it got there. The 'Look out for those tanks' line was deliberate, because we knew we would use those tanks later in the film to kill it. We had to say these things are dangerous — then let the audience forget about that until the very end."

A big jump comes in the finale when the shark crashes through the wall. "That is, again, successful use of subliminal expectations," the writer relates. "All through the movie, the boat has been a safe haven. They have a cozy scene in there, where they talk and have coffee. The boat is their little fortress. The terror comes from the fact that their fortress is being dismantled by the shark.

"The shark is such an elemental force that it can take apart their only shelter, which is the boat," he explains. "The thing that is so scary about being at sea on a boat, is you feel pretty secure, even on a small boat, until you go off the boat to go swimming. You paddle twenty feet away from the boat in the ocean and think, 'Oh, my God — that's all there is between me and drowning?!?' You realize how vulnerable a small boat is.

"What we did is make the *Orca* more and more vulnerable, the shark cracks the hull first; it starts leaking and fills with water. By the end, when it's just Brody against the shark in practically hand to hand combat, what was once a safe haven is now a trap that's gonna drown him. All of the sudden, it's like having your little blue security blanket turn around and start to suffocate you. Your sense of security has been violated, which makes it even more terrifying. Steven was co-author of all those concepts. We had conversations in the Vineyard as we were writing it on, 'How do we make it scary?'"

"I wrote the last line of *JAWS* to be a good last line, to be quoted in anthologies of last lines," Gottlieb says with pride. "Brody says, 'Would you believe I used to hate the water?' and Hooper says 'I can't imagine why.'"

That dialogue made it into the book *The Last Line*, about the best movie lines of all time. The *New York Times* praised "I used to hate the water" as "A snappy, ironic line to end a film full of bloody mutilations, a surefire candidate for the hall of fame of memorable last lines."

One of Gottlieb's more interesting alterations from the book was making Brody a stranger to the island. In the novel, he's a blue-collar local.

"Yeah," the writer states, "my favorite form of exposition is something done so subtly, you don't notice it. In the opening moments of the movie, a phone rings. You don't know who this Brody guy is. He gets up, there's a line about how the sun used to shine in here. His wife says 'Because we bought the house in January, now it's June'. So now we learn that he's a newcomer to the town. He's in his kitchen when the phone rings and we see he has two telephones. What kind of a guy has two phones?

"We still don't know he's police chief. When [his wife] brings his coffee to his car, you see the star and for the first time, you realize what he does for a living. That's really skillful exposition I'm very proud of."

Thematically, the screenwriter saw the film "as 'Enemy of the People meets Moby Dick.' The message of *JAWS* is, 'A man's gotta do what a man's gotta do.' It's also like *High Noon*: a lone sheriff and the town that won't help. *High Noon* was a blacklist era metaphor and *JAWS* is a diluted version of that … It's *High Noon*, pumped up!"

JAWS "was not iconic when it was made," Gottlieb says with perspective; "it was just a journeyman piece of work. *JAWS* was not a B-picture, because it had a much-better budget and the novel was a big bestseller, but nobody thought they were making art or history when we did the movie. Everyone was just trying to do their job. The fun of it was everyone did their job and then it became history — the highest-grossing film of [its] time, the model for summer movie releases!"

"Until *JAWS*, that was not how they released movies. We were the first summer hit. If you go back to when JAWS came out and look at the Top Ten money-makers of all time, it was *The Godfather*, *Sound of Music*, *Gone with the Wind*. That release pattern was totally changed with *JAWS*. It's historical for many reasons, not only for content, style and verve, but because of what it did to the business of distributing motion pictures. It changed that."

Has he kept in touch with any of his Amity comrades?

"I still see Ricky," he notes. "Dreyfuss and I were friends before it happened, I was instrumental in getting him to do the movie, and we're still friends. It was a seminal event for all of us — you gotta remember: Nobody was a star when we did it. *JAWS* was my first produced screenplay, Steven's second movie, Joe Alves' first big job as a production designer from being a television guy, so it was a big step for all of us.

"Ricky was not a big star yet, he had gotten an Academy Award nomination for *The Apprenticeship of Duddy Kravitz*, but he hadn't done anything spectacular yet. The most experienced actor in the company was Robert Shaw. He was the only one with a history because he was in the best James Bond movie, *From Russia with Love.*"

One impressive sequence, where Hooper performs an autopsy on Chrissie Watkins, the shark's first victim, manages to be frightening while showing very little. "I love the idea of her remains being in a baby bassinet, not even a full-sized slab," Gottlieb relates. "Just a box of body parts. It's terrifying — you didn't have to show anything when the guy comes out with that little box and that's all that's left of a human being!

"The other thing I like that's purely visual, was the first time they get the shark on the line. You see them floating there, in the doldrums. It's a flat sea, there's no breeze and you hear the ratchet on the reel of the rod go 'click'. Then 'click click click' and Shaw is the first one to understand what's happening, that the shark is taking the bait and he barely manages to strap himself in, when WHIZZZZ! you're off on a long, extended action sequence. That was like me writing…click. click click, WHIZZZ! That's a favorite bit of mine."

Gottlieb was amused by Benchley's own *JAWS* follow-up, the 'squid terrorizes town' novel, *Beast*.

"It's basically the movie version of *JAWS*," he laughs. "Peter just made all the cuts we made in his novel [*JAWS*] and incorporated it all into the squid book!"

Although he shares writing credits on two of the sequels, he freely admits "that I basically did *JAWS 2* and *JAWS 3-D* for the money! I came onto both of them quite late. They started without me in both cases, and came back and asked me to do it. It paid well, so I did them. When writing a follow-up, you know that you have to go on. If you get stuck in having done the biggest or the best of anything, you never work again, and retire.

"Now if I had an ownership position on *JAWS*, like Benchley, Zanuck and Brown, maybe I would have retired. I didn't, so I had to keep working, I had to make a living. If they ask you to do it and pay you good money to do it, you just hope it does well. *JAWS 2* did very well."

If he's writing in the middle of the night and *JAWS* is on television, does he watch it?

"Um, the truth is, no. I'll wait for a couple of scenes that I like, but I don't have the same view of it that other people do," he shrugs. "I haven't just seen it — I was *there.* I very often come across it on late-night TV, and I either go to sleep or surf the channels for something else!

"I was at a *JAWS* screening at the Arclight Cinema in Hollywood with Bill Butler, and I went out and paced around. I came back for the finale, but I'm like theater people with a play they wrote, unless you're watching it to work on it, you're done with it."

"On a purely selfish level, it gives me my little place in history," Gottlieb smiles. "I tell people I'm a screenwriter and they go 'Yeah? What have you written?' I can say 'I wrote and directed *Caveman*' and they'll say, 'That wasn't a big hit, was it?' I then say 'I wrote *JAWS*' and they go, [hushed tones] 'Ohhhh!' It's hard to one-up that one. Sharing the screenplay credit on *JAWS* is an accident; you can't plan those kinds of things. But it makes your place in history secure."

JOE ALVES: PRODUCTION DESIGNER

Joe Alves stands in the living room of his striking Laurel Canyon home, which he himself designed. It's a giant modular place, set on a cliff that overlooks the entire San Fernando Valley. The walls of his home are filled with trophies and awards for his work as production designer and director. There's an NAACP image award for having cast the African American actor Louis Gossett, Jr. in "a non-black" role in *JAWS 3-D* and a letter from Steven Spielberg in which the director personally expresses his appreciation for Alves' "imagination and devotion" during the filming of *Close Encounters of the Third Kind.* The soft-spoken, bearded Alves is not studying these reminders of a distinguished career; he is watching squirrels run by on his balcony.

"I can't keep 'em out of my apricot tree," he laughs.

Joe Alves has a special place in *JAWS* history. As production designer on the original film, he was responsible for finding the locations and designing the shark. On *JAWS 2*, he did second unit directing and producing chores (as well as production design), and made his directorial debut on the second sequel, *JAWS 3-D.* He also has the distinction of being the first person on payroll for the original *JAWS.*

"I had just finished *Sugarland Express* and had a very good relationship with Richard Zanuck and David Brown," he recalls. "So when David bought the galley sheets (the unpublished *JAWS* novel) from Peter Benchley in June of '73, they told me to read them. It was just galley sheets; it wasn't even a book yet. I started *JAWS* alone, because Zanuck and Brown were working on *MacArthur,* so I became the advance guy in getting the FX going and narrowing down the locations."

The designer immediately began work on the film's toothy terror.

"I started making sketches of concepts, ideas, little sequences in the book to [prepare for] when it became a script," he recalls.

To make *JAWS'* mechanical star appear realistic, "I went to the Scripps Institute and did research on great white sharks. While there, I met a young ichthyologist, Leonard Compagno, who was working on his doctorate at Stanford. I also went to the Steinhart in San Francisco.

"Steinhart loaned me a big set of shark jaws — in fact, they're in the movie (on the wall of Quint's shack). When the boat goes out to sea, there's a shot through the mouth of the boat.

They were flattered that we used them, but the second time I wanted them

Production designer Joe Alves with mechanical shark design. PHOTO BY PATRICK JANKIEWICZ.

(for *JAWS 2*), they wanted to rent it to us because we made so much money the first time," he laughs.

As he knew Steven Spielberg from previous projects, he was happy when the director came aboard JAWS. "I was the art director on *Night Gallery* and it was an exciting time, because I was fresh and young, working with new directors like Spielberg. I first hooked up with Steven on a show called *The Psychiatrist*.

"I got to know Steven pretty good on those shows. He was very, very young. When Steven got his first feature, *Sugarland Express*, I worked on it. That was fun because of Steven's enthusiasm and it was my real introduction to Steven."

Once reunited, the two "started to come up with conceptual ideas. When designing *JAWS*, Steven and I worked from the book, not the script. [Getting the job] was very flattering because I perceived it as a big picture, but the studio did not," Alves smiles. "If they did, they would have put one of their high-powered art directors on it, not me, because I was the youngest guy [in the art department].

"They looked at it as a two-million dollar horror movie about a shark," he says of the short-sighted studio. "The book hadn't come out yet, there was nothing other than Zanuck and Brown's name, because back then, even Spielberg was a nobody. Steven was just a young guy who had done this other picture [*Sugarland*], which was a moderate success, though it was an excellent movie."

It was difficult for the *JAWS* team to convince the studio how important the film was going to be. "We had a big meeting with the head of production at Universal and the head of Special FX. It was Zanuck and Brown, Steven, myself and all department heads. I make this big presentation, which is what the pro-

Alves' shark on production sign.

duction designer does — he's the first guy to get his head chopped off because he's got the sketches!"

"Everybody is talking in nebulous terms when you're saying, 'We want to do this, we want the shark to eat a boat in half and jump out of the water!' The head of the Special FX department said, 'We can't do that — It would take too long and be too expensive. Besides, we've got more important pictures, like *The Hindenburg!*'

"Marshall Green, then head of production at Universal, said '*JAWS* may be a bigger picture than *The Hindenburg.*' At this point, people started chuckling, because *Hindenburg* was their big picture. At the time, *Hindenburg* was a huge, sixteen-million dollar picture. I said "This is ridiculous — we just bought this book, now you're saying it's impossible? I think it *can* be done.'

"'They said, 'Do it. You go out and make the shark.'

"That was one of the first projects they allowed to be taken off the studio lot. All I had going for me was my naiveté."

The production designer remembers: "Steven and I decided we didn't want miniature sharks or studio tanks. We wanted a real ocean and a full-size mechanical shark. Maybe that was us being naive, thinking we could do it. A lot of the

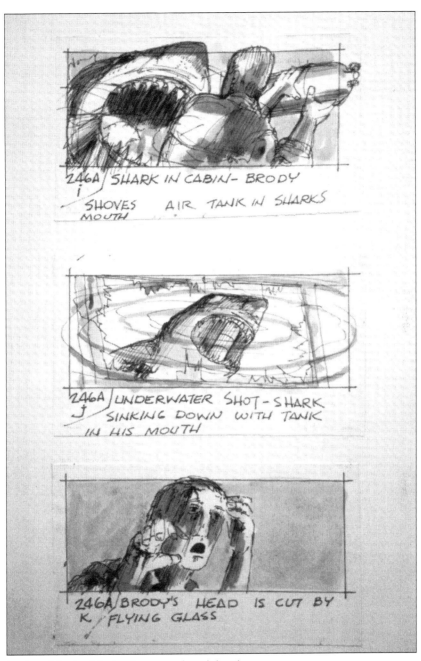

Brody and the shark in the climax, storyboards by Alves.

older, experienced people said, 'You can't do it'. They tried on a movie version of *The Old Man and the Sea*, where it was a total disaster.

"I ran into Steven at the mall a few years back and we sat down and talked for forty minutes," he says fondly. "We talked about *JAWS*. He was telling Kate [Capshaw, Spielberg's actress wife] how much of *JAWS* was really designed. We designed every frame of that thing. The third act, from the time they [Brody, Hooper and Quint] went out to sea after the shark, we followed [my sketches] shot by shot. Steven and I had a good working relationship."

"I was on *JAWS* a long time with just myself and Steven, who was also doing other things," Alves remembers. "I got nervous that Steven wasn't going to do [the film] for some reason. I enjoyed working with him, we had a good relationship, but he had mixed feelings about doing *JAWS* and there was a pirate movie he really wanted to do.

"Steven is very clever," says Alves. "When I first met him as a very young man, he always had a clear direction about his career and he wanted to make the right moves. He was being cautious about taking on a picture like *JAWS*. They had kicked around different directors, but I think primarily they wanted Spielberg. There was a period of time before Steven was set."

"My next step was modeling the shark," Alves explains. "That particular shark came from shark measurements by the Scripps Institute. In measuring these sharks and drawing outlines, I realized that if there really was a twenty-five-foot shark, they would grow in girth, too.

"They're really bulbous and ugly," he says of the fish. "I felt the shark should be formidable but still be sleek, so we actually took a twelve-and-a-half-foot shark, which is still young, and doubled it, so it didn't have all that heavy girth. If you've seen pictures of sixteen- or seventeen-foot sharks, you'll notice they're very fat.

"What I did first was, I went to a big empty room. I had a shark drawn at thirty feet. Then I drew an outline of a shark at twenty feet. Then I had all the Universal executives come in and I said, 'Let's make a decision.' When you do that, you know it's gonna end up being twenty-five feet, right? Which is right where I wanted it to be," Alves chuckles. "The thirty-footer looked awfully big and the twenty-foot shark didn't look that important, so we compromised and made it twenty-five feet."

From that point, "We decided how big the shark should be, and I did a model myself. The ichthyologist from Stanford came down and worked with me to make it right on the nose. I started going around trying to find somebody to make the shark. I went to Disney, and they said they would make it and just 'deliver it to us', but we would have to worry about it on location! That didn't seem to be a good idea.

"I talked to a lot of people who said they couldn't do it and then I met Bob Mattey, the retired head of the FX department at Disney. Bob Mattey was the most optimistic guy in the world," the designer says admiringly. "He convinced me he could do it. He made a little model and we talked about the mechanics and I sold the studio on the idea that he could do it.

"We started in my art department, drafting up all the mechanics, then Bob and I went out and selected, one by one, six specialists. The one that I still work with today and a very close friend is Roy Arbogast. Roy was my salvation on the picture, because even though Bob was a great engineer, Roy was really responsible for keeping it looking like a shark!

"Nothing against Bob Mattey, but he would be more concerned about the mechanics working — even if it meant changing the shape of the shark! I couldn't have that. I really had to stick to the shark's design. I had certain requirements that it do certain things: move its head, move its tail, that its mouth open and close and that it stay to the configuration that we modeled, which was done by a shark expert."

As that process was moving along, Alves' also had to find a real 'Amity Island'.

"I met Peter Benchley in New York and he told me all the various places that he had written for certain scenes," Alves recalls. "For this scene [Benchley would say], 'I had Montauk in mind…' I took a map and said 'OK, the location has to be on the New England coastline and it requires certain things visually for the town.'

"We also realized that, for this shark contraption Mattey came up with a barge that we floated out and sunk, with a big arm to move the shark back and forth, we needed a bay with a clear horizon and a depth of around twenty-five feet, with a very small tide change. About two feet of tide change (was needed), so we didn't have to deal with a lot of tide and could shoot there, but it would look like open ocean.

"We would have the protection of the lee of an island," he notes. "I was trying to combine that area where we'd shoot the shark with an area where we could do all the land things. Off of Montauk, we could do the tide change, but off of Cape Cod, there was too much tide change. You got six, seven, eight feet of tide change, so the shark would be out of the water too much or too far down.

"What I did was draw a map with all the tide tables, and went to all the places that Benchley suggested so I could get an idea what the visuals of the town were. I drove every mile of the coastline from New York all through Long Island and Cape Cod, all the way up to Portland, Maine. I didn't miss any little town on the East Coast of New England.

"I pointed to these islands of Nantucket and Martha's Vineyard to see if Benchley felt any of them could be Amity. Peter said 'Go to Nantucket and have lunch with my father' — Nathaniel [Benchley, who wrote *The Russians Are Coming, The Russians Are Coming*]. His dad was a real nice fella and Peter said, 'We should look at Nantucket as a possibility.'

"I said, 'What about Martha's Vineyard?'

He goes, 'Aw, there's nothing there!'"

Of course, Martha's Vineyard turned out to be the film's Amity.

"What's interesting is, I found out later that he'd never been to Martha's Vineyard," Alves says of Benchley. "People who live on islands don't go to other islands. It's either out of snobbery or 'Why vacation on another island,' but they pass right by it. I guess there's island rivalry.

"I did [my search] in the winter, so it was bitterly cold. I looked at beaches with snow on the sand. Steven recommended that I go see Marblehead, which is beautiful. I got on a ferryboat to see Nantucket and the seas were so rough, they had to turn back. I thought 'Well, I might as well see Martha's Vineyard since I'm right here anyway. Nantucket was a forty-five-minute boat ride; Martha's Vineyard was five minutes [away].

"Once I went to Martha's Vineyard, I saw it was perfect! It had all the elements and even a bay with the right depth of water. The shark could work there. I came back with my information and everybody thought Martha's Vineyard was great but worried it might be too difficult to negotiate with the town, because all these wealthy people live there.

"You had the Kennedy problem there, with Chappaquiddick and you had two factions there; the very, very wealthy who live on Martha's Vineyard for the summer and then you have five thousand permanent residents that live there all year round, who have to work as fishermen, carpenters, and merchants.

"They were all very excited that we would come there, but the population goes from five thousand to eight thousand when all the people come and open up their summer homes. If we could get in and shoot the movie before the summer crunch, we'd be in good shape," Alves says dryly.

"We were very optimistic! We compiled this information and started work on the shark. By that time, the book came out, which gave us some impetus to hurry up and make the movie, because the book was a bestseller.

"The studio [executives] said, 'This movie is not gonna go out unless it's four and a half million dollars.' Our budget was six million. They stopped the movie four different times. They didn't have confidence in it and didn't want to spend six million dollars. We made a budget accommodating the numbers they wanted. You do that. At a major studio — if it's realistic or not — you slot it in there."

Before JAWS began shooting, "We started making the shark. It was proceeding nicely, but we never tested it [in ocean water]; we tested it dry. We figured we'd ship everything back to Martha's Vineyard and test it in that water and do all the painting and finishing work there.

"I was also buying Quint's boat and designing sets, while Steven was working with [writer] Howard Sackler after two or three drafts by Peter Benchley. Carl [Gottlieb] didn't come on until we were on location. I was there from March 'til September."

Alves recalls the trouble of working on the ocean. Using a coffee cup as a boat and a pencil as the shark, he says, "If we had the boat here and had the shark come by here, it would take hours to anchor all this stuff. Boats go like this (He moves the cup around the table). You had to anchor them with four anchors.

"With the boat's shifting around, the crew would be out there for hours trying to get a simple shot of the shark going by the boat. We had the sketches, and I would go to the FX people and say, 'There's the shot, this is where it should be, the shark's got to be here.' The boat people could look at the sketches and say, 'The boat should be here.'

"It didn't give Steven that much flexibility," he explains. "Whatever idea he had, he had to come up with it and have it sketched. Because of the logistics, we kept it real tight. We were able to finish the movie [because of the sketches]."

To put it mildly, the Great White Shark proved to be a challenge.

"I was always involved with the shark. Whenever the shark was used, I was on set. I was doing continuity. Steven and I worked on the third act — The third act wasn't virtually written, but sketched," he says proudly. "We sketched the whole thing!"

"The ending was changed," he reveals. "What happened was this: while all this other stuff was going on, the shark was being built, rewrites were being done. Steven was working on it, but there was always one question: how convincing would the real shark be? We knew we could get the head shots, we knew we could get the side shots, even the left-to-right/right-to-left shark shots with the mechanical shark."

Filming the shark, "We had the mechanics on one side, so we knew we'd get some of the shark. We knew we could get some from the top, but we had nothing really from the rear end or a long shot, we needed a real shark for that.

"We got [undersea photographers] Ron and Valerie Taylor to do shark stuff for us. But how could we make the shark look big? (Instead of just shooting a regular-sized man next to a shark, the film needed a shark that would look like it was twenty-five-feet long.)

"That's when the idea came of putting a midget in the cage. We figured it all out, got a midget who could scuba dive and a miniature cage, but the miniature scuba tanks only held twelve minutes of air. If the guy got nervous down there, he could suck all that air up really quick. They went down there, got the midget in the cage, and then a real shark's approaching. They had just brought the midget up — he was panicking, so they brought him up, put the cage down, and the shark attacked the cage and broke the cage up.

"The footage was fantastic," Alves marvels. "But there was nobody in the cage. We said 'What the hell are we gonna do?' We gotta use this footage, it's so exciting, but Hooper's supposed to die in there', just as he dies in the book. We got it all sketched out, but we got live footage of the shark wrapped in this cage, tearing this cage to pieces but there's nobody in it.

"That scene was rewritten to where Hooper drops the bang stick, escapes from the shark and comes back later. That's why the ending was changed. It was a happier ending, too.

"There's no reason why Hooper should have died. Benchley wanted him to die in the book because he was having an affair with Brody's wife. That stuff was taken out. I think the script was more refined and more linear than the book. The book had all sorts of problems."

When Alves came onto the first sequel, he did production design, produced, and "directed one hundred days of *JAWS 2*, all the action stuff." Happy with his work, the powers-that-be "realized I could contribute more in other capacities."

This led to Alves directing the series' third entry, *JAWS 3-D*.

"The idea of doing it in 3-D was mine," he explains. "I met with [writer] Richard Matheson before we had a script. We had the general idea, and went to find a [Sea] theme park. I saw a 3-D underwater movie (*Sea Dreams*) and made a sketch [showing a shark's mouth with the words:] *Jaws 3-D 3-D 3-D*.

"I showed it to Sid Sheinberg and he got excited. My idea was to make it a successful part three — there hadn't been a successful part three yet. Along with *Rocky III*, *Superman III* and *Return of the Jedi*, we were one of 'the first 3s'. A second sequel just seemed too much before this, no one really had confidence in it, so I thought 'Making it 3-D would take the onus off it just being a second sequel'. I didn't know what I was getting into," he groans.

"It was hard to shoot because we didn't get a camera! For the first week or so, we were using the old 3-D stuff. It was a real headache and then Arriflex made us a camera."

Alves' tabletop shark prototype; the eye is a marble. (This prototype was broken and tossed out shortly after this photo was taken!) PHOTO BY PATRICK JANKIEWICZ.

ROY ARBOGAST: BRUCE BUILDER

Sitting on his expansive Valencia, California ranch with his dog nestled at his feet, mechanical FX wizard Roy Arbogast looks more like a rancher than a mad scientist.

"I love building monsters," he admits.

The kindly Arbogast has built a number of them, ranging from "Christine" (Stephen King's car from Hell) to John Carpenter's *The Thing*.

Of course, it would be hard to top his first one, the scary, unstoppable 'Bruce,' the malevolent Great White Shark from *JAWS*. The original table-top sized prototype — built by Joe Alves — is on display in Arbogast's workplace. One side of the model is the shark, the other bare wood. Every feature of the fearsome fish was crafted with loving detail, from its gills to its sharp teeth. Its skin may be faded, but it remains impressive.

"We do mechanical FX, no optics, no prosthetics, other than *JAWS*," he says of his shop's work. "On *JAWS*, we did the shark itself. With three *JAWS* movies and *Islands of the Stream*, I've done so many fish pictures that I forget which is which!"

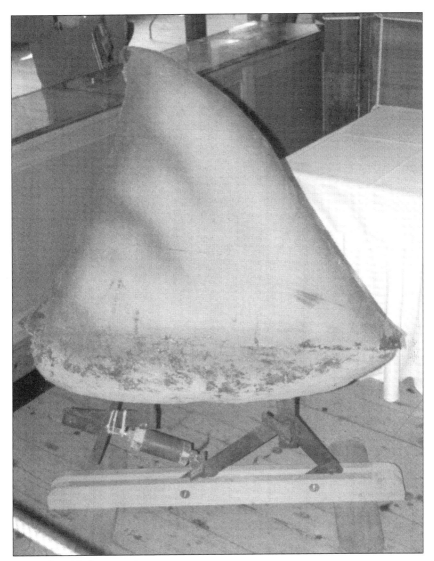

JAWS' dorsal fin by Roy Arbogast. PHOTO BY PATRICK JANKIEWICZ.

A self-described 'Backyard mechanic', Arbogast and his crew "build mechanical FX. This includes mechanical gags [Any special effect is called a "gag"], all the elements: wind, rain, fire, snow, dust storms and pyrotechnics, as well as breakaways. We did all the rubber props. Now it's more individualized. Everything is more characterized. Back then, we'd do everything and get a crew together; good mechanical people, divers, get everybody together and build this thing, then take it out and operate it. It was more in-house than it is today."

The Shark was made out of "Polyurethane rubber. We made Christine from the same material we built JAWS out of. 'Shore' is the hardness scale of rubber: JAWS was built out of a '30 shore. We had several sets of teeth for the shark, hard teeth and soft teeth," he reveals. Anytime somebody — a victim — was around the shark, the teeth were rubber urethane, the same material as the shark."

Arbogast came aboard *JAWS* "through Joe Alves and Bob Mattey. They were trying to get a team together and build the thing, because it was a big project. They wanted people who knew all the different aspects it would take to make the movie.

"Bob was the guy who oversaw the whole thing. He put [all the FX] together. Mechanically, he and Joe Alves did everything. I was brought in because I did a lot of rubber and prosthetics' work. We were the first to use big-time urethane material, before that it was all latex. It was very difficult."

Finding the shark's skin was a challenge.

"We spent a couple of months trying all different kinds of plastics, urethane and latex — we tried everything. We made a ten-foot section of the shark — the mechanical part, and we would 'skin it' with all different materials to see if it would work."

The shark was a mechanical marvel ("Even his tail could wag!"), but had a few kinks. Prior to Martha's Vineyard, we had dreams of this sucker doing everything — once we got there, all we wanted it to do was two or three gags and that was it! If we could get it to jump out of the water and bite — Great! If we could get it to surface and come down — that's fine. Your dreams are always ten times bigger than what it will ever do," he laughs.

"The hardest part to operate was the head. The eyes rolled back and his head could swing back and forth. We had a lot of trouble with the rubber urethane tearing right at the mouth. If any mechanical linkage broke inside, it would let the head swing too far and rip the gill sections. It was a nightmare!"

He remembers director Spielberg as "a wonderful guy. He was very excited. It was a first time deal, working with the shark. Spielberg was great because he faced it all. He had his problems; he was trying to direct the whole movie and Steve just wanted the shark to work. He is great to work for; you feel comfortable because you know how good he is. You never feel you're on a losing project with him. Steve is an excellent director and a very nice person."

"I was on 'the back end' of it, far removed from the set — we were busy trying to keep the sharks operating. I would stay in the shop while they took the shark out to sea to try and get him to operate. If he didn't work, they'd bring him back and we'd rebuild him. We worked 'round-the-clock, twenty-four-hour shifts in Martha's Vineyard to get him back out in the water for the next day of shooting."

There were three sharks in all, a full-size, full-figured shark, that could travel on a platform and rise, sink, bite, and move its head, and two half-sharks, one side would be shark; the other side hydraulics and pistons.

"The big platform shark was the hardest for everybody, because it was such a big piece of equipment," Arbogast explains. "The shark at the end that comes up on the deck was the platform shark. We just brought it up at an angle and it slapped right on board.

"With the platform shark, everything had to be perfect; Bob [Mattey] designed it for a certain depth of water. If you get a few feet variation, such as with the tide, you had problems.

"To float this big mechanical shark and sink it, hold it under and have it come out of the water, was terribly difficult! For the change in weight, you have to bring it up and empty all the water out of the shark's head — tremendous mechanics. All of that was Bob's genius."

Arbogast has nothing but praise for the man who brought him onto *JAWS*.

"Bob Mattey was a mentor to me and a lot of other people. As long as he saw you were working hard and trying, he would teach you anything he could. Anytime a problem came up, he would come up with ten different ways to solve it."

As Mattey also built the monstrous squid for *20,000 Leagues Under the Sea*, did he find *JAWS* a difficult project?

"Bob really did," Arbogast remembers. "He brought that up many times. He was the guy who said we could do the shark and we did it, but there were times when we were in the middle of it that he wished we had done it optically somehow!

"He was such a wonderful person," Arbogast continues. "He came out of retirement to do it [work on *JAWS*], and we'd be so tired, dragging our asses because we could hardly stand up, and we were thirty years younger than he! Bob would walk over to us, jump up, kick his heels twice in the air and say, 'Come on, boys — we got work to do!' He had an incredible amount of stamina. If anybody lost their temper, it should have been Mattey."

As difficult as making *JAWS* was, Arbogast feels "Bob Mattey was under more pressure than anybody on that whole film.

"He's the guy who put the thing together, the guy everybody was pointing fingers at!" Arbogast emphasizes. "Spielberg was under pressure, but it wasn't his fault the shark didn't work right, he did a wonderful job directing the movie, Zanuck and Brown produced a wonderful picture, but poor old Bob Mattey, he's the guy out there walking the plank and I don't think he ever got the credit or respect he deserved for hanging in there and making that thing work.

"I personally don't know of anybody else who could have pulled it off back then, even on his crew. I don't think anybody wanted to make a better movie than Bob Mattey — I'd say that about anybody on *JAWS*. He was the proudest person you could ever meet, in wanting to do good, wanting to please and wanting his work to be the best."

Filming on Martha's Vineyard was anything but a vacation.

"I worked five months straight with one day off!" Arbogast recalls. "Twelve-hour days were the minimum. It was a long haul. Looking back on it now, *JAWS* was a great experience — but at the time, there were a lot of tense days out on the set. We had our hands full just trying to keep this thing going.

"We knew if we couldn't get the shark working, there was no movie. It was important for us to just put our heads down and keep on working, re-welding or re-patching it for twenty-four hours. There were nights when Bob Mattey and I went out to sea, after working fourteen hours, because the shark ripped out in the ocean. It would have taken days to get it off the platform and bring it in, so

Bob and I went out and worked all night on it, just the two of us standing on a rubber Zodiac [raft], with the shark sticking up out of the water. We did patchwork all night so they'd have something to shoot the next day."

Another hero on the film was Joe Alves.

"Joe's a guy who can work twenty-four hours a day and only wants to do his best," Arbogast says admiringly. "Under the most adverse conditions, he can

Arbogast and Alves. PHOTO BY PATRICK JANKIEWICZ.

keep struggling. Bob Mattey, as great as he was, was so tied up with the mechanics of the thing, that when the going got tough, he was just thrilled it worked! Whether the shark had its rubber head on or not, 'it's fuckin' workin', what more do ya want?' When the shark jumps on deck to eat Quint, it jumped out of the water, but the head was not on it!

"Joe and I became good friends because I was in the background and not getting beat on by anybody! Everybody was being nice to me so I could just do my work. I had my own crew, so we just did our best. Joe found me as a go-between him and Bob. Joe sculpted the shark model. We worked very hard to make sure that shark looked like a real shark, to scale, to the eyeballs rolling back and the lips snarling. I admired Joe for being there all the time, for not just walking away from it and saying, 'That's not my job, that's special FX!'

"Between Joe and Bob, those guys wanted that shark to work so much … If it wasn't for them, it wouldn't have. I would work for Joe on whatever movie he did, because when he's production designer, he literally designs the production. I would answer to Joe over anybody. Let him do all the footwork, deal with the directors. He's mechanically inclined and artistic; I am happiest when I've got my nose down filming a great gag, whatever it might be."

With *JAWS*, they were building a creature that the Universal Studios FX department deemed 'Impossible'.

"Universal was not excited about this picture," Arbogast remembers. "*The Hindenburg* was the one they put everything into. They left us out there to die."

Fortunately for the *JAWS* crew, "Zanuck and Brown were behind us 100%. They never beat on us. David Brown would come down to the [shark] shop and always have a good word to say, like 'Boys, don't give up!' or 'Keep up the good work. We'll be here till we get it, just do your best.' They were wonderful guys."

Arbogast's work on *JAWS* called for him and his crew to build different objects. Besides the shark and Quint's boat, "On the first one, we also built a miniature shark cage and miniature dive tanks for the one shot where the real shark attacks the cage [with a little person standing in for Richard Dreyfuss]."

They used two half-sharks (one half to show to the camera; the other simply hydraulics), because "You take a five-gallon bucket and push it underwater. It takes a lot of force. Now you've got all this force pushing against something you don't need anymore. Now pull it up full of water. The full head would be too heavy to get up, it tears the skin off.

"The whole head came loose a couple times when it leaps out of the water to eat Quint. What usually happened was, when you went to suck it back down, you'd get this thing which was like a balloon that would pop everything. You take that much cubic feet of air and you're displacing thousands of gallons of water. Think of the power against a rubber skin. It doesn't take a rocket scientist to see what a problem that is, with currents going against you and rough seas."

JAWS had many tricky FX to pull off.

"One of the toughest things on that picture, which you'd never guess, is when the barrels were being towed by the shark out in the open sea and then you would see them go down," Arbogast explains. "When you have a barrel full of water, the amount of power it takes to pull it down is tremendous. They wound up putting chunks of concrete in so they would sink. To watch the movie, you would never guess it."

Another difficulty was the shark's 'fish eyes': "The eyes were on little mechanical cylinders and if they got over center, the eyeballs would get hung up in the rubber [skin] and stick up," he recalls grimly. "The pressure in the head would change so much [that] the sockets for the eyeballs would get squished and go haywire.

"In some parts of *JAWS 2*, you can see smoke coming out of his eyes — it was horrible! They were big-budget films of the day, but nothing compared to today's films. We didn't have all the time and backing that some pictures do today. Back then, you had to kiss somebody's butt just to get a new eyeball cylinder."

The Montana-born Arbogast came out to California at age six, with no desire to be in film. As a college student 'who went into construction', he entered the film business on a fluke. A friend's father "came to me while I was building race cars and Baja buggies. He said 'You should go to the studio, they'd probably like you.' I went to the studio and signed on a Friday and they called me to go to work that Monday. I started as a stagehand on a Rock Hudson/Doris Day picture. I liked it so much I never went back to school or construction!"

Because of Arbogast's involvement with *JAWS'* first sequel, he missed out on working with Spielberg again.

"I was on another picture when they started *JAWS 2* — I was gonna do *1941* with Steve. *1941* got postponed, so David Brown and Joe [Alves] called me and said, 'Please come help us with the shark'. They were having problems with the skin again.

"Joe said, 'Just get us going and as soon as Steve starts up *1941*, you can leave and do that'. *1941* kept getting pushed back. By the time it finally started and

Steve called, I was so involved in Florida on *JAWS 2*, I couldn't go. I had taken a big part from Bob Mattey and it was *too* big. *JAWS 2* was a much more difficult picture than *JAWS*; there was more shark, more boats, and I don't think it was anywhere near as good as *JAWS*.

"The first shot of the movie was the shark coming into Amity Harbor right in Martha's Vineyard. We were very proud to get the first day shooting *JAWS 2* with the shark, which we never did on *JAWS*. We shipped the shark from Pensacola, Florida, myself and three guys, took it to Martha's Vineyard, got it all rigged and got the first scene."

Overall, Roy Arbogast is happy to have been part of the Amity experience.

"*JAWS* is still a great film. It was a lot of work, but it paid off. If it [hadn't been] a big hit, I wonder if the FX in all the big movies would be what they are today. Let's face it, money talks and when *JAWS* made so much more than anybody ever dreamed of, they opened up their pockets so we could make more movies."

BILL BUTLER: SHARK CINEMATOGRAPHER

Iowa-born Bill Butler is such an easygoing, laidback guy that you almost forget that he's also one of Hollywood's hottest cinematographers. A man with a sharp photographic eye, Butler worked with Spielberg, Francis Ford Coppola, Mike Nichols, Milos Forman and William Friedkin. For many of these people — "I shot their first movie," he says. "I even shot Jack Nicholson's directorial debut."

Butler enjoys working with such filmmakers because "If you work with good talent, the inspiration of someone whose soul is on fire inspires you."

As Director of photography on the original *JAWS*, Butler created some of the terrifying tricks that brought Spielberg's vision to the screen.

"The goal was to have Amity in *JAWS* resemble an Andrew Wyeth painting," Butler explains. "We did a lot of original things on *JAWS*; I'm so proud of what we did with the camera. They hadn't shot a sea picture in a long time when *JAWS* came along and Spielberg asked me if I could shoot day for night on the ocean. That was a very difficult thing to do. On land it's very simple, because you simply don't show the sky. Shooting on the ocean, you have to show the sky. I told him I could do that, but I really didn't know if I could. I wanted to shoot the picture.

"A Director of photography does a lot of things," he adds. "As the title implies, you're really responsible for the look of the picture and when you're responsible for the look, you're responsible for a lot.

"My position is partly mechanical, partly art," Butler states. "You're taking a very tricky mechanical device that you must know well: the camera. You're using film which is a laboratory chemical and you must know that, because there are many different kinds. Most importantly, you must get the result that you want onscreen. You must have taste and the level of your taste has a lot to do with the level that you reach as a cinematographer."

Butler has worked on a lot of blockbusters, but "*JAWS* was the first one to go over the 100 million dollar mark. I can hardly say 100 million dollars because it's so much money," he smiles.

He wound up on *JAWS* through a close encounter with the director.

"I had worked with Steve before and we had a great relationship. Before *JAWS*, we had worked on several television shows together. I worked with him just before he did *Duel*. He picked me up on *JAWS* when I happened to be in the parking lot behind his office one day as he came out and we started talking.

"It was just a chance meeting in a parking lot. He had been looking for someone to shoot *JAWS*. They told him he had to have a cameraman from New York and he didn't want to do that. He got them to agree on someone from L.A. and was probably talking to someone else, when he saw me. We had so much fun together [in the past], we just clicked. A lot of what a director looks for is just to have a good time while they make their picture."

Cinematographer Bill Butler. PHOTO BY LISA ORRIS.

Butler was able to give the film his talented touch. "I brought a lot of new things to the picture, such as handholding the camera. In the old days of making sea pictures, they used a gimbel (a giant arm that holds the camera steady), which weighs roughly four hundred pounds and is slow and hard to set up, but does keep the camera level.

"I found, just by experimenting, that I could handhold the camera on an ocean-going boat and keep it level simply by using my knees. That eliminates a lot of equipment and makes things much faster and more original. I told Steven that I had this idea about shooting the picture hand-held and he just about fainted," Butler laughs.

"He didn't think it was possible and wanted everything on a tripod. I showed him that it worked, and a majority of *JAWS* was shot handheld, the first time a sea picture had been shot that way! We didn't use a gimbel at any time. Most of it was handheld simply because we could keep the horizon level so people wouldn't throw up as they sat in their seats!"

The cinematographer feels "Everybody has an opinion of how to make horror work. In the case of *JAWS*, the thing that's exceptional about the way Spielberg handled it, was he did not show you the shark until well into the picture, but he let you know it was right under the water.

"We had several things that allowed us to shoot underwater: an underwater camera, a waterbox, which allowed us to work 'dry'. If we were in water that wasn't too deep, we could simply stand on the bottom (which we would not show on camera) and the camera could shoot above the water and below the water at the same time."

A waterbox, Butler explains, is "nothing but a box with a glass front in it. Panavision made this particular one for me especially for this picture, and it allowed us to do a lot just under water level. A lot of the legs dangling in the water or kids swimming were done fairly close to shore, with us hand-holding the camera and standing on the bottom. We did a lot of things, new and original, while shooting this all on location in Martha's Vineyard."

Because of this lighter-weight Panavision camera, Butler was able "to work right at water level. It was very effective in a subconscious way, because you could see the water right there. Regardless of what was on top of the water or what was happening in the scene, the fact that the water was right on the bottom edge of the picture told you, 'There's something down there — There's something under the water'. We're constantly telling you there's something dangerous there, something's gonna happen. So when it does happen, people jumped right out of their seats!"

Butler recalls when he first realized the film would be a hit.

"I knew *JAWS* would be successful the first week we ran over [schedule]," he laughs. "Universal had a policy that a director did not run over. If he ran over a day, they would warn him that they don't do that at Universal. If he ran over two days, there was somebody else sitting in his seat. They were very serious about it.

"We're out on Martha's Vineyard and we're running over the first week. Spielberg came to me and said, 'What do you think?' Trying to get some opinions, because he knew the rules as well as I did.

"I said to Steve, 'I'll tell ya something — It's been a week and we're still here. You have absolutely nothing to worry about.'

"He says, 'Whaddaya mean?'

"'They must think we've got a great project going here or we would be gone, because we're over further than any picture at Universal has ever gone over!' We went six months on a picture that was only supposed to be three months. We also made them more money than they'd made on any picture, ever."

The cinematographer remembers being very impressed with 'Bruce.'

"The shark was very difficult but so cleverly made; a huge mechanical device. It had a vertebra, and each length of vertebra was a foot long, with a rib-like pipe coming off of it. Everything worked — it could wiggle its nose and roll its eyes! The shark was so real that if the guys working on it everyday were swimming out to it and someone wanted to scare them, they would hit levers and make the creature move, and the guys would always jump. They couldn't help it — that thing was so believable.

"They would roll up sponge rubber and put it under the shark's skin so the skin would feel right! The lengths they went to make that shark work properly was amazing — those people deserve all the credit," Butler insists.

The only ones making the film who couldn't leave the island during the film's long shoot were director Spielberg and Butler.

"We were there for six months on an island," the cinematographer recalls. "We never got off that island, except once and that was to go to another island!

"It was very tough. I remember on the last day of shooting — what we hoped would be the last day of shooting — we were trying to shoot this scene where the creature blows up. We were blowing a bunch of squid into the air and the shark head. It was a prop shark head, made just to blow up.

"They rigged and rigged and rigged, the special FX people took all day, as they often do. Pretty soon, the sun's going down and I've got four cameras lined up, some of them high-speed. I finally had to turn to Steve and say 'Steve, we're not gonna make it today — they're taking so long that we're losing the light and I won't be able to run the high-speed cameras.'

"Steve turned to me and [said], 'I'll tell you what, you do it, I'm leaving!'

"He was ready to go home that night. He did not change his plans and got on the plane and left. I shot the explosion the next morning. That was the very last take; people couldn't stand to stay on that island any longer. We all had Cabin Fever very badly."

(Spielberg considered this incident to have brought luck good luck to the production. So, to this day, he lets someone else oversee the final shot of whatever film he is making.)

Butler cannot pick out any scene in the film as 'The most difficult', because, he says, "They were *all* difficult! We had to make the ship appear to tip over as if the shark were hitting it from underneath. I tied a line into a bolt under the water, ran it under the boat to a speedboat and just sent him off until it got to the end of the line. We did that a couple of times; it would rock the boat as if it were being hit by the shark.

"It was also pulling the board out that it was fastened to. The ship started sinking! As we stood there and watched, the ship was going down to the bottom of the ocean with all our talent [the actors] on board! That was a bit of a scramble, but we got everybody off and got the speedboat back and started towing the *Orca* to shore, until we got it into shallow water where it finally sunk. The mast was above water so we could find it and save it."

Butler remembers *JAWS* as having a rigorous shooting schedule.

"We would ride to work before the sun was up in a boat with salt spray hitting you in the face all the way out and then we'd work all day till the sun went down and you'd come back in the same situation with salt spray hitting you in the face," he says with an involuntary shiver. "We rode in a Boston Whaler, not a very big boat, and we would always be the last ones back. Day in and day out, it's pretty tough work. You're so exhausted and your concentration so great, you don't remember it as being a lot of fun, you remember it as being a lot of hard work."

At the end of the film, when the Great White Shark attacked the boat, he also attacked the camera.

"He drowned one of our cameras," Butler chuckles. "We had the special FX people bring the shark up to show us how much the boat would go down when he flops onto the deck of the *Orca*, so we would know where to set the cameras. When they got to the actual [shot], they gave it a little more '*Oomph*.' The

Bruce attacks the Orca — and the camera!

shark came up so hard, the boat went much lower than they told us it would and drowned one of my cameras! To be safe, I had put the camera in a waterbox, but it went over the top and flooded it. Salt water is hard on cameras and that camera went underwater and got salt water all over it.

"We pulled the [film] magazine out and put it in a bucket of fresh water to rinse the salt water off. We kept it in the fresh water bucket, sent it to New York by airplane and took it right to the lab. They put it in and saved the film!"

Butler also has good memories of the *JAWS* ensemble: "Roy Scheider and I became good friends on the picture," he says. "I didn't get to know Robert Shaw that well, because he tended to drink a lot and I'm not a drinking person. Dreyfuss was becoming successful at the time, so he was feeling his oats. Shaw would put him down pretty good, telling him what an old actor can tell a young actor. They had that debate quite a bit, and I'm sure Dreyfuss benefited from it."

Sadly, the 1970s film stock used on the picture has warped some of the film's color scheme.

"Back when we did *JAWS*," Butler explains, "film wasn't as stable as it is now. Film has improved, so it's more stable. This was back when they weren't paying as much attention to that. The colors aren't as good today on that original piece of film as they could have been simply because Kodak is now paying more attention to making film last.

"It's disappointing to see it go. I had an occasion to re-time the picture when they were going to put it on laser disk and I was disappointed to see [the print was] not as good as I would have liked to see it. The film stock is much better now."

The underwater look of *JAWS* was done to match real sharks. "Before the film ever began, Ron and Valerie Taylor shot real white sharks in Australia, before we even started," Butler states. "That meant we were locked into what the water looked like [in that footage] and it wasn't perfectly clear, it was kind of murky.

"The very end of the picture, the final scene of the shark, was shot in the pool in MGM. The very last shot of it, where the shark sinks to the bottom of the ocean, was a smaller shark made to look big."

"Something like *JAWS* works because of the little details you put into it," Butler explains. "The subtle little touches you're giving it, like having a camera right at water-level, and not some sensational underwater shot, that isn't what makes a picture work. It's how you use it. It's what you don't do or are doing just enough and not too much. You can't just throw the book at them [the audience] and expect it to be successful. It's the little things, the touch, the taste, the talent. Spielberg had it and hopefully I did, too."

JEFFREY KRAMER: DEPUTY HENDRICKS

One can't say that Jeffrey Kramer has forgotten his roots. In the handsome Emmy-winning producer's giant office, there are pictures of friends and family, as well as mementoes from shows he produced, including *Ally McBeal*, *Chicago Hope* and *The Practice*. And, of course, on the wall closest to his desk, Kramer has proudly framed a poster of *JAWS*. It was in that classic film that he made his big-screen acting debut as Len "Lenny" Hendricks, Brody's eager-beaver deputy. In his first big moment, he finds the remains of the Watkins girl on the beach and promptly throws up.

It was Hendricks who has to put up the 'BEACHES CLOSED' signs, but Brody tells him, "Let Polly do the printing."

Hendricks whines, 'What's wrong with my printing?"

Brody repeats, "*Let Polly do the printing!*"

"Hendricks is a local guy who is kind of a sweet, loving bungler," Jeffrey Kramer explains. "He's the guy who grew up on Amity Island and he's gonna stay there his entire life, maybe eventually become Chief of Police ... There wasn't a lot of complexity to Hendricks; he was a sweet, simple man."

JAWS came Kramer's way when "I was an actor in New York and I knew that Steven [Spielberg] was casting this film in The Vineyard, because I read about it in the *Village Gazette*! I knew the Island well, because my Mom was born there, so she's a real islander. I came in the summers and ran a summer theater, where I produced it and played all the best 'young men' roles.

"When I heard they were gonna shoot in The Vineyard, I called my agent and said, 'Can you get me an appointment with Steven Spielberg?' He did, in Boston. I flew into Boston, on my own buck, to meet Steven. After talking to him, it's the only time I ever said to any-body after an audition, 'I know I'm gonna get this!' Somehow, I just knew it. Ten days later, I was shooting a commercial in Vir-ginia, when I got the call that I got *JAWS*! I didn't have any great expectations. I was just so pleased to be there. The first day of principal photography was the day I found the first body and threw up!"

Jeffrey Kramer meets JAWS 2! PHOTO COURTESY OF JEFFREY KRAMER.

To simulate throwing up, "I just threw up! I was so nervous anyway, I could have thrown up anywhere," he admits. "My God, I was nervous! Also, the head of the girl the shark killed looked very realistic, and there were crabs crawling all over it, which was pretty creepy. I blow the whistle and come down into frame. I knew Jonathan Filley [Chrissie's date] from before we did the movie. They laid these huge dolly tracks on the beach."

"We were all babies when we made *JAWS*. I was not in the main group, because they all stayed in the same place, but I loved it. I was just so grateful to be work-ing! I was happy to be there and prepared. We were all lovable eccentrics! I loved Lorraine Gary; Carl Gottlieb was a good guy and I knew Lee [Fierro] from the Vineyard. She was active in community theater and children's theater.

"I was also very close to Murray Hamilton [Mayor Vaughn]. I loved Murray! He used to keep a bottle of gin in my boot," Kramer says fondly. "He was the best, I just loved him. You know he got skunked, right?" *Skunked*! He was walk-ing home one night, after we'd all had a few cocktails, and he sees this cat. He goes 'Here, kitty, here kitty!' and *SHOOMP!* He got sprayed — it wasn't a cat, it was a skunk! We had to bathe him in tomato juice!"

For the scene where Brody and Hendricks pose with the guys who caught a shark, "They used a tiger shark for the scene where the hunters catch a shark.

They tried to find one in the waters off the Vineyard and couldn't, so they finally had to go to Florida to get it and fly it up to us. Boy, it really smelled after three days! Whew, what a stench!

"Steven Spielberg was still 'Steven' then, just a nice young guy — kind, decent, always respectful to me. I remember helping carry his parents' luggage up to their room when they came to the set. Steven and I were just nice acquaintances, we were not best friends, I didn't hang with him, but he was always pleasant and decent. I spent more time with Richard Dreyfuss than Steven, and Richard is Godfather to one of my kids, Jeremy.

Kramer in his office. PHOTO BY PATRICK JANKIEWICZ.

"Richard and I became friends when we made *JAWS*; I knew his first wife. Richard's great. When Richard and his wife were pregnant, we were pregnant. We all had dinner together and I brought chicken from Greenblatts in West Hollywood. The next day, Richard's wife delivered and twelve hours later, we delivered and we always blame it on that chicken! Richard and I have been friends forever; I was thrilled when he went on to do *Close Encounters* with Steven."

"We never shot tons of takes on *JAWS*," Kramer recalls. "Three takes each scene, tops. Steven knows what he wants; he gets it and moves on. He's not one of those guys who shoots and shoots and shoots. There were rumors all through filming that it was over budget and Universal was gonna pull the plug, but they didn't. None of us knew *JAWS* was gonna be so huge when we were doing it. You just get into it and do the best you can. Who knew?"

In the Benchley novel, the character of Hendricks is involved in more of the action.

"I hadn't read the book," Kramer confesses. "Once I did, I was surprised how much my character did. In the book, Hendricks meets the shark when he tries to save a victim, but when he tries to pull the swimmer to safety the guy's arms come off in Hendricks' hands! I read it long after I got the part. In the *JAWS* movies, I never had a scene with the shark! The closest I come is in *JAWS 2*, when I'm on the boat and I snag something ... You think it's the shark, but it turns out to be the electric cable!"

One of Kramer's highlights "happened one day on *JAWS 2*. I'm in my Amity Police uniform, sitting and talking to Sid Sheinberg, the head of Universal. I remember thinking, 'Oh my God, I'm talkin' to the President of Universal!' This woman comes up to me and says, 'Sir, you look so familiar — .'"

"I thought this would impress Sid, when she suddenly says, 'Are you in a bowling league?'

"I ran into Sid and Lorraine in New York not too long ago. When I became an executive, I called Sid up and he had lunch with me and was so encouraging. I was a young exec and he was the President. They're great people. They and their kids support my charity, The Tourettes Syndrome Champion of Children.'"

JAY MELLO: SEAN BRODY

As Sean Brody, Jay Mello has some of the biggest laughs in *JAWS* — especially the scene in which he imitates all of the actions of his father.

Brody then says, 'Give us a kiss.'

"Why?" the little boy asks innocently.

"Because I need it," his father answers.

Mello is also in one of the most intense scenes in the film, when the shark nearly kills his older brother.

"I really shouldn't have been there for that," he laughs, "It really scared me!"

Now a carpenter on Martha's Vineyard, Mello remembers "that I was six years old when

Jay Mello, The original Sean Brody! PHOTO BY PATRICK JANKIEWICZ.

we made *JAWS*. Chris Rebello who played my big brother, Mike Brody, was six years older than I was; he was 12. I'm in my thirties now and I had no idea [the film] was gonna be a classic. Playing Sean in *JAWS* was fun; it was hard, but fun, especially for my mom, who had six other kids to watch over. My parents also bought a business at the time, so there were a lot of challenges. I would get up at six a.m. and go to the set, then come home at eight or nine o'clock that night, going straight to bed and doing the exact same thing the next day."

Did he understand what was going on?

"Yes, I did … Actually, they were pretty amazed that I could comprehend what was happening at my age in doing Sean Brody. Steven Spielberg was a very energetic guy. He had a real 'get up-and-go' energy, to say, 'This is what I want, this is how we're gonna do it and now let's have some fun with it.' He was a very fun guy. He didn't really take things seriously — until they were really to the max and things had to be absolutely done that day. I loved his dog, Elmer … The dog and I only had one scene together — but I really liked playing with Elmer!"

Mello was also quite fond of his father in the film: "Roy was like a father to me while making *JAWS*. He was very kind, but he made the point that when things had to be done, they had to be done. If he had time to socialize with the rest of us, he would take that time to sit down with me and Chris and say, 'You boys did really well today, let's try to be even better tomorrow.' If we did better the next day, he'd say, 'That was fantastic!'

"He'd have coffee, while Chris and I would have chocolate milk. We took walks with him all along the beach shore, we talked, and he was a sweet, generous man.

Lorraine Gary shares a scene with Elmer Spielberg.

"My favorite scene was the one at the dinner table. Roy and I really bonded by the time we shot it, but not in an actor/actor way — it was more like a father and son relationship than acting. That's why it's my favorite scene. The way that came about is Steven Spielberg asked me if I could copy what Roy Scheider was doing at the dinner table, so I said, 'Yes I can,' and that's how it came about. I love when Hooper comes over and Roy says to me, 'Get out of here!' They just told me what to do, what to say and how to say it. I didn't really have a script to go by, they would just ask me, 'Jay, can you say this? Can you do this?'"

Watching the shark eat estuary victim Teddy Grossman "was very scary — That was really too intense for me," he admits, smiling. "It scared me, watching that. I was too young to see that! I didn't go into the water until about three years after the movie. They actually shot that scene twice. In one version, Teddy saves Mike Brody, by pushing him out of the way while he's in the shark's mouth! That was pretty bloody!"

There's also a scary shot of Mello building a sand castle, singing "Do you Know the Muffin Man?" as the shark passes him by in the water. "I remember that, because when the shark cruises into the pond, they asked me if I knew any songs that I could sing. I said, 'Yes I do,' because my first grade music teacher had just taught me that 'Muffin Man' song, so I did that for them!"

"My family has always been ecstatic that I'm in *JAWS*. Chris Rebello, who played my brother Mike, passed away in 2000. We were really close, so it was a terrible blow for me when he died. Our families were very tight even before we did the movie together. I have a family of my own now, two daughters and a son. My kids love the movie."

SUSAN BACKLINIE: CHRISSIE WATKINS

In the opening of *JAWS*, actress/stuntwoman Susan Backlinie is the pretty college girl who leaves her beach party to take a midnight plunge in the placid waters off Amity Island. During her swim, we follow a point-of-view from the ocean floor of a Great White Shark. The woman is savaged and dragged under as the waters return to their normally placid state.

While millions of moviegoers have watched the scene in horror, one views it with pride. Susan Backlinie, who played the unfortunate Chrissie, has fond feelings about *JAWS*.

"It will always be a classic," she states. "It's great to have been in that movie."

Sitting in a seaside restaurant near her Ventura, California home, the charming blonde believes she knows why her scene unnerves audiences: "My death is like the *Psycho* shower scene; it freaks you out. People always make the comment, 'You kept me out of the water for a long time!'

"I always say 'Yeah? I made myself nervous, too,' because when I dive, that's all I ever think about now!

"It works just like *Psycho*; because it's a pretty girl having a violent death. It's a terrible situation, really … Something coming up from the depths of nowhere," she shudders. "Having a girl torn apart by something will give anybody the creeps."

JAWS first came to her attention when she heard, "They were looking for a girl who could do underwater work. I was working with animals in Canada and just went and interviewed for it. [*JAWS*' production manager] Bill Gilmore, the gentleman who interviewed me, looked at my portfolio. Because I had one nude photo in it, I didn't even have to take my clothes off. All Bill said to me was, 'Let me stipulate: I don't want to get you all the way down to Martha's Vineyard and then have you decide you don't want to take your clothes off. That's all I ask.'

I said, 'No problem.'"

Was she nervous about being nude?

"Yeah," she confides. "But when you start working, your mind goes to your work. You're too busy concentrating on what you're doing. Steven was very sweet; he would close the set when I was naked … Of course, it's amazing how many people can get on a closed set! It's just human nature; though; if there was a naked man on the set, I might be there, too!"

She was the first! Susan Backlinie today. PHOTO BY LISA ORRIS.

The actress, who has worked as an animal trainer and stunt-person, was perfectly suited for her watery role.

"I was a mermaid," she confides. "I grew up in Florida and worked at Weekee Wachee Springs, a place where they do underwater shows. I was a mermaid there and would drink a soda pop and eat a banana underwater.

"When I started on *JAWS*, I just went in and swam. Steven asked me, 'What else can you do?', so I did a leg lift! That was from Weekee Wachee; I used to do water ballet shows as a kid."

Backlinie enjoyed working with Steven Spielberg: "When I first met Steve, he was a little bit stand-offish," she recalls. "It made me nervous because I had heard that he wanted an actress, not a stuntperson. Steve thought it was necessary for the shot to have an actress. Bill Gilmore kind of pushed me down his throat, so I was really nervous when I met him! When I did my first shot, it wasn't even a water shot — it was where I was just sitting on the beach, staring into space. As we shot that, we got along fine.

"Steven Spielberg reminded me of a kid; he enjoyed what he was doing, which made it better. I remember looking down the lunch table one time and Steven was sitting with a styrofoam cup in his mouth acting like a camera! I thought 'Now there's a distinguished director,'" she giggles. "I really liked Steve because he was considerate. He's a perfectionist in what he wants, he knows what he wants and I enjoyed working with him."

One of the most impressive things about her attack is that the shark is never seen. "They never, ever considered showing the shark," she confides. "That's exactly how Steve wanted it filmed. He told me, 'After your scene, I want the audience — all of them — under the seats with the popcorn and bubblegum!'"

She has nothing but praise for her unseen co-star: "When I was there, the shark wasn't even in the water yet. The only part of the shark that I saw in operation was the fin, for the scene where it came through the estuary to eat Teddy [Grossman]. That was all being pulled behind a boat, with the fins attached to hoses.

"Before it went in the water, I saw the shark and was just amazed; it looked so real! I climbed under it. I'm into boating, so I'm hip to what the sea does to things. I noticed that under the shark, there was all this shiny metal. I thought 'Boy, is electrolysis gonna do a number on this thing!'

"They put the shark in the water and did some scenes. The next time I went under the shark, he was lined with zinc, because zinc is a less porous metal. Electrolysis eats the zinc before it eats other parts. All boats have zinc on them so it doesn't eat anything. Next time I saw the shark, he was covered with zinc! He was amazing. I have a lot of respect for special FX, because stunt people work really closely with them."

"When I was there," Susan continues, "everybody was thinking 'It's gonna be a bomb', 'It's not gonna make it', 'It's not gonna work'. They called the movie, 'Flaws'! We didn't know if the shark would work ... I think [the finished film] was a surprise to a lot of people; I don't think any of us knew it would be so big. By the time I had done my scene, they hadn't even put the shark in the water yet. They really worried that it wouldn't work or look right.

"They say the hardest things to work with are kids, animals and water and JAWS had all three. The water was the most difficult challenge for them — they had so many situations to deal with: the boats, the current, chop, shadows and the water changes. It's not a constant situation, as the water changes all the time."

While the fluctuating weather often held up filming, "It didn't affect my scenes because we were on the lee side of the island; not the ocean side. The water was really flat and calm there. We were between Martha's Vineyard and the mainland."

Ironically, Backlinie was "attacked" by the shark on two different coasts, in two different oceans. "We shot my actual attack in Martha's Vineyard — all the above-the-water stuff, the beach with the picket fence and the party, as well as my stripping off all my clothes and running across the dunes was all done in Martha's Vineyard. The shark's point of view was shot elsewhere.

"The only thing that wasn't Martha's Vineyard was the underwater shot, that Point of View of it coming up underneath me. We actually did that off Catalina Island in Southern California because the water in Martha's Vineyard was 'no good'; it was too dirty. They couldn't see anything, so we came down here to Catalina.

"They flew me to Catalina; I was there for a half hour and they flew me back. In Catalina, I wasn't in the water for more than ten minutes. Back East, in Martha's Vineyard, I was really cold! All the guys were in wetsuits, but I had to be naked. I did have a pair of wetsuit bottoms on underwater because Steve wanted me as high in the water as I could get for when the shark pulls at me."

To simulate her shark attack, "I wore a pair of shorts underwater with metal sides, like the kind they fly people in for movies like *Peter Pan* and *Superman*. That's what they dragged me around in. I was then hooked up to cables coming out from the beach going through pylons. I was between the pylons, with four or five guys on each cable pulling me back and forth. I felt like I was just along for the ride!

"When they pull, they pull you underwater, even if it's just barely underwater, so I also put on the wetsuit bottoms and fins for more buoyancy; anything to help me stay up. I had to kick as hard as possible to stay up because they had a

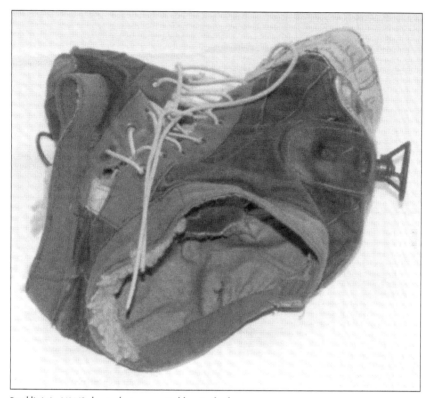

Backlinie's *JAWS* shorts that connected her to the harness. PHOTO BY PATRICK JANKIEWICZ.

tendency to pull me under! It took a lot of energy and I got very cold. That's a fake buoy I'm grabbing when the shark yanks me down."

The first time the shark pulls at her from underwater, it appears to be a neck-jerking attack.

"It really wasn't a big 'pull down,'" Backlinie states. "None of the movement they did was violent. I could feel my hips moving by what they were doing, so I would throw my arms and make it look really violent. They could get me from one side to the other and pull me down underwater.

"Steven Spielberg was the one who did the big pull-down," she reveals. "When Chrissie is unaware of what's going on and all of a sudden she gets pulled down? That's the one that he did! Steven had the line and he pulled me down himself. It didn't take much energy and I told him 'When you tug,

I can feel you tugging. I know what you want.' The rest was done by the guys on the beach."

She remembers that "Shooting began at sunrise and I was back in the hotel by 10:00 a.m. every morning in a hot bath, just layin' there in the tub," she smiles. "I was only back there for two weeks and when I was working, I was in the water most of the time.

"As I was off by 10:00, I usually hung around the hotel in case they called me back or I just roamed the island, went swimming, watched some of the filming and didn't do much of anything," she says happily.

"After I was there for two weeks, they told Steve, 'You have enough footage'. Steve kept filming and filming, when Bill Gilmore said 'We've got the footage, send her home!'"

One wonders if she was surprised to see her character on the film's poster or to be the first scene in the movie.

"I knew it was the first shot in the movie, but it kind of surprised me that it was the main shot for all the posters; they kept that from the novel. I didn't expect that, it was just another part in another movie."

Backlinie's Buoy. PHOTO BY PATRICK JANKIEWICZ.

Riders on the Universal Studios Tour frequently hear about how the actress in *JAWS* broke her ribs or hip shooting her scenes, but —

"Nothing happened to me," she grins. "I didn't get hurt. My mom took that tour and she stood up and told that lady tour guide on the tram that I didn't get hurt! I've never been on the tour myself."

"There're all sorts of rumors about me being injured, but I didn't get hurt. The only time I came close was when they pulled me during rehearsal without telling me. I was just hanging onto an inner-tube, I hadn't even started yet, and they were getting ready to pull me back and forth. They pulled me off without letting me know, at which time I sent word back to the beach — Do Not Pull until there is a cue — because I am totally relaxed and if you jerk someone when they're totally relaxed, they end up getting hurt. That's where that Universal tour story came from."

Did she ever fear being set upon by a shark?

"Oh yeah," she professes. "I worried about being attacked by a shark a lot while filming. They hunt at first light. I've always been into sharks and read a lot about them. One book, *Sharks: The Silent Savages*, was about experiments to attract sharks.

"One experiment had a man go into the water, flail around until a shark came in — because that sort of movement calls them in — and then exit the water and go back in and start again. That experiment was found to be very dangerous and that's exactly what I was doing. I was in the water, sitting on that line, flopping, floundering and stopping, flopping and stopping. So yeah, I thought a lot about sharks! I used to joke about what a great ad it would make: 'Lady eaten off cable for *JAWS*.'

"Somebody said, 'Yeah, but I hope we get our footage first!'

"I said, 'Gee, thanks'!"

Although she filmed in the morning, all her scenes are set at night. "Except for the land scenes at the beach party, which we really shot at night, all the scenes of Chrissie swimming were shot 'day for night,'" she explains. "One time I had to go into the water when the sun was really low and I was the only one in the water. I didn't like that because I'm one of those people who, as much time as I've spent in the water, I don't like being the only one in it.

"It's always nice to have company in there. The crew was on the beach, but a lot of good that does if something attacks me! People on the beach won't do me any good," she laughs.

When she began her shark encounter, "I said to Steve, 'Give me an hour in the water with special FX to let me feel the rigging. I know what I'm doing, so when you come to shoot, I'll be ready. I'll know how to move my body to give you what you want.'

"They sent me down to special FX, who weren't really pleased about having to do it. Bob Mattey (head of FX) wanted to put me on an electric winch and I said, 'No' — I wanted to do it with manpower. I said, 'What if that electric winch overrides? I'm out there in the water, you have an override in here and I'm screaming and flailing. Nobody would ever know if I was really in trouble until it was too late.'

"Mattey wanted to just screw me into these things and I learned a long time ago as a stuntwoman that nobody ever screws you into anything or ties you in. Period. How many people have been hurt that way? I bought all kinds of special releases so that no matter what happened, if I was in trouble, I could get myself out by pulling a release and being totally loose.

"When I told Bob Mattey I wouldn't use the electric winch, he got mad at me. He had made a special anchor that laid flat on the sand for the 'jerk down' scene and he was so mad at me, he pulled it out of the water," she marvels. "I now had no way to be pulled down. I had a stake hammered into the bottom of the ocean floor with sandbags put on top of it, so when they pulled me down I wouldn't be impaled on this stake. By the end of the show, Bob and I were fine."

For her death scene, Backlinie did some horrifying things. Besides her choked, waterlogged panting and moans of 'God help me' and 'It hurts!', "I was supposed to say The Lord's Prayer — actually, the Right of Penance. I'm Catholic and so were four of the crew. With five Catholics on the set, in Boston no less, none of us could remember it! I felt like a terrible Catholic!"

When it came time for her to dub her agonizing attack — "They put a basin of water in my lap and put me in front of the microphone, so I just put water in my mouth and started screaming. Richard (Dreyfuss) came in and just sat there for a minute. I would put the water in my mouth, gurgle and scream. He looked at the screen, looked at me doing this, looked at the screen, looked at me and said 'God, I gotta get outta' here — I'm gonna be sick!' He was really funny."

"The crew was great. Teddy Grossman (the stunt coordinator and the shark's rowboat victim) helped me out a lot. Teddy's a great guy, a lot of fun and a hard worker. His death was pretty good, too, very nasty! I'm not into 'getting eaten' — any time you get eaten, it's bad," she jokes. "Having worked with animals, I can't imagine anything more terrifying than being torn apart by one."

Not all of Backlinie's work on *JAWS* was limited to filming. "I did a nude spread while I was [in Martha's Vineyard]," she reveals. "It was very nicely done — tasteful, not nasty — and Universal was gonna sell it. Universal told me they put in a file and locked it up, which was good for me. When I was in Australia, somebody had a magazine they had found in a barber shop that printed those pictures! Universal didn't do it, but I have a feeling that it was the photographer who took the shots. They were supposed to have been locked up."

When *JAWS* opened, "I was working on [the Gene Hackman/Burt Reynolds movie] *Lucky Lady* down in Mexico. Nobody knew *JAWS* would be big, 'til it came out and — Woo-Hoo — it was really huge," she enthuses. "I saw nothing of it until I came back. When I returned, it had been out almost a month."

Immediately upon her arrival stateside, friends took her to a theater to see it. "I'm very critical of things I do, so I sat there and thought, 'Oh, I could have done that better and I could have done this better'. Everyone else in the theater was terrified. I liked it and thought it was excellently done, but you always see something you could have done a little bit better. Still, it's a good scene and I feel proud that I did it — it's good to have something like that in your life."

The film frightened her family. "My mother asked me not to tell her about things like [*JAWS*] because it makes her nervous," she chuckles. "Mom liked *JAWS*, but she hates sharks! [And my death scene] gave her a few worries!

"My daughter was only five when *JAWS* came out and we lived on a boat. She really wanted to see it and I thought 'Should I let her go see it? She's pretty young.' I hoped it wouldn't bother her, so I let her go. It scared her to death, but the next day she was in the water on a raft.

"She even came home with a *JAWS* joke about me that she heard at school. She said 'Did you know the woman from *JAWS* had dandruff? They found her Head & Shoulders on the beach!'

"My mother and my daughter weren't unnerved, but [the movie] gave my family the creeps. The guy I'm going with now, it gives him the creeps every time he sees it. Steven did a great job with it."

She realized firsthand how popular *JAWS* was when "I got a crew jacket and somebody stole it on the very next set I worked on! I also had the original crew shirt from *JAWS* that shows the shark with a wide open mouth. When the shirt finally wore out, I clipped out the shark and saved it!"

"After *JAWS*, a few agents came to me said 'You don't say anything in the film.' And with a [New York] accent like mine, if you have a lot of dialogue, you're pretty much set to an area unless you go to dialect school and get rid of it. I didn't push it because I really enjoyed working with animals and doing stunts. I didn't have a huge drive to be a movie star."

She did appear in other films in the seventies, including *The Great Muppet Caper* and the "nature strikes back" movie, *Day of the Animals*. "I was called to do the animal work and Billy [Girdler, the director] was excited that I was Chrissie in *JAWS*, so he put me in. He wanted me to be the first victim in his films *Grizzly* and *Day of the Animals* because I was first to go in *JAWS*! It was great fun, because I did all the girl stunt-work/animal work and the acting," she grins. "I had three different paychecks coming in, but it was exhausting."

Backlinie was even reunited with Steven Spielberg on his World War II comedy, *1941*, which began with a *JAWS* parody. Once again, she does her signature beach run and swim, but this time she's lifted out of the water by a massive submarine.

"*1941* was actually harder to do than *JAWS* because it was difficult riding the periscope of the submarine!

"Steven wanted you to be able to recognize who it was and what it was. He had someone call me up because he said 'I'd like to use her for a take-off on *JAWS*.' That was a hard show for him; [there were] a lot of problems. He had a lot to do.

"We shot *1941* up in Oregon, where the water was really cold! I did the dive and hit the water and it was freezing. I said, 'The instant my head goes under the water, is that a cut?' they said 'Yes'. It was fifty degrees and the place we filmed had a long sandbar so you had to run a ways out before you could actually hit the water and get underneath it. I hit the water, turned around, came up and ran for the beach. I only had to do it twice, thank God!

"The rest of that shot in *1941* was done in a soundstage. The crew was in vests and jackets, while I was soaking wet with no clothes on. The minute I got out of the water, they had a fan going (To simulate a windy beach)!"

As far as her nudity, *1941* was tricky, because, unlike *JAWS*, her sequence takes place in broad daylight.

"Steven was very careful about that. He told me, 'Look, when you're on that scope, turn yourself because I don't need an R-rating!'

Backlinie is pleased by director Spielberg's ongoing success, especially his Academy Award for *Schindler's List*. "I was so happy for him; he's a very talented man," she says fondly.

In the early eighties Backlinie turned her attention to training animals for feature films through her company, Lion Wild Animals Rentals. That was *her* tiger trying to eat Frederic Forrest in *Apocalypse Now* and those were *her* ostriches in *Blade Runner*.

"It's hard to train wild animals, to always have something with big teeth looking at you. Everybody bitches at work when you have to do something you don't want to do. Animals do the same thing with a snarl. They learn quickly. It's strange working with an actor that has four-inch fangs."

As someone with experience with wild animals, did she feel her shark attack was accurate?

"Some of the shark's actions at the end of the movie may not be, but I think my attack was very well done. It was like an attack we had out here In California; a guy disappears, pops up, yells and is gone. That's exactly how it happens."

Perhaps the most amazing thing that Susan Backlinie did after *JAWS* was leave the country. "I continued to work animals and do stunts. I had always wanted to go cruising around the world on a sailboat; it was my dream. When I had the opportunity, I had the boat and so my old man and I untied the lines and left!"

"I cruised foreign countries for eight years. I lived in Australia for two years. I built a 54-foot Catamaran. We spent twenty-one months building it and the two of us then spent five and a half months just bringing it around to the East Coast of Australia. I left the Hollywood scene and never really got back into it. I knew when I went cruising that I probably would not get back into it, which doesn't really bother me."

Susan Backlinie is proud of her involvement in *JAWS*. But what is her opinion of the film's many sequels?

"They made *sequels?*"

THE SEQUELS

"I think we've got another shark problem!"

BRODY (IN *JAWS 2*)

Like any productive fish, *JAWS* spawned several sequels of varying quality.

The first *JAWS* made the three leads — Scheider, Shaw and Dreyfuss — incredibly popular with moviegoers. Unfortunately, Shaw's character was killed off and, because Dreyfuss's character was supposed to die in the original, no one thought to lock him in for a possible sequel (Matt Hooper's absence was conveniently dealt with by a reference to his "being away at sea on the *Aurora*" — the boat trip he had supposedly passed up in the original.) This left Roy Scheider as the only member of the ensemble who was contractually obligated to return to Amity.

JAWS 2

Release date: June 16, 1978
Tagline: "Just when you thought it was safe to go back in the water..."
Produced by Richard D. Zanuck and David Brown
Directed by Jeannot Szwarc
Written by Carl Gottlieb and Howard Sackler
Based on characters created by Peter Benchley
120 minutes

Cast

Police Chief Martin Brody	Roy Scheider
Ellen Brody	Lorraine Gary
Mayor Larry Vaughn	Murray Hamilton
Len Peterson	Joseph Mascolo

Synopsis

Two divers discover the wreck of the *Orca* off Amity Island. They take pictures and are quickly attacked by a new shark. Their camera snaps one last shot as it hits the sea bottom. Amity has been in a recession since the events of *JAWS*, and is finally on the verge of a recovery, with a new hotel and investors coming in.

Brody joins his wife Ellen, Mayor Vaughn and her boss, shady developer Len Peterson (who seems fond of Ellen) at an opening party for the new Holiday Inn. Meanwhile, in Amity Harbor, a huge dorsal fin glides in.

There's fun in the sun, as swimmers, sailors and tourists take to the beaches. A killer whale is found on the beach, badly mauled.

A water skier is chased and eaten by a Great White Shark. The driver of the ski boat looks for her missing friend ("Teri!" she calls).

The fish rams the boat and starts to sink it. The driver spills a can of gas all over the boat and, to prevent herself from being eaten, shoots a flare gun at the shark, immolating herself and half the shark's face. There's a huge explosion, but no one can tell Brody what happened.

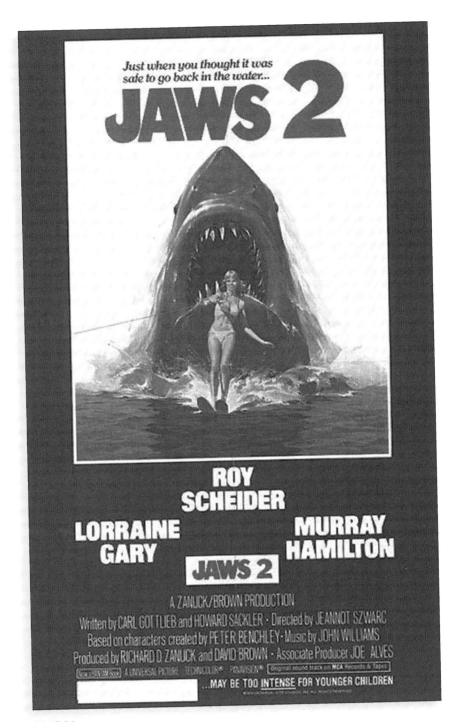

JAWS 2 Poster.

Brody is convinced another shark is at large. He makes poison-tipped bullets, just in case. Coming across the wreckage of the water skier's boat, and treading into the surf, Brody discovers the driver's burned corpse. When Ellen and Len take some potential investors to the beach, they're embarrassed by the shark spotting tower Brody sits in. When Brody sees a dark shape heading into the swimming area, he charges in firing his gun. It's just a school of minnows. Mortified, Ellen leads the investors away.

The shark cruises through Amity Harbor, attracted by splashing. It tries to attack a swimmer, but the victim is yanked out of reach — he's paragliding. The shark heads to a different part of the beach. When the divers' camera is finally recovered, Brody shows the Mayor what he thinks is a picture of a shark's eye (It is), but Vaughn and the Selectmen are unconvinced. Instead of closing the beaches, they fire him. Brody goes home and gets drunk.

Brody's sullen teenage son Mike and his friends go on a boat race. Sean threatens to wake their parents if he doesn't take them, so he does, albeit reluctantly. During the race, the shark attacks stragglers Tina and Eddie. Eddie is eaten. Brody and Ellen rescue Tina. Brody sends Ellen and Tina home with Hendricks

FISH FACTS

▶ Verna Fields was up for the directing job on the sequel, but was ultimately turned down when the Directors Guild of America would not grant her a waiver to do it.

▶ *JAWS 2* Editor Neil Travis later won the Oscar for *Dances with Wolves*.

▶ Cable junction, where the shark is killed, was a floating set.

▶ Gary Springer, who plays wise-cracking fat kid Andy, was a production assistant on *Taxi Driver*.

Shark vs. sailboat in *JAWS 2*.

and sets out to rescue Mike. At sea, the shark eats several teenagers, a Shore Patrolman and his helicopter, nearly eats Mike and Sean, before being tricked by Brody into biting an electric cable, which causes the shark to burn itself up.

JAWS 2 benefited from a great poster (which showed a gorgeous water skier with a large shark looming behind her) and the best tagline a sequel has ever had ("Just when you thought it was safe to go back in the water…" — this was conceived by the brilliant copywriter Andrew Kuehn). The film's biggest problem was that it wasn't *JAWS*. It's more of a depressing, beat-for-beat remake than a sequel, lacking the full impact of the Spielberg original. Worse, there were behind-the-scenes problems and a malfunctioning shark.

The film re-stages every shock from the first film with minor alterations (there's a burned-up corpse instead of Ben Gardner's head, a water skier instead of a nude swimmer, etc.), even minor incidents from the first film are redone (Instead of a Kung Fu school karate chopping fences, townsfolk are upset about a kid on a CB radio) and — most damning of all — the shark is obviously fake.

Despite the poster's promise, the shark never actually comes out of the water to eat the water skier. Instead, you see the water skier let go of the rope and then cut to an underwater shot of the real shark from *JAWS*.

"Using that shot of the shark was Verna's idea," Jeannot Szwarc states, "because the mechanical one wasn't working."

The water skier on the poster "was a blatant rip-off of the Chrissie scene in *JAWS*," Carl Gottlieb confesses. "Everybody on *JAWS 2* was excited, because they had the shark's Point of View this time. Instead of just swimming around, he was gonna chase somebody and it was gonna be a big water skiing scene. It also made a good poster for the movie — It's like teenagers in horror movies … If you have sex, you're gonna die. In *JAWS* movies, if somebody attractive goes in the water early in the movie, she's outta' there! A girl in a bikini? — Kiss her goodbye!"

Ironically, when scoring the death of the water skier, composer John Williams does not reprise his shark motif.

Even mentioning the water skier gives *JAWS 2* director Jeannot Szwarc flashbacks.

"Ohhh, that was the most difficult shot in the whole film," he recalls. "I was obsessed with getting a POV of the shark going after the girl skier. We went everywhere to find someone who could help me get that shot. I said, 'I *will* get that shot!' I investigated getting a mini submarine, talked to the U.S. Navy and the Japanese. They all told me, 'Because of the inertia of the water, that shot can't be done.'

"I was depressed at a bar on Saturday night and an old grip named Dino said, 'Jeannot, do you really want that shot?'

"I said, 'Boy, do I want that shot! Can you do something?'

"Dino said, 'Give me a warehouse, a week and three guys, but I don't want any interference.'

"I said 'You got it!'

"He *did it*! Dino took a catamaran, put a space crane on it and at the end of the crane, he put a plastic bubble. We had the catamaran behind the skier and using the bubble meant we never had to deal with the inertia! We had the water skier going at minimal speed, which meant she kept sinking, but we finally got the shot! Universal used that shot everywhere — every trailer, every clip on TV!'

"The scene after that was also hard," he continues. "The woman who was driving the boat pulling the water skier was a very nice stuntwoman. She's looking for her friend, when she's attacked by the shark. Just having that shark smash into her boat was amazingly difficult to do. Getting the shark to ram the boat was almost impossible!"

"That water skier was a stuntwoman and those elements — a woman water-skiing while being chased by a shark [was] too difficult to produce at the time," explains Kevin Pike, who helped with the shark FX for *JAWS 2*. "There was no way to have a shark jump out of the water and eat her like the poster showed! That was *not* gonna happen. Today, you could easily have a CG shark eat a water skier, but this was the 1970s."

The shark "was never in the same location with the water skier — except for that one shot with the fin," Pike explains. "The water skier was shot inland, in the harbor, in a lagoon, with turbulence and air mortars, but the full-scale platform shark was done in the open ocean, outside Pensacola. Joe directed those sequences, of the shark attacking the water skier and boat."

Steven Spielberg had no desire to be associated with *JAWS 2*, telling the *New York Times*: "I'm not interested in sequels in general and the *JAWS* sequel specifically. The original idea was an important one, but it was a once and only shot. Why not make four new movies rather than rehashing one old one?"

Sequels, he told an audience at the San Francisco Film Festival, were little more than "a cheap carny trick"

Spielberg practiced what he preached, as he began work on *Close Encounters of the Third Kind*.

Gottlieb also decided against returning to the *JAWS* franchise (He later changed his mind), so uncredited *JAWS* co-writer Howard Sackler came up with several scenarios. One involving a prequel about

▲ In a cute visual gag, The Brodys' porch has a planter made from one of the barrels used in the original *JAWS*. (This same planter was found in the town years later by a *JAWS* collector.)

▲ There were originally going to be an additional water skier, played by Richard Zanuck.

▲ Marvel Comics' *JAWS 2* adaptation (like the novelization) was based on the aborted Hancock/Dorothy Tristan screenplay.

▲ The TV version adds several scenes, including Ellen spiking the punch at the Holiday Inn opening and telling a waitress to "Smile." Also, the shark actually attacks the pilot after sinking the helicopter. There is also a scene in which Vaughn and the city council debate whether to fire Brody (In a nice touch, Mayor Vaughn is the only one to vote to let Brody keep his job).

▲ Ellen blasts Brody for excessive smoking in *JAWS 2*. He and Mayor Vaughn smoke like fiends all through the original film and nobody says a thing.

Quint's horrifying experiences after the *Indianapolis* sank was dumped in favor of doing a more direct sequel.

There was a false start for *JAWS 2* with director John Hancock. Howard Sackler, who took no credit for his work on the original film, did the first draft of *JAWS 2*. John Hancock was hired to direct, after doing such suspense films as *Let's Scare Jessica to Death*, but Hancock was fired a month into filming. Report-

Roy Scheider and *JAWS 2* director Jeannot Szwarc.

edly, he made *JAWS 2* a darker horror film than the studio intended. He also had his actress wife, Dorothy Tristan, rewrite Sackler's script. This was considered an insult, as Sackler brought Hancock to Universal's attention.

That said, the plot for Hancock's *JAWS 2* was actually scary, with a higher body count than the finished film. The shark bit one kid in half, and was much more ambitious than this Great White. Hank Searls' *JAWS 2* novelization is based on the Hancock/Tristan draft. (Learn the whole story in the "Submerged Sequels" section of this book.)

After Hancock was fired, Carl Gottlieb was brought in to rewrite the script into something more manageable. Hancock was replaced by director Jeannot Szwarc. The clever, French-born Szwarc saw *JAWS 2* as "a Godzilla movie" because — as he explains it: "They are both about creatures from the ocean floor that attack a town."

JAWS 2 was a rigorous shooting schedule, involving six months of location work. The film also switched Amity Island from Martha's Vineyard (where a second-unit crew obtained matching shots of Scheider) to the warmer waters of Fort Walton Beach, Florida.

Like Spielberg, Szwarc also started at Universal Television, directing episodes of Rod Serling's *Night Gallery*. Szwarc's episodes were extremely clever, showing him to be skillful at stretching the budget and his imagination.

"I knew we had to get the film made," he states.

Despite his efforts on *JAWS 2*, *Newsweek* declared: "Szwarc comes nowhere near Spielberg's blend of kinetic drive and comedic touch." To be fair, he was handed a much weaker script than the original *JAWS*. When Szwarc came aboard, "Joe Alves knew him from *Night Gallery* and he was really excited when the announcement was made," says Kevin Pike. "Joe said that Jeannot could take a cheesy two-wall set and make it look like a palace onscreen! Joe said Jeannot had a lot of ingenuity in shooting."

Director Szwarc had no idea he was about to take the reins to the sequel to the highest-grossing film of all time.

"I had just finished a pilot for Quinn Martin productions," he remembers. "They wanted me to do another TV pilot, when Joe Alves comes to my house and gives me the script for *JAWS 2*. I read it and tell Joe, 'I think the action is pretty good, but some of the dialogue is weak.' He leaves.

"The next day, Joe calls me and says, 'We want you to come to Universal. [*JAWS* editor] Verna Fields says to me, 'We need you to prepare a reel of your work very quickly. I do, and still have no clue they want me to do *JAWS 2*. I keep telling them I need to prepare this pilot," he laughs. "I go to Universal, and they start bombarding me with questions. Then they ask me, 'If you were doing *JAWS 2*, what would you do?'

"I said, 'I would start with a big action scene while the dialogue was rewritten to give the characters a little more substance. I go back to Quinn Martin. What I didn't know was the picture was a disaster; after ten months of preparation, Verna Fields shut it down. They needed someone who could start it right away.

"They went to twenty directors and no one would touch it," Szwarc continues. "No one wanted to try to follow up the biggest moneymaker in history. They needed someone who could step in under pressure. Joe and the [assistant director] both said, 'I know a

▲ Spielberg explained to the press that he directed *The Lost World: Jurassic Park* sequel "because I didn't want another *JAWS 2* on my hands!"

▲ The studio apparently worried that viewers would think the sequel was a re-release, because they stamped "ALL NEW *JAWS 2*" on all the posters and products.

▲ Ever wonder what happened to the unfriendly mechanical fish from the *JAWS* movies? Shark-maker Roy Arbogast reveals that "They were trashed — I had them all hauled out as scrap!"

guy' — *me* — because they had both worked with me on *Night Gallery*. I was told at Quinn Martin that Zanuck and Brown wanted to see me.

"David Brown told me they had dropped the ball and they needed me to start immediately. They wanted me to use as much of the previous director's work as I could. I looked at all the footage and only ended up using an eight-second shot of the shark coming in the harbor. The material was unusable. There would be a scene where you couldn't see the head of the person talking! He would improvise [weird] things and this is before we started with the shark!

"Verna Fields was smart — she shut down, which took a lot of guts. Her theory was, 'If they're in this much trouble now, what will happen when the shark starts?' I had made a movie called *Bug* that opened the same day as *JAWS*, and *JAWS* killed it. *Bug* was a little $500,000 movie. Verna liked the earthquake sequence I did at the beginning of the film. When she heard I shot it in a day, she thought it looked better than *Earthquake* and told the *JAWS 2* producers, 'That's the guy,'" he says happily

Director Szwarc hit the ground running: "All I had to do was get a beginning, middle and end," he jokes. "I had four units shooting at the same time. Do you know how easy this movie would have been if we had CG? We started shooting on the open ocean — and everything shot on water is a nightmare! I got the idea of shooting [shark scenes] in a lagoon to turn things around.

"I love Jeannot Szwarc," Jeffrey Kramer professes. "I think he's a visionary, talented, and one of the most wonderful human beings I have ever met in my life. He came in under circumstances that would have killed a lesser man. Three units shooting simultaneously and some days, they didn't get a single foot of film! Boats dragged, a storm came in, a nuclear powered aircraft carrier cruised into the background and we had to wait 'til it passed. Kids, too, lots of kids, running around. We were there for nine months making *JAWS 2*. Marriages of twenty years broke up on this, because we were on location so long.

"On *JAWS 2*, I was hired on and then the initial director [John Hancock] cut my part into two deputies," Kramer recalls. "I said, 'I don't wanna do it. That's not what I signed up for!' and I left. Jeannot Szwarc came in and asked, 'What happened to the guy who played the deputy? I really liked him.' He combined the two roles again and I came back. I wasn't privy to why Hancock was fired, but I think they spent a lot of time and the studio wasn't happy with what they saw. If they thought it was a darker take, they should have made a move earlier, but who knows?"

Carl Gottlieb "came onto *JAWS 2* quite late," the screenwriter says. "A director named [John] Hancock and his wife had been hired to do the picture and had rewritten the script extensively. I think Sackler did the first draft again and they [the Hancocks] misbehaved artistically and were replaced two weeks into principal photography."

"The company took a week's hiatus to regroup and they looked around for someone to do it," Gottlieb explains. "My name came up and I had an approach for them. They had all these kids they hired and I said, 'Don't junk the kids, they're good actors and if the kids are in jeopardy, it takes it off of Scheider — he's not gonna get in the same shark jeopardy twice.

"I came up with the concept of the kids being like cruising valley kids. Instead of cruising in cars, they would cruise in suped-up sailboats, kind of 'an East Coast' thing. For *JAWS 2*, we invented this sailboat culture which I don't think exists," Gottlieb laughs.

One wonders if it was challenging for him to write the sequel to what was then 'The highest-grossing picture of all time'.

"*JAWS 2* was difficult," he concedes, "but you've got to remember the nature of a sequel. Sid Sheinberg put it best. He said, 'People come to your house, you give 'em fried fish for dinner and they love it. You invite 'em back to your house, you don't give 'em a barbecue — you give them fish again. Give them what they liked the first time.'

"Something people forget about *JAWS 2* is that it was the most successful sequel in the history of the movies up to that point," Gottlieb states. "Part of that was because it was so similar in theme, because it was a retread. That's the nature of sequels. You look at the second Andy Hardy movie and the fifteenth Andy Hardy movie and they're very similar — it's the 'sequel syndrome.' The worst sequels are the ones like *Exorcist II* and *III,* which stray fatally from their central characteristic. You can't abandon the thing that made the movie in the first place."

The writer has fond memories of scripting the sequel.

"I went on location for *JAWS 2*. One of the great moments is when they shut down production. They would resume in a few days, so I was in a room writing what they were gonna shoot. I was isolated, locked in a suite typing — no computers in those days — and I'm just typing away.

"I would go out for a break, just walk around the hotel or go to a coffee shop. I would run into members of the crew. Because the company was idle, there were 120 people there: grips, cameramen — the whole crew. Everybody, out of nothing but good feelings, would say 'How's it coming?' I'd go, 'Fine.' I would walk another fifty feet and someone would say, 'How's it going?' I get to the coffee shop and the waitress would say, 'You're the writer aren't you?' 'Yeah.' 'How's it going?' There would be this chorus, so I'd flee back to my room and keep typing."

Many of the actors hired by Hancock were let go and the roles recast.

"John Hancock had hired Ricky Schroeder to play Sean Brody in *JAWS 2*," explains Marc Gilpin, who played Sean in the Szwarc version. "Nothing against Ricky Schroeder, but he apparently couldn't pull off the job. They needed a kid to cry, scream and freak out. When Jeannot came on, Ricky didn't make the cut, so Shari Rhodes, the casting director, said, 'We've got to get Marc out here, because that's who I wanted to begin with.' I waited for two weeks to meet Jeannot, because he was under such a tight schedule in taking over *JAWS 2*, it took him that long just to get the time to meet up with me.

"We had about ten minutes together and he decided that I was right for the part. The very next day we go out on the water, my very first scene, Martha Swatek was being eaten alive to protect me from the shark. They threw me on the turned-over boat and said, 'Okay, Martha's being eaten. We want you to react in horror at this shark.' That was it, trial by fire! They wanted to see if I would hang tough. I passed the test and stayed on.

Director Szwarc notes that "Ricky Schroeder was a nice kid, but he came off kind of whiny as the Sean Brody character. I also didn't think he looked like the son of Roy and Lorraine."

"Even at ten, I could tell it was a troubled production," Gilpin states. "There was a lot going on. I remember the shark breaking down quite a bit ... The hydraulics gave them all kinds of problems ... We would wait all day for them to get it fixed, divers worked on the hydraulics underwater ... They would try to figure out how they could get the shark to rise. A lot of days, we were out on the water in treacherous weather when we really shouldn't have been, with fifteen-foot high waves and a hammerhead shark even circled us!

"I also turned eleven during production.

"We shot *JAWS 2* all the way into late November, early December of '77. We wore flesh-colored wetsuits because it was so cold. We had to put ice cubes in our mouth all the time because it was so cold and we didn't want to show our breath on camera, because it was supposed to be summer. The next spring, we did pick-up shots in Long Beach, California, for two months. I was on the *Queen Mary* as we shot it."

When it was time for *JAWS 2* to film, the first film's cinematographer, Bill Butler, opted not to return to Amity Island and did the film *Grease* instead. *JAWS 2* was shot by David Butler (No Relation). "They asked me to do the second one, but I felt if I did the second one, there should be some compensation because of the success of the first one, probably over and above what they wanted to pay," Bill Butler states.

JAWS 2 lacked the documentary look of the first film.

"I felt the other Butler did a fine job photographically on *JAWS 2*," Bill Butler diplomatically continues. "There was some nice underwater stuff. I used David Butler on my helicopter work and I think some underwater photography on the original *JAWS*. The reason *JAWS 2* didn't look like the original film was due to the fact that Spielberg didn't direct it and I didn't shoot it. You try to hand the same project to two other people and it just doesn't work as well because they don't realize what you were doing on the original film ..."

There were behind-the-scenes controversies. Scheider was contractually obligated to do the film (reportedly, when Universal exercised its option for him to do the sequel, he had just quit the title role in *The Deer Hunter* and he clearly knew he was making an inferior product). To sweeten the pot for him on *JAWS 2*, Universal agreed to let the film count for the two films he owed them.

According to *The Making of Jaws 2*, controversy erupted when Scheider refused to kiss Lorraine Gary in a scene. (Her husband was Universal CEO Sid Sheinberg, so this was apparently Scheider's way of sending a message). When a fight started between Szwarc and Scheider, Verna Fields ended it ... by sitting on both men!

"I had heard Roy Scheider really did not want to do the film, but Universal made him," says Gilpin. "He may not have wanted to do it, but once he was here, he was a consummate professional. Roy was there to get the job done. He didn't act up in front of me. Whatever problems he had in doing the second film, he wasn't vociferous about it. Lorraine Gary was a sweet, lovable lady — very personable, very sweet. Lorraine went out of her way to have silver cups engraved for the entire cast."

Jeffrey Kramer says, "Roy *had* to do this movie and didn't really love being there. He sat in the sun so much, he got so dark from the sun [that] they had to color-correct him! He was terrific on *JAWS*, but this time, he was distant. I didn't take it personally, that was 'his thing.' There was not a lot of love between Roy and Lorraine, and Lorraine Gary is a professional — she's terrific, warm and open — always encouraging to all of us, but [she] and Roy ... David Brown is a gentleman — ask *him* about Roy on *JAWS 2*," he grins.

Jeannot Szwarc, the target of Scheider's wrath, confirms that "Roy truly did not want to do the movie. He was an angry guy about it. Roy attacked me, so I responded. I had my hands around his neck — David Brown and Verna Fields had to pull us apart! He was being a pain in the ass, but he was a very good actor.

"While we wrestled, Roy and I both started laughing and I got the truth. I said 'Roy, what's going on?' It had nothing to do with *The Deer Hunter* or us — he told me he had just done the William Friedkin movie, *Sorcerer*, the remake of *Wages of Fear*. He was punishing us for his experience on *Sorcerer*. We laughed and he was fine after that. One night, we were watching a championship prize fight on TV. Roy turned to me and said, 'I thought *we* were better!'

"We were really limited on what we could do on *JAWS 2*," Szwarc explains. "We didn't have Robert Shaw or Richard Dreyfuss; the studio hated Roy Scheider and Roy Scheider hated the studio, so I said, 'The only thing we can do is do more things with the shark."

Some POV shots he attained by putting the camera on the shark's back are excellent.

"We put a cowboy saddle on the shark's back to get that," laughs the director. "I wanted to do that shot all along. The first thing I said is 'I want to see the shark' and it was a disaster, it didn't work. Sometimes it would work, but not very much. That shark was on a platform that you had to synchronize.

"There was a second shark that we pulled and it worked pretty well. I told Joe Alves that we should get this shark to open its mouth and that shark saved our ass! Roy Arbogast was a great guy who worked so hard on those sharks ..."

Although only a child at the time, Gilpin was touched that "Lorraine and Roy went out of their way to spend time with me and make sure I was comfortable. When we did scenes together, Roy added his own direction for how we should play off of each other. Talking to Jay [Mello, the original Sean], I found out that he did the same thing with him, too."

The brutality and body count of the Hancock version were toned down, although "I was actually on the 'kill list,'" Gilpin reveals. "They heavily debated whether or not Sean Brody would get munched ... They pulled the plug on that idea, but they considered whether or not I would be killed off. Eventually, a shark does get Sean in the last *JAWS* movie! I heard that the John Hancock *JAWS 2* was more of a bloodbath, but they pulled the plug on that."

Spielberg's clever way of establishing an uneasiness of the ocean from the first film is replaced by bored expectation ("OK, where's the shark?"). Spielberg's style simply could not be duplicated. At this writing, the only other Spielberg-inspired film to be made by another director is *Jurassic Park III*, although Spielberg did serve as the film's producer and supervisor.

The shark is more of a plot device in *JAWS 2*, creaking along to keep the story moving. It looks realistic until half its face is burned away, and then it looks ridiculous, like the half-burned bear from *Prophecy*. It loses the sleek look of the shark from the first film. Ironically, *The Creature Walks Among Us*, the last and least of the *Creature from the Black Lagoon* trilogy, has a similar scene where the monster attacks a boat, only to have someone set him on fire and alter his appearance.

One of the main problems with *JAWS 2* is it doesn't bother to humanize the victims. In the original *JAWS*, Steven Spielberg took the time, however briefly, to familiarize viewers with every victim. We see Chrissie flirting and having fun at the beach party; Alex having a moment with his mother; the estuary victim is seen at the beginning taking boy scouts out for laps to earn their merit badges; and Ben Gardner extends a moment of kindness to Matt Hooper ("Hello back, Young Fella").

Even Tippit the dog is seen scampering playfully with his owner on the beach before he's eaten. Spielberg takes a moment to set up why we should care about each victim, before these characters are killed.

JAWS 2 fails to do that — the two divers eaten in the beginning are faceless nobodies underwater in scuba gear. The water skier and the woman driving her boat are just stuntwomen — we know nothing about them, we are told nothing about their backstory and they hardly say a word — viewers couldn't care less when they are eaten.

This mistake is made in all of the *JAWS* sequels.

Roy Scheider and Lorraine Gary, who gave the earlier film realism as the determined husband and his caring, worried wife, are shunted into supporting roles, despite their top-billing status. Murray Hamilton seems to be mistakenly reading his dialogue from the first *JAWS* (He wonders why beaches should be closed) and because the film's leads are all teenagers, the movie feels juvenile. There are too many teens, none of them get killed and they're all bland. The painful part of using them is they date the film terribly. The Tab Generation's dated bell-bottom pants, angels' flight collars and Farrah Fawcett hair-styles give viewers even more reasons to laugh at the dull film.

Sharp-eyed viewers will spot actor/future director Keith Gordon in a small role ("He was fun to be around," says Szwarc) and B-movie actress Donna Wilkes, star of the '80s cult exploitation film, *Angel* ("High school honor student by day — Hollywood hooker by night!").

John Dukakis, who plays 'Polo', is the stepson of former Presidential candidate/Massachusetts' Governor Michael Dukakis. (Kevin Pike remembers "When Dukakis visited the set of *JAWS*, his boat accidentally hit the *Orca* ... You can see the dent on the *Orca* in the film!")

"I was a kid, so all the teenagers seemed very worldly to me," laughs Marc Gilpin. "I liked Keith Gordon; a great, down-to-earth person. John Dukakis was nice; I don't know what happened to Donna Wilkes ... I heard she had a lot of trouble over the years. I remember Donna had a lot of pressure, because she's the one who had to freak out so much in that film. Donna kept to herself on *JAWS 2*, because she had to constantly psych herself up. I don't remember her enjoying *JAWS 2* so much, because she had such a heavy load on that film.

"It was amazing how many times I walked in on Mark Gruner and other cast members smoking pot on the set!" Gilpin recalls. "He was always [saying], 'Dude, be cool — don't say anything to anybody!' so I did keep a few secrets. Mark dropped off the face of the Earth after that film, but he was great."

"The beautiful blonde Cindy Grover and I formed a very close bond," Gilpin continues. "I was eleven and she was nineteen, but I truly fell in love with her. She knew it was puppy love, but she didn't crush the crush, which I was grateful for. We stayed in touch for a long time, but I unfortunately lost contact with her. Cindy, if you read this book,

Marc Gilpin, the second Sean Brody. PHOTO BY PATRICK JANKIEWICZ.

please contact me! Last I heard is that she got married to a guy from Sweden. She'd be in her late forties by now."

Actor Billy Van Zandt played 'Bob' in the film: "I made it from the Hancock version to the Szwarc *JAWS 2*," he says happily. "Carl Gottlieb told me the reason my name was 'Bob' is because I was bitten in half in the original script for *JAWS 2*, the kid is bitten in half and his torso 'bobs' in the water!"

The crew also helped provide victims.

"Roy Arbogast and I built the dead whale with the bite out of him," says Kevin Pike.

"Oh, the dead whale," smiles Jeffrey Kramer. "That dead whale was made out of styrofoam. I think at one point, they got in trouble for taping the bird's feet to the whale!"

A couple of plot points from the original novel are brought in, though to little effect. Joseph Mascolo, who usually plays mafia types, is a possible romantic rival for Gary, reviving the Ellen Brody/Matt Hooper romance angle and the Mayor

Joseph Mascolo and Roy Schieder.

Vaughn/Mafia connection from Benchley's book, but neither is developed. He is linked with the Mafia in the Hancock/Tristan version and provides more of a romantic threat for Ellen in *JAWS 2*.

A scene where the shark eats a helicopter, complete with pilot, is so silly that you wonder why it's even in the movie. Worse, it taxed the filmmakers to the limit.

"*JAWS 2* was three times the size of *JAWS*, production-wise," Roy Arbogast sighs. "That picture was the toughest thing anyone had ever done. We had weather against us, bad seas, so much work at sea. Two units going all the time, and the tail-end of a couple hurricanes hit us and just wiped us out. It was very, very tough. I was there the day [director John Hancock] got fired, right after they showed *JAWS 2* dailies in Martha's Vineyard.

"Getting the scene where the shark eats the helicopter was just ridiculously hard," attests Arbogast. "We were out on the set of *JAWS 2*, at sea, because it was so big. Bob Mattey had a whole crew trying to get the platform shark to do a couple of gags. It was incredibly difficult, so we were working with two sharks and that helicopter scene was hellishly hard."

Marc Gilpin agrees, recalling "The logistics of the hydraulic shark eating the helicopter was a nightmare, as you can imagine! That was an actual helicopter pilot, playing the pilot in the movie. That was a huge amount of work, expended for that one scene. I sat on the barge, watching them try to do that."

Kevin Pike adds, "Yeah, that helicopter scene was murder, but we were thrilled by the shark on *JAWS 2*. He was better built than the first one, a big improvement on the first shark, with better skin, so we didn't have as many problems with him as we did on that first shark. The movie doesn't have the magic of *JAWS*, but we were really happy with the shark!"

In director Szwarc's defense, he was brought in at the last minute after Hancock was fired and he makes *JAWS 2* work a lot better than it should. The opening scene, for instance, suggests real menace: the shark's dorsal fin glides into Amity harbor to the strains of John Williams' always effective music. Szwarc knows he can't hold the shark back, so he shocks the audience by placing the shark where it shouldn't be: lunging out of a clump of seaweed, coming through the bottom of a boat, rising unexpectedly at inopportune moments. It works, but *JAWS 2* still plays like a schlocky B-movie.

Szwarc was able to prove he could do better than *JAWS 2* with his touching cult hit, *Somewhere in Time*, written by *Duel/JAWS 3-D* scribe Richard Matheson.

Production designer (and the film's associate producer/second unit director) Joe Alves feels "*JAWS 2* was the biggest film I've ever been involved with. It was a bigger movie than *JAWS* in terms of FX. We were there (in Florida), forever shooting it, and we attempted to do a lot more with the shark and fight the ocean. It was like a war."

Carl Gottlieb, brought in to 'punch up' the film, does an admirable job on Martin and Ellen Brody. Both are good characters, but, unfortunately, they are stuck on the sidelines.

Scheider manages to stand out in the scene in which he sees the shark's silhouette enter swimming waters. After pulling everyone out of the water, he fires his gun into it, only to find that it's merely a school of fish. He turns to see everyone (even his wife) staring at him as though he were crazy. It is a fine moment.

There is also a very suspenseful sequence where the fish attacks a teenage couple alone on the ocean, knocking a boy overboard. He desperately tries to swim back to the boat (He doesn't make it.) The scene is taut, scary, and achieves the standard of the original *JAWS*, which is why it was the only clip used to promote the film on television.

JAWS 2 received an unprecedented wave of merchandising from Universal, much of it aimed at kids — posters, albums, beach towels, toys, T-shirts, coloring books, comics and cups.

"I was on the *JAWS 2* bubblegum cards," Marc Gilpin recalls. "But I had to go to the store and buy them ...You woulda' thought they would have sent me some! Because of *JAWS 2*, magazines like *Tiger Beat* were calling me all the time to do articles. I also got a lot of weird letters because of *JAWS 2*...Although I was eleven, I got a lot of mail from twenty-year-old girls offering to 'pop my cherry' for the first time! They sent me nude photographs. At first, my parents let me open my own fan mail, I got two thousand letters a month, but when I said, 'Wow, Mom — this girl wants to go out with me!' Mom and Dad started screening it."

As with the first film, anticipation for the upcoming *JAWS 2* was so great that numerous TV shows started finding ways to rip it off. *Happy Days*, a sitcom set in the 1950s, suddenly came up with a multi-part episode in which the popular character Fonzie — wearing a leather jacket and water skis — jumps over a shark! This plotline was so ludicrous, it coined a catchphrase. Whenever a long-running show passes the point of credibility, it is now referred to as "Jumping the Shark."

Left: JAWS 2 bubblegum card. *Right: JAWS 2* coloring book.

There's also a lot of advertising in *JAWS 2* — something Spielberg didn't do in the original. The Brody boys are shown enjoying the Atari video game Pong. When Eddie and Tina are out at sea, a Coca-Cola cup is prominently displayed and at the Brody kitchen table, a box of Cheerios is lit as carefully as a member of the cast and plugged by name. Sean Brody whines that he wants Fruit Loops (a Kellogg product) and Ellen replies, "You'll get Cheerios, mister!"

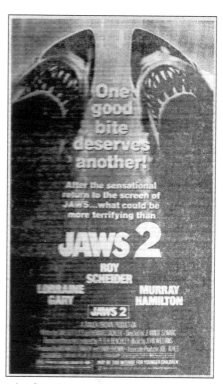

A brief *JAWS 2* re-release.

JAWS 2 opened in 640 theaters to a then-whopping $9,866,023.00 and went on to gross a robust 40% of the original's take, making a *JAWS 3* all but a certainty. The summer of 1978, *JAWS 2* opened against several rip-offs, most of which were more entertaining than the sanctioned sequel. These included Joe Dante's *Piranha* and the Italian squid epic, *Tentacles*.

Non-derivative competition included John Travolta's *Grease*, Ryan O'Neal's *Oliver's Story* and the Elliot Gould boxing kangaroo bomb, *Matilda*. *JAWS 2* came out on top. It would, in fact, be the highest-grossing sequel of all time until *The Empire Strikes Back* in 1980.

The box-office bonanza must have been a terrific victory for director Szwarc, as his feature film directorial debut, the horror movie *BUG!* had the misfortune of opening June 20, 1975, the same day as the original *JAWS*. (Yes, it was crushed like a bug!)

Amity, for a town, really gets around. It's Martha's Vineyard in the original JAWS, but "*JAWS* was shot all over," Carl Gottlieb states. "There was real underwater stuff with real sharks in Australia, stuff we shot in the MGM tank (where 'Million Dollar Mermaid' Esther Williams made her films), and there was stuff shot off Catalina for the opening (of the shark's POV in seaweed) and in the Universal backlot."

Because *JAWS 2* shot in Martha's Vineyard and then Florida, you literally change states when you watch Brody drive into town in the first minutes of JAWS 2. "I'm sure I spent more on sets for *JAWS 2* than I did on all of *Close Encounters of the Third Kind*," says Joe Alves. "We made a little town in Pensacola, Florida look just like Martha's Vineyard; we built things like The Lighthouse and the island that the kids swim to at the climax. We only shot in Martha's Vineyard for two weeks, but for the rest of the movie — the majority of shooting — we completely redressed this Florida town and nobody ever noticed!"

"*JAWS 2* was shot in Pensacola and Fort Walton Beach, Florida, with a few weeks footage in Martha's Vineyard for continuity," Gottlieb explains. "All the beach and ocean stuff was shot in Florida because the water was warmer there. By that time, we had learned about shooting on the water!"

Catalina Island, one of several Amity locations. PHOTO BY PATRICK JANKIEWICZ.

JAWS 3-D

Release date: July 22, 1983
Tagline: "The third dimension is terror!"
Produced By Rupert Hitzig
Directed By Joe Alves
Written By Richard Matheson and Carl Gottlieb
Based on a story by Guerdon Trueblood
and suggested by the novel "Jaws" by Peter Benchley
97 minutes

Cast

Mike Brody . . . . .Dennis Quaid
Kathryn Morgan . . . . Bess Armstrong
Phillip FitzRoyce. . . . . .Simon MacCorkindale
Calvin Bouchard . . . . .Louis Gossett, Jr.
Sean Brody . . . . .John Putch
Kelly Ann Bukowski . . . . Lea Thompson

Synopsis

A team of female water skiers are performing maneuvers in the open ocean. The familiar *JAWS* theme pipes up as the girls return to their Sea World theme park, a dorsal fin surfaces and a Great White Shark secretly follows them in. Mike Brody, Sheriff Brody's son, now grown, is the park's construction foreman. His boss is Sea World owner Calvin Bouchard and he's dating Dr. Kathryn Morgan (Bess Armstrong), a dolphin trainer. Mike's younger brother Sean (John Putch) arrives. Terrified of the water because of his history with sharks, Sean is a college student and self-styled Colorado cowboy. Sea World is about to unveil an undersea attraction that allows customers to look out into the middle of their aquarium.

Sean may be afraid of the water, but Kathryn's water skiing friend Kelly Ann Bukowski (Lea Thompson) helps him overcome his fear with a make-out session in the lagoon. An even bigger shark cruises into the park, knocking the gate off the tracks and eating Shelby, one of Mike Brody's employees. Kathryn and Mike realize that the first Great White is a baby and hiding in a fake shipwreck. They catch it and put it on display against Mike and Kathryn's wishes. It swims one lap around the observation pool and quickly dies, as Great Whites have a poor track record for living in captivity.

The bigger shark — the baby's 35-foot mother, comes after its pup and smashes through the park with a vengeance. In the process, she damages an undersea observation deck full of tourists. The tourists' oxygen is running out, so Mike, Kathryn and photographer/shark hunter Phillip Fitzroyce plunge in to distract the fish and spot-weld the damage.

JAWS 3-D — the third dimension is terror!

The mother shark eats Fitzroyce and tries to get Mike and Kathryn, who are saved by plucky dolphins, Cindy & Sandy. The mother shark attacks performing water skiers. Unlike *JAWS 2*, this shark doesn't catch anyone. Kelly Ann convinces Sean to overcome his fear of the water and go out on the Bumper Boats. The shark attacks, biting Kelly Ann with such force that she's lifted out of the water. Despite being bitten by a 35-foot Great White, Kelly Ann only suffers a little nip on the leg.

FISH FACTS

➤ Original plans for the film were to use real sharks, and mechanical people. (This concept was eventually scrapped.)

➤ James Cummins sculpted the shark used in the film.

Bumper boat horror for Lea Thompson and John Putch!

Bouchard decides to suffocate the shark by cutting off all the oxygen in the park's water tanks. This will kill all the fish. Not to be outdone, the mother shark rams the observation glass to get Bouchard, who escapes. Mike sees the shark hasn't finished swallowing Fitzroyce, whose head, arm and torso are still in its mouth. He sees that the dead man's arm is still holding a hand grenade, so Mike manages to set it off and the shark blows up. Mike and Kathryn happily watch their dolphin friends do victory somersaults.

One of the smartest decisions made on *JAWS 3-D* was to bring in screenwriter/novelist Richard

➤ Lea Thompson's shark attack on the bumper boats is a playful shot-by-shot steal from the estuary victim's rowboat attack in the first film.

➤ Dennis Quaid's mad dash across the park is a take-off on the climax of Robert Wise' *The Andromeda Strain*.

Matheson. A master of horror, Matheson has written such films as *The Pit and the Pendulum, The Incredible Shrinking Man, The House of Usher,* and *The Legend of Hell House,* as well as many classic *Twilight Zone* episodes. He also wrote the classic science fiction/horror novel, *I am Legend,* which has been adapted to film three times.

Matheson devised a scary, plausible scenario — in the water park, the shark would be a frightening, unexpected adversary. Matheson also added the angle of two sharks. "I thought that would increase the suspense," he says. "You realize that there [are] two of them, because this creature has come into the waterpark to give birth.

"I had the idea that the shark would give birth in the tunnels ... This is when it was believed that a shark had to keep moving or it would die. It goes into the tunnel so water will pass through its gills while it gives birth."

The writer decided to do *JAWS 3-D* "When they offered it to me and I thought, 'With the second one, you had to continue directly from the first. You're stuck doing a rehash. With the third one, you could make a complete break', which

Legendary writer Richard Matheson. PHOTO BY LISA ORRIS.

I did. I wrote a very good story, but the script was revised, not to my liking," he states.

"It was not my idea that the Sheriff's sons would be in it. The [idea of the] two guys being Brody's sons was forced on me; I thought that was ridiculous — they go all the way down to Florida and have the same damn shark problem down there?! The fourth one [*JAWS THE REVENGE*] was really inadequate, it was like the shark had been to Oxford — he was now smart enough to chase them all the way down to the Bahamas!"

"I wanted to make the shark menacing," Matheson muses. "In the [undersea] tunnels, you would never really be sure where it was. They wanted to make it the same shark from *JAWS 2*! The same shark all burned up! I thought the audience would hoot that off the screen. That would have been horrible but, thankfully, someone regained their sanity and they decided not to do that!"

Mike Brody explains to Kathryn that Sean is afraid of the water because of "that shark attack I told you about when we were kids." This single line of dialogue seems to negate the events of *JAWS 2*. One assumes if Mike were talking about *JAWS 2*, he would be more specific, like "That shark eating the helicopter when we were kids!"

Having the shark in 3-D was a brilliant gimmick, harkening back to '50s 3-D movies like *Creature from*

◤ Sandy Berman gets credit for doing 'Special Shark Sound Effects,' including the Shark's roaring. This is impressive, as sharks have no vocal cords and make no sound.

JAWS 3-D's roaring shark!

the Black Lagoon. It's a credit to Universal Studios that the film's Arrivision 3-D is quite terrific. Unlike previous 3-D movies, they would only need one camera to film it. Joe Alves' production designer background serves him well, as he exploits the 3-D to its fullest extent.

Opening credits note the film is "Suggested" by Peter Benchley's *JAWS*. What in the classic book suggests a shark attack at Sea World is anyone's guess. *JAWS 3-D* actually owes its plot to a couple of popular '50s monster movies. The idea that the shark is only a baby whose mother comes to rescue him is straight out of the giant monster epic, *Gorgo*. The rest of it, with a monster running amok in an aquatic theme park comes from Universal's *Revenge of the Creature*, a 3-D sequel to *Creature from the Black Lagoon*. In *Revenge*,

◤ Mickey Rooney was originally announced as cast in the film as a clown, but neither he nor the clown character appear.

◤ Dennis Quaid told *Movieline* the lowest point in his life came when a pimp in Times Square recognized him from *JAWS 3-D*.

◤ John Putch ('Sean Brody') became a director. In 2005, he helmed a TV remake of *The Poseidon Adventure*.

the Creature is captured and placed in the Marineland water park, where it eventually escapes, causing a full-scale panic.

The scene where they catch the baby shark in *JAWS 3-D* is incredibly similar to the one where they catch the Creature in *Revenge*, as is the follow-up sequence where they walk the baby shark around the tank to keep it alive by getting water through it's gills. Ironically, these scenes with Kathryn and Mike are the only time in all four *JAWS* movies where we see anybody trying to save a shark! You hear a child cry when the baby shark dies, which adds a touch of pathos to the scene.

Screenwriter Carl Gottlieb (again brought in to 'punch up' the script) felt that any similarities to *Revenge of the Creature* were unintentional.

"It certainly wasn't in my consciousness. I don't know what was in Joe Alves' mind, or Richard Matheson's, who wrote an early draft of the film. It was such a hodgepodge by the time I got to it, that I just did what I could."

"I tried to make Dennis Quaid, Lea Thompson and Bess Armstrong's characters believable and fun," Gottlieb explains. "I tried to work with the cast and write for them, because by that time, I knew who was gonna be in the movie. That's a luxury for a writer because sometimes you don't know who's in the picture. If you know who you're writing for, it's easier and more fun."

"At the water park, they showed Joe Alves and me a 3-D movie called *Sea Dreams*," Matheson recalls. "Joe made a drawing of the shark coming out of the water with its big mouth opening and the words *JAWS 3-D*, which he thought of. It was such an obvious title — "JAWS 3 in 3-D"! Periodically in the script, I would try to indicate where I thought the 3-D should be used, writing something like, 'The shark rushes right at you.'"

JAWS 3-D is also the goriest sequel in the series, with severed arms, rotting heads and other limbs, all coming at you in three dimensions. The gimmick is used most successfully in the opening, in which we see a fish bitten in half, as its head (with mouth still gaping) floats directly into the audience. It was a cheesy effect, but it effectively sets the tone for some goofy cinematic fun. The film's cardboard 3-D glasses came with a shark on the bridge of the nose.

Unfortunately, Universal didn't issue a 3-D version on video or TV. They simply called it "JAWS 3" and a lot of the film's original charm is lost. (The ending, where the exploding shark's jaws shoot out at the audience for almost a minute, is usually cut for TV. Without the 3-D, it's pretty pointless, as are the endless shots of Cindy and Sandy, the leaping dolphins.)

Airing without the 3-D crutch, *JAWS 3* usually looks blurry when it airs on basic cable networks. Director of photography James Contner was a camera operator on the original *JAWS* and directed his own man-eater movie, The Hallmark Channel miniseries, *Shark Swarm*.

Polarized 3-D has not been developed for a mass market TV format yet. The ending, with the wild POV from *inside* the shark's mouth — was a shot Alves' designed for the original *JAWS* (the one with Hooper being attacked in the shark cage). Spielberg opted not to use it, so Alves resurrects it here.

As *JAWS 3-D* takes place at an underwater park (with fake sunken ships) the filmmakers can do a lot with the big fish and its ability to travel in the spooky, dark tunnels. When it explores the fear of encountering a man-eating monster in such tight quarters, it's mildly effective. Unfortunately, *JAWS 3-D* takes the banal approach of saving tourists from suffocating, which brings to mind all of the '70s disaster films.

Another strike against *JAWS 3-D* was that it had been beaten into theaters by a number of cheapjack 3-D movies: *Spacehunter: Adventures in the Forbidden Zone, Parasite, Friday the 13th Part 3* (in 3-D), *Amityville 3-D*, and Empire Pictures' heavily hyped but terrible *Metalstorm: The Destruction of Jared Syn.* As their visual FX were not half as good as *JAWS 3-D's,* some looked blurry and gave viewers eyestrain, which helped wear out the gimmick's welcome before Universal's big fish had a chance to prove itself.

"The 3-D all boils down to the glasses; whether you do the polarized glasses or red and blue glasses," states *JAWS 3-D* location manager Carl Mazzocone. "I think there was a lot of politics over which 3-D camera system to use. There were some people involved who were able to profit on the glasses by cornering the market. There were a lot of politics over that."

Shark builder Roy Arbogast devised a new form for the fish.

"We had two sharks, as well as a tail section, a rear section and side section," he explains. This way, the filmmakers could just operate a fin, without having to move the whole shark. "I think *JAWS 3* was a thirty-footer and the whole picture was done underwater in one big tank."

Director Alves' gets as much mileage out of the story as he can, and, as this was his directorial debut, it's impressive in terms of unusual camera angles and pacing. He also resurrects such popular 3-D tricks from the *Creature* movies as fish swimming at the camera, spear guns, and of course, cavorting dolphins and other undersea life.

Ironically, *JAWS* was given the 3-D treatment over a proposed remake of *Creature from the Black Lagoon.*

Director John Landis (*Animal House*) spearheaded the *Creature* remake: "Jack Arnold [director of the original *Creature* film] came to me about doing a *Creature from the Black Lagoon* sequel, and I thought it was a good idea — it would make a really great movie,"

◣ This was the first *JAWS* film not produced by Richard Zanuck and David Brown.

◣ *JAWS 3-D* composer Alan Parker later did the score for the acclaimed *What's Eating Gilbert Grape?*

◣ Rexford Metz, who did some underwater photography on the original *JAWS,* handled the 3-D visual FX cinematography.

◣ The film was originally announced as "JAWS '83"—in the tradition of the *Airport* movies.

◣ In December of 1982, a fiberglass *JAWS 3-D* head fell off a Universal Studios billboard in Studio City and smashed a VW.

◣ The Brody boys no longer have Cheerios for breakfast — now, apparently, they have Wheaties.

◣ While Deputy Hendricks is *not* in the film, he can be heard. Actor Jeffrey Kramer "did some looping on *JAWS 3-D* because my friend Joe Alves directed."

◣ In 2008, *JAWS 3-D* was #20 on *Moviefone's* "25 Worst Sequels of all Time" list. They added, "Dennis Quaid can use those cheesy 3-D glasses to hide his shame." Ouch.

Landis recalls. "Jack was gonna direct it, and we were gonna do it in 3-D. We did a 3-D test that looked great. Sid Sheinberg, head of MCA, saw the test and said, 'What a great idea! But why [remake] the *Creature*? Let's do *JAWS 3-D!*' Our little movie was cancelled and they made that piece of shit!

"I feel very bad because Universal treated Jack really poorly," Landis says sadly.

John Landis. PHOTO BY PATRICK JANKIEWICZ.

The Creature From The Black Lagoon, a film that influenced JAWS.

Director Joe Alves had spoken with Jack Arnold when both men were preparing their projects, little knowing they would be in competition.

"I met with Jack on *JAWS 3-D*. There are shots in the first JAWS, like the Chrissie scene, that are similar to *Creature*," he notes. "I wasn't aware of that until Jack showed me an original 3-D print of *Creature from the Black Lagoon*. When they decided to make *JAWS 3-D*, Jack was trying to do another version of *Creature* and he lost out."

Alves felt fortunate that, for his directorial debut, "I had such a great cast. It was Lea [Thompson]'s first big part, a real breakthrough for her. Lea was cute and a very good actress. I also had Dennis Quaid, Lou Gossett, Bess Armstrong and Simon MacCorkindale.

"*JAWS 3-D* was an opportunity for me to direct and I think we did as good a job as could under the circumstances. I wish I had been closer to Steven [Spielberg] at the time, to get some advice from him, but he was off doing other things."

"Shari Rhodes, who cast the original *JAWS*, also worked on *JAWS 3-D*," notes Carl Mazzocone. "They were looking for a fresh face to play the water skier Sean Brody dates. I said 'You should look at that girl in the Burger King commercial!

Next thing I know, the girl from the Burger King commercial is hired and it's Lea Thompson! I always felt I had a little something to do with that."

Lea Thompson appeared in *JAWS 3-D* before she co-starred in the Spielberg-produced *Back to the Future* trilogy.

"Dennis Quaid was in his party mode in those days. He showed up with his wife, this beautiful girl from *Stripes* [PJ Soles]. I remember meeting her and then, the next thing you know, he had an illicit affair with Lea Thompson," Mazzocone marvels.

John Putch, who played Sean Brody in *JAWS 3-D*, remembers, "Lea was beautiful and a great person. It was her very first movie. She was fresh out of Pittsburgh, where she had been a ballerina. She came straight from a dance company. She seemed very excited to be doing *JAWS 3-D* — I know I was! You kiddin'? We all thought it was gonna be 'The Big Thing'! I didn't know it was terrible when I made it," Putch professes. "I was only twenty years old and happy to be in a movie!

"I had never made so much money before, it was in 3-D and I was acting with Dennis Quaid, Lou Gossett and all those great movie actors! I have gotta believe some of the other actors had to know it was bad. I hope your book is poking fun at certain things when you're supposed to," he adds. "Make sure it's noted that *JAWS 3-D* is absolutely, positively the worst movie I have ever been in! I'm so happy to be part of it. People argue with me and say '*JAWS 4* [*JAWS THE REVENGE*] is worse and I say, 'There's no way that was worse than *JAWS 3-D!* We're fighting a shark in Sea World, for God's sake!"

As for the third Great White in the series, Putch remembers, "That shark was huge! I remember all of the FX guys including Roy Arbogast in the water with scuba tanks, to keep that shark running. Lea Thompson and I are attacked by the shark while riding the bumper boats and the shark bites Lea! I remember the shark head was huge.

"It was the same kind of thing they have on the Universal Studio Tour, a giant shark head on a hydraulic arm. It would be pushed forward and up. The shark head only went halfway down the body, so all you got is the head and mouth coming out and then it would pull back in. It was pretty impressive. To your eye, it looked like a scary animal. But you know... there was the movie part of it ..."

"My all-time favorite scene in *JAWS 3-D* is a huge laugh and a scene I'm not even in," Putch adds. "It's at that point, toward the end, everyone else in the film is either gone or dead, but there's a shot where a submarine is coming at the camera. It banks to the left in the foreground and it completely disappears because the green screen key was so bad! The fucking top half of the submarine just disappears and they released it in theaters looking like this! That was the funniest thing ever."

Alves concedes that "It was a real difficult project to make as your first feature. It was a big picture with all the normal and mechanical problems you have on a *JAWS* movie. I had to work with whales, dolphins, and mechanical sharks," he laughs. Particularly difficult for Alves was when "I had a scene where the mechanical shark was fighting real dolphins underwater!"

Putch and Thompson put 3-D to good use.

Kevin Pike "got to visit Joe and Roy while they were making *JAWS 3-D* and it was the best shark on any of the *JAWS* movies — it worked great and did whatever they needed him to do! The sharks that Roy Arbogast made for *JAWS 3-D* were the finest sharks ever made. Their skin, their design — they were just the most perfect sharks you could ever make! Every time Roy had to make a shark, it was a quantum leap over the last one he did."

"Watching them build the shark was like nothing I had ever seen before," Carl Mazzocone remembers. "They used these giant molds that Roy Arbogast and his crew made to put these sharks together; [it] was amazing to watch. Many of the crew [members] had worked on Steven Spielberg's *JAWS*, so they were the best of the best — a bunch of amazing pros! I feel so lucky to have known them, from Joe on down. We really bonded ... I think I drank my paycheck with them every week at the bar, with these great New York grips, electricians and [*JAWS 3-D* actor] P.H. Moriarty! They were the kind of group where, if you had a birthday, they all took you out. I never had more fun on a movie — we were like a family."

"I loved P.H. Moriarty," he continues. "When he did *JAWS 3-D*, he had been in a great gangster movie, *The Long Good Friday*, and after it, he starred in *Lock, Stock and Two Smoking Barrels*. This guy is a phenomenal friend of mine, I just adore him. He played Simon MacCorkindale's sidekick. Off-camera, Simon MacCorkindale was a bit of a loner — you never saw him — but P.H. and I became great friends!"

Director Alves explains that on *JAWS 3-D*, "I chose to do most of the work in a tank to keep it controllable. Because of that, we were able to keep on budget and on-schedule."

Screenwriter Gottlieb never went out of his way to add 3-D scenes.

"The problem with 3-D scenes is they have to be planned so meticulously in advance that I think *JAWS 3-D* is a movie that was sunk from it's planning," he admits. "They organized the whole picture around the concept of a theme park because they wanted to control costs and didn't want to shoot on the open ocean. It made sense as a logistical idea, but it was tough to execute.

"They had this idea of an underwater floating control chamber and after all that conceptual work was done, sets were built and the scenes of the shark swimming at the camera had been planned, sketched and storyboarded, so you couldn't change that," Gottlieb adds. "There really wasn't much you could do, they had all that stuff laid out, it was like, 'This is what you got,' so you had to write around that. It's like a Roger Corman movie where he's got footage of the riot or the plane exploding and four days of footage of Transylvania and he says, 'Here, write a vampire movie around it!'"

Roy Arbogast recalls that "I had fights with the powers-that-be at Universal after *JAWS 3-D* and I never went back. They gave me problems and I wound [up] being black-balled at the studio. On *JAWS 3-D*, we never held up shooting once. We never had a malfunction with the shark, not one single time. That should have made it a breeze to shoot. Unfortunately, one person there didn't like independent FX people — he wanted all the FX to be run in-house through the studio.

"There were several political battles going on and I just wanted to do the movie and get out. We did it all in Florida and on the last day of the movie I went to the producer and said, 'What are we gonna do with all this equipment and the shark?' I was sick of it all and just wanted to go home. Nobody has an answer!

Putch teaches Thompson French.

"The day I was done, I packed my trailer with my equipment and left, the shark was still in the water. Everything was still there and I could give a shit what they did with it! I came home and got accused of stealing the shark," he says with disgust. "How could I get it home, for God's sake? I wanted that shark like I wanted a hole in the head."

John Putch found the whole experience to be surreal: "I was just some kid doing summer stock and now I'm in a *JAWS* movie," he laughs. "I remember shooting in Florida was fun; lots of fun. Dennis Quaid was cool, Orlando was nice and warm and there were always a lot of girls in bikinis running around — that part was fantastic!

"Whenever I see that movie, I look at the people in the background, because they were the animal handlers. They were all Sea World employees and they did ADR [Automatic Dialogue Replacement], so they all had lines put in their mouths in post. They were sweet, nice people who really loved their dolphins. When I catch *JAWS 3-D* now, all I think is, 'I was so thin and I had hair and I was acting up a storm.'"

"Yeah, it was great," agrees Carl Mazzocone. "*JAWS 3-D* was not the best movie, but it was an amazing experience. All these beautiful water skiers! There was this one girl there we used to complain about because she used to smell like Shamu! We couldn't believe it; the hottest girl there and she has to smell like the whale!"

Actor Putch adds, "I loved Joe Alves — he worked really, really hard — a sweet man. He was the production designer of the other films, but I don't know

The *JAWS 3-D* cast. From left: Simon MacCorkindale, Putch, Thompson, Dennis Quaid, Bess Armstrong, P.H. Moriarty and Lou Gossett.

how he wound up as director. I love Joe, he got a bad rap for *JAWS 3-D*, but the real problem was that cheesy script. In the bar scene, where I meet Lea Thompson, I'm playing that 'push'/takedown game with a big bearded guy — that's Carl Mazzocone, who was the location manager and built the tank that we shot in. Carl's great, a big producer now."

Ironically, the film's major plot point — a shark breaking into Sea World "was impossible, because Sea World Florida is landlocked in Orlando," laughs Mazzocone. "The shark couldn't get in there if he tried! I had to find a proper seaside opening that looked uninhabited by condos and TV antennas, to bring the shark into the park with the water skiers.

"I sat on the edge of the shark tank and made a deal where I got the governor of Florida's helicopter to find that location. People were so excited to hear we were shooting a *JAWS* movie, they would help us in any way. There was nothing we couldn't do and nothing we couldn't get — I called it 'Cinematic Immunity'!"

Lou Gossett was filming *JAWS 3-D* after he won the Best Supporting Actor Oscar for his role as a tough drill sergeant in *An Officer and a Gentleman*. "He was very fun to be around," Putch says. "Whenever we had a crowd scene with extras, Lou Gossett would start doing his character from *An Officer and a Gentleman*! Lou would look at somebody and do one of his classic lines like, 'Don't you eyeball me, Boy!' He did it for fun and we all loved it!"

Putch, Armstrong and Quaid at Sea World.

As a former lifeguard, he was qualified to meet a shark, but Gossett didn't see Calvin Bouchard as his most challenging role. As he told *Films in Review*: "The shark doesn't get me — [I] guess he doesn't like soul food!"

The film's use of 3-D really paid off, as it opened to a robust $13,422,500 on 1,300 screens with a healthy $10,325 per screen average. Ultimately, there was a worldwide gross of $87,987,055. This was an impressive amount, considering that it was a "threequel" in a summer crowded with such fellow three-timers as *Superman III*, *Rocky III* and the finale of the original *Star Wars* trilogy, *Return of the Jedi*.

"*JAWS 3-D* had a huge opening and did a lot of business — It may be Dennis Quaid's most successful movie," Carl Mazzocone observes. "He's been one of those guys who never really had a hit..."

In spite of its commercial success, *JAWS 3-D* was nominated for five Razzie/Golden Raspberry Awards — including Worst Picture, Director, Supporting Actor for Lou Gossett, Jr., and a nod for Worst Newcomers, for Cindy & Sandy (which The Razzie Committee described as "the shrieking dolphins")!

"I had no idea they were even nominated," Putch jokes.

"After it was finished, Bess Armstrong and I went down to The Hitchcock Screening Room on The Universal Backlot to see it," Putch recalls. "They gave us 3-D glasses and there were only twelve people in there, all Universal execs including Sid Sheinberg and Joe Alves was there. Bess and I were sitting in the back, totally excited — and then we watched it! When we came out, we were standing there trembling — not knowing what to do with each other.

"Bess goes, 'This is it, our careers are over!'

"I agreed and said, 'There's only one thing that we can do now.'

"Bess said, 'What?' — and I laugh, 'Let's go get drunk!'

And we did! We finally felt better after that. It was a career low at the time, but now I point to it quite proudly as one of the greatest 'worst movies' ever made!"

JAWS THE REVENGE — the new shark eats some poor dummy.

JAWS THE REVENGE

Release Date: July 17, 1987
Tagline: "This time it's personal!"
Produced and directed by Joseph Sargent
Written by Michael de Guzman
Based on characters created by Peter Benchley
89 minutes

Cast

Ellen Brody . . . . .Lorraine Gary
Michael. . . . . .Lance Guest
Jake . . . . Mario Van Peebles
Carla . . . . .Karen Young
Hoagie. . . . . Michael Caine
Thea. . . . . .Judith Barsi

Synopsis

It's Christmas on Amity Island. This year is tougher than most, as Chief Brody has died of a heart attack (His picture can still be seen, hanging on the wall). Things get worse when son Sean, now a cop, has to go into Amity Harbor to remove some debris from the shipping lanes.

As he puts a winch into the freezing water to tow it out, a Great White shark lunges out of the water and rips his arm off. As the shark repeatedly attacks him, Sean's screams are drowned out by the high school choir singing Christmas carols. The shark then sinks his police boat.

Devastated by the loss of her husband and son, Ellen Brody flies to the Bahamas to join her marine biologist son Michael, his wife Carla, a sculptor, and their daughter Thea. Once there, Ellen has repeated nightmares of being attacked by the shark and begs Michael not to go in the water. Carla is prepping a statue for the town's grand celebration.

Ellen insists that the shark killed both Sean and Martin Brody.

"Dad died of a heart attack," Michael protests.

"No," Ellen insists, "he died from fear … Fear of that shark!"

Lightening up a little, she begins to fall for devil-may-care pilot Hoagie.

Meanwhile, the shark swims to the Bahamas, where he attacks Michael and his Jamaican friend Jake. They manage to slap a tracer on the shark and track it by monitor. After close calls in a sunken ship and a mini sub, Michael and Jake come to the only conclusion that makes sense to them: the shark only wants to eat members of the Brody family(!). They use the transmitter on the shark to know when it's in the area.

At the grand unveiling of Carla's statue (the movie's version of *JAWS'* Fourth of July celebration), Ellen is cajoled by Thea into letting the child go on an inflatable banana boat ride.

As the boat goes through the water in slow motion, the massive shark surfaces, determined to get Thea. As it leaps from the water to devour her, an island woman shoves Thea out of the way and dies in her place, as the shark munches her in full view of the children.

Distraught and convinced the shark has specifically targeted her family, Ellen Brody pilots a ship out to sea to give herself to the shark and end the 'curse' once

Bruce hits The Bahamas.

and for all. Piloting Michael and Jake's boat by herself, she taunts the shark, screaming, "Come and get me, you son of a bitch!" When they realize what Ellen has done, Mike, Jake and Hoagie jump into Hoagie's plane, determined to rescue her.

When they see it attack her boat, Hoagie rams the fish with his plane, crashing it in the water. Miraculously, all three swim to the boat before the shark can get them. Jake and Michael rework the transmitter in the Great White to hit it with a painful series of electrical shocks in an attempt to kill it.

To show his displeasure with this plan, the shark leaps out of the water and eats Jake before coming after Mike, Ellen and Hoagie. With the fish bearing down on them, the trio decides to dive overboard (!), just as the fish jumps out of the water and impales itself on the prow of the boat. The curse over, they head for shore. Hoagie is going to fly Ellen home to Amity and a possible life together.

With its Bahamas setting, a single parent mourning the death of a son at Christmas, a shark and a character sculpting metal, *JAWS THE REVENGE* is a radical reworking of Ernest Hemingway's novel, *Islands in the Stream*. Both Michael Caine's boozy Hoagie and Mario Van Peebles' Jake can be seen as take-offs on the novel's drunken Eddie and Joseph, the black deckhand. Ellen Brody's grieving parent is clearly based on Hemingway's protagonist, Thomas Hudson.

The only problem is: screenwriter Michael de Guzman is no Hemingway.

FISH FACTS

🐟 Steven Spielberg sent Joe Sargent a jokey letter when he landed the job, telling him how miserable and lonely he would be filming a *JAWS* movie in Martha's Vineyard.

Brody Family '87. From Left: Karen Young, Lance Guest, Lorraine Gary and the ill-fated Judith Barsi.

JAWS THE REVENGE is the worst in the series; just a giant mess. Even the title stinks. (Wouldn't THE REVENGE OF JAWS be a bit more grammatical?) The idea of the shark chasing Brodys for revenge is also ridiculous. The filmmakers apparently didn't listen to the lady scientist in *JAWS 2*, when she told Brody "Sharks don't take things personally."

JAWS THE REVENGE is so ridiculous, that when Sean Brody is attacked, they cut to a still photo of the shark's mouth and zoom in and out to simulate movement. When the shark bites the boat, the boat gushes blood. (Yes, you read that right: *THE BOAT GUSHES BLOOD!*)

Another absurd moment comes when Ellen has a flashback from the original JAWS of Brody fighting

🐟 *JAWS THE REVENGE* marked Michael Caine's second encounter with Peter Benchley, as he also starred in *The Island*.

🐟 When Caine crashes his plane into the water, he surfaces completely dry!

🐟 Lance Guest starred in another disappointing sequel to a horror classic, *Halloween II*.

🐟 Fifty-one slabs were made to create a fake graveyard for Sean's funeral.

the shark — she 'sees' Brody clinging to the mast, muttering 'Smile, you son of a — ". The only problem is that Brody was alone at sea when it happened, Ellen wasn't there — so no matter how vividly he may have described it to her afterwards, she should not be able to see it.

Director Sargent provides three shocks that tell you how good the movie could have been, had everyone tried a lot harder. The first is when Lance Guest

Shark Attack!

is underwater in a submersible craft, and Sargent pulls back to show the shark's head right next to him.

The second is the film's best jump: Mike Brody, in a sunken ship, encounters a Moray eel. It's a small jolt, but the most frightening thing in a JAWS movie should not be an eel!

Lastly, in the film's best executed sequence, the shark goes after an inflatable banana boat loaded with children. The scene is intense, with the shark bearing down in slow motion on a small child. A woman (Diane Hetfield) pulls the child out of the way and goes into the fish's maw instead.

The shark then begins chewing on the woman as the banana boat circles. As the boat pulls away, we can still see the monster eating its catch — a truly chilling moment.

The shark now resembles a long, grey concrete slab, and the way they dubbed in tiger growls for the shark is extremely silly — it's even worse than the growling shark from JAWS 3-D. What's more, the shark spends most of the movie traveling *on top* of the water! The model that Joe Alves designed so perfectly and Bob Mattey brought to scary life has been reduced to a silly-looking caricature.

In *JAWS THE REVENGE* press notes, Henry Millar, head of the FX on the film, said he started on the film "we didn't even have a script ... But as the story developed they started telling us all what they wanted. I knew this wasn't going to be like any other shark anyone had ever seen."

Lance Guest Today. PHOTO BY PATRICK JANKIEWICZ.

Well, he was right about that!

Seven sharks were built for *JAWS THE REVENGE*, two were fully articulated, one for ramming, two for jumping, one was a half shark and the last one was only a dorsal fin. The two 'hero' sharks had fully movable jaws, sharp teeth and had 22 sectioned ribs. The 'skin' was flexible latex, they weighed 2500 pounds and were 25 feet long.

"The Great White Shark was actually in different pieces...There was a 'Front Shark,' a 'Middle Shark', a 'back shark' and a whole shark — it was kind of like a big puppet," Lance Guest reveals. "I was never afraid of the shark while working in the water with it — Not at all! That shark broke down a lot. In fact,

▲ Lynn Whitfield (Jake's wife) won the Emmy Post-*REVENGE* for the title role in The Josephine Baker Story.

▲ Hoagie's backstory of being a gambler was cut from the film. The TV version adds one deleted scene of him in a casino.

▲ The late comedian Richard Jeni did a routine on *JAWS THE REVENGE*. He got his biggest laughs by simply recounting the plot.

▲ Mario Van Peebles' father, film director Melvin Van Peebles (The Watermelon Man) has a cameo as Mr. Witherspoon.

▲ Joe Sargent directed the heist classic The Taking of Pelham One Two Three, starring *JAWS'* Robert Shaw. He also helmed The Marcus Nelson Murders, the TV movie that inspired Steven Spielberg to cast Lorraine Gary as Ellen Brody.

▲ After the critical drubbing she took for *REVENGE*, Lorraine Gary never made another film.

▲ When the shark dies, the background cyclorama of the sky (Which still exists, in Falls Lake on the Universal backlot) is so shamefully bad, that at times you can see waves slapping against it. Yes, you can see the "ocean" slapping against the horizon.

it broke down all the time! It's hard to do, because to make the shark work, you had hydraulic jacks on the bottom of the ocean floor manipulating it and they had a hard time with the ocean; I remember having to go home a lot of days because the shark just wasn't working. But since we were 'home' in the Bahamas, that wasn't bad."

JAWS THE REVENGE "was a lot of work," Lance Guest insists. "I was pretty much on the set for that all of the time. I had no days off, because the days I wasn't acting, I had to do the underwater unit scenes fighting the shark, scenes where I'm diving and everything. They had to certify me and I did a lot of the underwater stuff."

Michael Caine suffered the most from his involvement. Due to a prolonged Bahamas shooting schedule, he missed picking up his best supporting actor Oscar for Woody Allen's *Hanna and Her Sisters.* In his autobiography, Caine claims "I have never seen it [*JAWS THE REVENGE*] but by all accounts, it is terrible. However, I have seen the house that it built, and it is terrific."

Despite missing the Oscars, "Michael Caine was a good and generous actor, as well as a wonderful guy," Lance Guest praises. He also has kind words for Lorraine Gary.

The *JAWS* franchise returned to Martha's Vineyard for the first day of principal photography, on February 2, 1987. On February 10th, filming continued at Nassau in The Bahamas. While Steven Spielberg had it in his contract that Universal Studios could not use clips of his work in other films and TV shows (He was offended by the unauthorized use as footage from *Duel* being used in an episode of *The Incredible Hulk*). *JAWS THE REVENGE* uses various clips from the classic original and then tries to clumsily re-create those scenes. Because of this, a bad film suffers even more by immediate comparison.

One cast member of the first film didn't mind at all: "I was happy they did that, it meant a lot to me that they took something of mine from the original *JAWS* to use in another JAWS movie," notes Jay Mello, the original Sean Brody. "I was especially pleased because it was my favorite scene — the one of Roy and [me] at the dinner table. I was happy about that, but of course, I was sad that Sean finally got eaten by the shark...I didn't like that at all!"

Sharp-eyed viewers will spot Mrs. Kintner (Lee Fierro), whose son Alex was eaten in the original *JAWS*, comforting Ellen Brody at her son's wake.

"I really don't know how I wound up in it," Lee Fierro laughs. "They just got a hold of me and asked me to be in it, so I said okay. It was supposed to be a good movie; they had anticipated that it would be really great. Lorraine Gary, who starred in *JAWS* and *JAWS 2* agreed to be in it, so it was a project they all seemed excited about, but you know the end result of *JAWS THE REVENGE*! I am gonna reserve my personal comment on the film."

Fritzi Jane Courtney also returns as Mrs. Taft ("I don't think that's funny — I don't think that's funny at all!"), the hotel owner from *JAWS* and *JAWS 2*. Phil Dubin, who played Amity Selectman Mr. Posner is upgraded to Mayor for the final film and the roles of Brody's secretary Polly and Deputy Len Hendricks are both recast from the original.

Because Lorraine Gary is the wife of Universal's then-CEO Sid Sheinberg, it's astounding that he would put her, the mother of his children, in such a terrible movie and leave her to the mercy of the critics. Worse, she's dressed horribly, with her big asymmetrically styled hair and huge '80s shoulder pads that make her look like an extra on *Dynasty*.

Amazingly, the film originally planned to use Chief Brody himself. Roy Scheider was asked to reprise his role as Brody with a brief cameo at the beginning. The filmmakers wanted it to be Martin Brody who gets eaten by a Great White Shark at the beginning of the film. Why they thought any lover of *JAWS* would want to see Brody eaten is anyone's guess.

Scheider asked for a then outrageous one million dollars to return as Brody for nine days' work. When Universal balked, he was dispatched with an offscreen heart attack and Sean Brody was chomped in his place. Scheider's *JAWS 2* headshot hangs on the wall of the Amity Police Department.

Mario Van Peebles (who described his character as "a black Richard Dreyfuss") is eaten by the shark in the original 1987 release. It leaps out of the water, grabs him, and we see a bloody shot of Van Peebles struggling underwater in the shark's mouth. The TV version, however, shows him swimming to shore. After *JAWS THE REVENGE* flopped stateside, Universal hastily shot an ending where Mario Van Peebles' character lives.

"The day after the film opened, Joe called me up," *JAWS THE REVENGE* star Lance Guest recalls, "It was my birthday, because Joe Sargent and I have birthdays one day apart — Joe calls me up and says 'Lance, what do you think of coming up to Malibu to re-shoot the ending?'

"I said 'Joe, the movie's already out!'

"We were re-doing it for the foreign release and TV. We wound up shooting it in a tank instead of Malibu, where Mario Van Peebles lived, after the shark got him. In a strange way, it was like just another day at the office when we did it, because we had spent the last month and a half of shooting in that tank (on the Universal backlot), now we were back and re-shooting four days *after* the movie came out!"

The ending — with the shark leaping out of the water and impaling himself on the broken prow of the

▲ That Falls Lake locale is also where Jim Carrey crashes his sailboat at the end of *The Truman Show* and the same spot Hulk battles mutant dogs in Ang Lee's *Hulk*.

▲ The filmmakers originally planned to re-tool the mechanical whale from *Star Trek IV: The Voyage Home* to use as the shark. This plan was abandoned.

▲ Michael de Guzman's original screenplay had a cameo by Matt Hooper (Richard Dreyfuss' character).

▲ *JAWS THE REVENGE* composer Michael Small also did Roy Scheider's *Klute* and *Marathon Man*. His soundtrack for *REVENGE* wasn't released until 2000!

▲ Murray Hamilton was asked to reprise his role of Mayor Vaughn, but died before filming began.

▲ As part of the opening was shot in the *JAWS* pond from Southern California's Universal Studios Tour, the *Orca* can be seen in the background — despite having sunk in the original!

▲ Karen Young, Brody's daughter-in-law Carla in *REVENGE*, played Roy Scheider's girlfriend in the 1988 slasher film, *Night Game*.

Mario Van Peebles feeds the fish.

boat — is so confusingly shot that you're not quite sure how the shark has been defeated. Film critic Roger Ebert notes how stupid it is "That the shark would stand on its tail in the water long enough for the boat to ram it [or] that the director, Joseph Sargent, would film this final climactic scene so incompetently that there is not even an establishing shot (of the shark's death), so we have to figure out what happened on the basis of empirical evidence."

In an alternate ending seen in the TV version, when the shark is impaled, his head blows up in a shower of gore. Why is the ending so abrupt and why does having his head speared make the shark explode like a grenade?

"I have no idea," Lance Guest laughs. "Nowadays, they would have CGI'd in a lot of nifty stuff in that scene with the shark, and you would know exactly how he's killed off, but in those days, they were not able to get a lot of those shark shots.

"I remember being in a tank at Universal, trying to get that big ending filmed … It was a pretty tall order: the shark has to come out of the water, you stab the shark with the bow of the ship, the shark whips around and trashes the boat. A lot of stuff that doesn't usually happen in real life; sharks *do not* come out of the water to attack boats like that. They usually don't target members of the same family either!

"They had a hard time 'selling that' as something that was really gonna happen and actually getting the shot of this giant shark jumping out of the water was impossible, which are both the reasons why that scene is cut so abruptly.

"In the end, it was hard to get that shot and 'sell' to the audience what the shark was doing," Guest acknowledges. "It was a shame, because they did have CGI at that time, but it wasn't as expeditious as it is now, where you can have anything that's called for, from aliens to dinosaurs. In those days, CGI had to be done painstakingly, frame by frame."

"I was a fan of the *JAWS* movies when I landed *JAWS THE REVENGE*," Guest states. "I didn't see the first one when it originally came out because I was a water guy and I just didn't need to know about sharks eating surfers! I still go surfing in areas where there actually are sharks, so it's freaky..."

▲ Judith Barsi, the spunky child actress who played Ellen Brody's granddaughter Thea (and provided the voice of a baby pterodactyl in Steven Spielberg's *The Land Before Time*), was murdered by her father on July 25, 1988, before he shot her mother and himself. "I felt really bad when Judith was killed," says her *JAWS THE REVENGE* co-star, Lance Guest. "She was a nice kid, a sweet kid."

▲ *JAWS THE REVENGE* is in The Internet Movie Database (IMDb)'s 'Bottom 100' of the 100 worst films of all time.

The TV version also tries to cover the film's various plot-holes. Critics laughed because the shark chases the Brody family all the way to Jamaica, so the TV version adds a voice-over trying to explain the film: "Since time immemorial mankind tries to judge actions as 'fate or circumstance.' As to whether the shark's actions are due to 'fate or circumstance', the narrator leaves it "for you to decide."

It's silly and adds nothing to this muddled effort.

"The first *JAWS* movie by Steven Spielberg is *so* great, you really can't remake [it]," says Lance Guest. "You don't know what the kismet was that made that movie so good. We tried to make a family drama movie with an outrageous premise — a shark wants to eat the whole family! You had to buy that the shark's gonna follow them all the way to The Bahamas and do all that stuff? That's a hard buy — I think a lot of people refused to buy it — and the fact that the shark is only going to attack members of this one family? The first one didn't have that — it just had this shark that did what sharks do; swimming and eating. They tried to explain away our shark by adding that narrator at the beginning, with all that 'fate or circumstance' stuff.

"That narration was used in one of the previews for the movie — it was *not* in the script. We shot through most of the acting part of the film in about three weeks, so the acting and dialogue portion was shot pretty quickly, in less than a month. I remember there being a lot of problems when they changed the order of scenes — I had a problem with that, too. Character development wasn't as clear to me as it was when I first read the script."

The shark traveling from Amity to The Bahamas in three days to hunt the Brody family is the biggest problem for viewers. In the novelization for *JAWS THE REVENGE* by Hank Searls, we follow the shark in his quest to The Bahamas. The shark is also believed to be a voodoo curse — there's even a scene with a witch doctor, out to get Mike Brody and his family. There are indications of this in the finished film when Ellen seems to 'see' through the shark's eyes and the witch doctor is apparently out for 'the revenge' in the title. Michael Brody addresses this when he tells his mother 'Come on, sharks don't commit murder! Tell me you don't believe in that voodoo."

Amazingly enough, Mike and Sean Brody, almost incidental characters in Benchley's original novel, are the only ones to appear in all four JAWS movies. (In the novel Brody had three sons, Michael, Martin, Jr. and Sean. Martin, Jr. was eliminated for the sake of clarity; having two characters named Martin might have proved confusing). In the original film version of *JAWS*, Mike and Sean are innocent kids. One is nearly eaten while the other watches in horror. In *JAWS 2*, Mike Brody is a "cool '70s high school student" and Sean is now a brat. In *JAWS 3-D*, Mike has become a construction worker, and in *JAWS THE REVENGE*, he's now a marine biologist. Apparently, the character switched professions (and faces) between movies.

"I thought that too," laughs Guest. "I'm Michael Brody in *JAWS THE REVENGE*, taking over for Dennis Quaid. When I was cast, I thought it was kind of strange. I said 'Wait a minute, you want me to play Dennis Quaid's part?!

The audience will know the difference, guys!' They had no problem with it, so I thought, 'Oh well!' I mean, how many Batmans have there been?"

The press kit for *JAWS THE REVENGE* attempts to flush *JAWS 3-D* down the Memory Drain, referring to *JAWS THE REVENGE* as "the third film in the remarkable JAWS trilogy." This is ironic, as *JAWS 3-D* made a similar attempt to write *JAWS 2* out of continuity.

Joe Alves recalls that "When they came out with *JAWS THE REVENGE* press materials, they were knocking all three previous *JAWS* films, including the first one! They said, 'This is gonna be the greatest and all the others were a piece of shit.' It was very offensive; you don't do that to fans who had gone to three of them. They were all financially successful and I don't regret doing any of them."

JAWS THE REVENGE opened on July 17, 1987 with a combined box-office take of $7,154,890. While that matches *JAWS* then-astounding opening in 1975, *that* film was on only 409 screens — *JAWS THE REVENGE* opened in 1,606, and dropped like a rock after that. Its domestic gross a paltry $20 million — which was the budget for the film's expensive Nassau shoot. Foreign was marginally better, taking in $31,118,000.

Despite their best efforts, the studio could not prevent bad word of mouth. The reviews amounted to a fish fry. *Films in Review* critic Scott Rose asks, "What happens to a fish that stays out too long? You get the idea."

Many critics noticed the shabby look of the shark. Movieline's Joshua Mooney commented that "The mechanical shark, which continues, inexplicably, to look less and less realistic each time out, is noticeably rubberized." Rose noted "Three sequels is more than enough to devote to a rubbery, mechanized prop."

The most damning review came from Deborah J. Kunk of *The Los Angeles Herald Examiner*. Referring to the fish as "Jaws, the Styrofoam Float," she wondered if "Universal keeps cranking these things out to keep their studio tour attraction halfway current".

JAWS THE REVENGE had more than its fair share of Razzie Award nominations: Worst Screenplay, Worst Director, Worst Actor ("Bruce" the shark), Worst Actress and Worst Picture. Henry Millar actually won, for Worst Special Visual Effects.

In 1989, Spielberg proteges' Bob Zemeckis and Bob Gale made a funny *JAWS* reference in their film, *Back to the Future Part II*. Set in the future of 2015, Michael J. Fox encounters a holographic shark coming out of a movie marquee to attack him. He screams, crouches in fear and then quickly adds, "The shark still looks fake!"

EATING HABITS

The *JAWS* movies gave us some of the most fearsome undersea creatures ever seen on screen. But who was the toughest? Who ate the most? What was the most impressive carnage they caused? This chart will help.

JAWS

Vital Statistics: 25 feet, 3 tons,
Nickname(s): "Bruce" (after Steven Spielberg's lawyer); 'You son of a bitch' (by Brody)
Most Memorable Havoc: Rams, smashes, jumps onto and sinks the fishing boat, *Orca*.
Star Turn (how the fish upstages cast): Eats Robert Shaw.

Body Count:
- Chrissie Watkins
- Tippit the dog (offscreen)
- Alex Kintner
- Ben Gardner (Fisherman, offscreen)
- Man in rowboat ("Estuary Victim")
- Quint

Cause of Death: Scuba tank exploded in its mouth.

JAWS 2

Vital Statistics: Approximately 30 feet
Nickname(s): "You fat fish!" (by Brody);
"Turkey" (by the crew)
Most Memorable Havoc: Chomps and
pulls under moving helicopter, with pilot.
Star Turn: No important actors eaten.

Body Count:
- Two divers
- Killer Whale (Offscreen)
- Terri the Water Skier
- Skiboat Driver (This one's a toss-up, because she actually blows
  herself up trying to kill the shark)
- Eddie (Horny teenager)
- Helicopter pilot
- Teenage Girl

Cause of Death: Electrocution. Bites electric cable.

JAWS 3-D

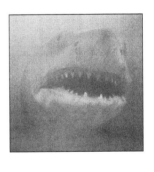

This one is a split, as JAWS 3-D *has a
mother/son combo.*
Vital Statistics: Mother: 35 feet, 3 tons,
Son: unspecified.
Bite Radius: "A yard wide"
Nickname(s): "Goddamn fish!" and "Some
fish's mutha" (Lou Gossett); "Big Bitch!"
(Bess Armstrong)
Most Memorable Havoc: Trashes
underwater amusement park.
Star Turn: Bites Lea Thompson and eats Simon MacCorkindale.

Body Count:
- A big Grouper (That's a fish)
- Shelby (Construction worker)
- Two Coral Thieves
- Phillip Fitzroyce (Shark hunter)
- One Sea World technician

Cause of Death: Explosive in its mouth is detonated.

JAWS THE REVENGE

Befitting its reputation as the worst of the series, *REVENGE* also has the lowest body count of all the films, and the smallest shark of the series. In fact, the shark hardly gets a tooth in edgewise among the rather boring sub-plots.

Vital Statistics: A paltry 23-feet (according to the press notes).

Most Memorable Havoc: Finally eats a member of the Brody family. (It only took 4 movies!) While he doesn't eat that many people, the shark deserves props for swimming all the way to The Bahamas!

Star Turn: It almost eats Oscar-Winner Michael Caine (Notice the fish never gets to eat Oscar-winners? Richard Dreyfuss, Lou Gossett and Michael Caine all escape unscathed!)

Body Count:
- Sean Brody
- Ellen Brody (in a dream sequence)
- Woman on banana boat
- Jake (who survives in the TV version, despite having been chewed up on camera)

Cause of Death: Suicide. The shark clumsily impales itself on the prow of the boat. (In the TV version, he impales himself…and then explodes!)

SUBMERGED SEQUELS

While *JAWS* inspired three sequels, there were many sequel ideas that were bounced around, before they settled on the ones they made. Some of them were more interesting and audacious than the ones that reached the screen. Original sequel ideas for JAWS 2, 3 and 4 (!) are now revealed.

One *JAWS 2* idea sounded promising. It was about Quint's experience when his ship the *U.S.S. Indianapolis* sank, as sailors in the water fought off sharks. This true-life story was the basis for several great books (including *Abandon Ship*) and a riveting TV-movie starring Stacey Keach (*The Mission of the Shark*). This came from Howard Sackler, who introduced the *Indianapolis* backstory into the original film. Reportedly, this was the only *JAWS 2* pitch that Spielberg sparked to; it could have been the basis for a gripping *JAWS* movie (with not one but dozens of Great White sharks), but was apparently too downbeat. As it was an actual historical event, there was no way this could provide a Hollywood happy ending, other than the characters' survival.

"That story about Quint's time on the ship was something Spielberg proposed," *JAWS 2* director Jeannot Szwarc says. "Steven Spielberg said he would do it, if they would wait until after he finished *Close Encounters of the Third Kind*, but they couldn't do that, because they had a solid release date set."

Other *JAWS 2* scenarios came from Peter Benchley, who suggested using a prehistoric megamouth shark (something Roger Corman and director Chuck Griffith did in *Up from the Depths* and is a creature used in the yet-to-be-filmed potboiler horror novel, *Meg*), while *2001: A Space Odyssey* author Arthur C. Clarke devised a *JAWS 2* pitch about a giant squid attacking an oil rig — which is weird, because squids have beaks, not jaws.

Instead of the truly terrible *JAWS THE REVENGE*, Universal could have made a wild action/comedy *JAWS 4*, scripted by Steve DeJarnatt (writer/director of the cult classic, *Miracle Mile*).

He explains: "I wrote a draft for *JAWS 4* that had nothing to do with the one that came out in the Bahamas. My script was set in Malibu, California, with surf punks. I had an Australian surfer protagonist and just had fun with it. It was outrageous and fun, but I wrote it for [former Universal head] Frank

Price. Sid Sheinberg threw it out and came up with something his wife could do."

DeJarnatt's script opens in what appears to be the Middle Ages. A medieval princess heads for the water and we see she's wearing a Walkman radio. She's not a princess at all — she's working at a Renaissance Faire in Malibu. In a parody of the original *JAWS*, "She goes swimming. There's a shark coming up towards her, then, all of a sudden, a shark ten times bigger bites the first shark in half." In

Filmmaker Steve DeJarnatt. PHOTO BY LISA ORRIS.

the climax, the shark swallows the Australian surfer's girlfriend, "so he surfs the shark onto the beach and cuts his girlfriend out of the stomach," DeJarnatt shrugs. "You use concepts and play with them."

The strangest *JAWS 2* scenario had Quint's son come to Amity to collect his father's $10,000 bounty for killing the shark. He teams up with Brody's son, Mike, to pursue another killer shark.

The two most discussed unmade *JAWS* sequels were the original *JAWS 2*, which was directed by the soon-to-be replaced John Hancock, and the proposed horror comedy, "National Lampoon's Jaws 3, People 0."

JOHN HANCOCK'S *JAWS 2*

WELCOME TO AMITY!

Once known as that "summer destination for beachgoers out for fun in the sun," it is now a ghost town. Windows are boarded up, businesses are closing and even the Amity billboard of the smiling girl is peeling from neglect. The shark attacks of three years ago have left the island teetering on the edge of bankruptcy.

Sheriff Martin Brody "has the look of a survivor, rather than a resident. He will NEVER shake off the memory of what he survived." Kids mock Mike and Sean about their Dad's shark obsession. The town's residents have increased by two — a mobster and another Great White Shark.

Welcome to John Hancock's *JAWS 2*, a darker, more ambitious version that never saw the light of a movie screen.

Hancock, who directed Robert De Niro's touching *Bang the Drum Slowly* and the thriller *Let's Scare Jessica to Death*, landed the coveted job of directing *JAWS 2*. He and screenwriter/wife Dorothy Tristan came with the intent of making a dark, serious horror movie. A month into shooting, the pair was relieved of their duties. Ironically, their story, used for the film's best-selling novelization and comic, was more interesting than the beat-for-beat remake of *JAWS* that was released in theaters.

John Hancock wound up on *JAWS 2* because "I had known Dick Zanuck and David Brown since my first film, an Academy Award-nominated short about businessmen playing touch football in Central Park. After *Bang the Drum Slowly* did well, they came to me with *JAWS 2* and I wanted to do it. I was surprised to get the job, but it was a sequel and I really liked the first film.

"My *JAWS 2* was darker than the first *JAWS*. I thought, 'This Island has suffered a terrible calamity and we ought to show the residue of that.' We really got into it and took it seriously. We treated it as if *JAWS* had really happened and these are the repercussions on the community. The economy is ruined because no one wants to go to Amity after the shark. Roy Scheider's Brody is haunted by it. He has nightmares, and sees sharks everywhere."

Dorothy Tristan notes that Brody "suffers post traumatic stress from the events of the first film. I would, wouldn't you? You have a person who's already kind of ragged as a result of what happened and facing it again makes it even worse and adds to his pressure — but of course, he comes out on top!"

Director Hancock "wanted to make a scary movie. We wanted to really give you the feeling of what it was like to be bitten by a shark. I wanted the picture to have a different look and feel than the first *JAWS*. Grittier, edgier and more haunted — to show the impact of the first picture on the place and the people. We had Joe Alves, a wonderful art director who had done the first picture and *Close Encounters*, and he really achieved that look."

Before he accepted *JAWS 2*, "I had lunch with Steven Spielberg," the filmmaker reveals. "He wasn't 'SPIELBERG' yet, just another director around town with a big grosser who was seen as lucky at that point. He wasn't a demigod yet, but he just had wonderful ideas. He had a whole series of things, like the shark coming into the harbor, he described it so vividly and I used that in the film — I was very impressed at how friendly he was and how filmically he thought. He was helpful, he said, 'Trust Joe Alves,' and I did.

"Steven said, 'Re-shoot things that don't work.' He said most of the shark scenes in the first movie were the second or third re-shoot of it. They re-shot, re-shot and re-shot everything with the shark until they got it right. Steven felt of all the sharks, 'The tow one works real well'. He was right — it was such a simple thing; a bag that filled with water with a fin on it and a wooden board that would enable you to submerge it with a rudder device — like a puppet in liquid. Michael Chapman, the camera operator, got a lot of credit from Steven for [filming] difficult stuff on the boat. We tried to hire Michael Chapman, but he wasn't available."

Not everyone wanted the dark tone. "When she saw the dailies, Verna Fields said, 'It's so contrasty and blue, can that be changed if we decided to fix that in post [production]?' The cameraman said 'Absolutely!' That didn't become a problem — the problem really was the power struggle between Zanuck and

Sheinberg over the overages on the first picture and 'who was the better man' — that kind of thing."

To prepare the story, "They had a draft by Howard Sackler, who had done certain writing on the first *JAWS* and it was terrible. Dorothy sat down and she re-wrote it on spec. They [Zanuck and Brown] loved it and that's the script they finally went ahead with."

Tristan recalls that "John was directing it and Howard Sackler did the first draft of it. I knew Howard and I think he felt that it was beneath him. He scribbled out this script and just threw it at the producers. I looked at this and said, 'What is this?! If he's not interested in it, I have some ideas!' I was very naive, in terms of the political aspects of Hollywood. Both John and I were. I told Zanuck and Brown my ideas and they said, 'Let's go for it.' We didn't look down on *JAWS 2*. We wanted to make it really, really scary and exciting and did the best we could."

Reportedly, Sackler brought her and Hancock in. "That's true," she says quietly, "and I rewrote him. He felt betrayed and rightly so; I would have felt betrayed, too. It was one of the things that we did. It was ignorant and blithe, but what he turned in was crap — It never went anywhere and he wrote it out in longhand! It was a mess, terrible — I argue that it was an insult. When I read it, I thought, 'If he thinks so little of this, I'll fix it!' My attitude was, 'If you don't want to do this, get outta' the way and let me at it!' I was gung-ho and excited, because I love spooky stuff."

The girl water skier surfaces in the Hancock/Tristan *JAWS 2*,

Marvel Comics adapts Dorothy Tristan's *JAWS 2* script. ©1978 MARVEL COMICS.

and became the film's central image on the poster and marketing of the movie.

"That was a real contribution by Dorothy," Hancock notes, "The whole climax of the picture was hers, the way they kill the shark. And Dorothy *never* got screen credit!"

Tristan thought of the water skier "because if you think about it from the shark's point of view — it goes zoom, zoom overhead, so it would seem interesting," says Tristan. "That's why I went with the boat race. To a shark, a catamaran would look like two seals going along the surface, plus the kids legs dangling down — how could he resist?!"

Unshot scene from John Hancock's *JAWS 2*. Art by Gene Colan. ©1978 MARVEL COMICS.

If the director had his way, the sequence would have been much more elaborate than the finished film.

"We had *two* water skiers in the script and the sequence was much darker than it wound up being — a man and a woman, but the shark gets them both, and he eats them slowly. It was bloody and grim — and it would have been a good sequence. I really missed getting to shoot that. I tried to talk Zanuck into being the male water skier, but he said 'Oh, that's all I need!'

"We went to Acapulco to learn how to scuba dive, so I could film the underwater sequences. That's where we figured out how to kill the shark, by having him bite the cable. We didn't really have a climax to the picture before that. We were breaking our heads over how to kill the shark, when Dorothy said, 'The electrical cable would kill him!'"

Dealing with the shark was tricky: "I got that shot of the shark coming into Amity Harbor our very first week — the one Spielberg suggested, because that was just the fins, not the big mechanical shark," recalls Hancock.

"We didn't shoot any shark attacks because we didn't have a shark yet," he explains. "Bob Mattey had done the mechanical shark for the first picture, but it never worked! They had terrible problems with it. Sheinberg insisted on hiring him for the second picture on the theory that 'His shark worked enough to make a lot of money.'

"Instead of using the same sharks from the first one, he wanted to re-design it so it could do more things like go up and down, side to side and a much more elaborate set of controls. They never made it work when I was directing. We were constantly waiting for the shark to be ready. Zanuck did not want to use Mattey on *JAWS 2*. He knew the guy was a flake and had been a terrible problem. This was another issue between Zanuck and Sheinberg. I think they were looking for a reason to shut down until the shark was ready," Hancock reveals.

One of his favorite *JAWS 2* scenes came about by accident: "We were on our way to film something else and I saw these guys on a sailboat, hanging from rubber bands on yard arms and dipping themselves into the water. I saw some of that and grabbed it. It was incredibly beautiful with the color of the sails and the ocean, I thought it would be a great sequence, where the shark keeps trying to get the guy, but he'd be yanked away."

Tristan added a Mafia element. "I took that from Peter Benchley's book," she explains. "I thought it wouldn't hurt to have one more threat. The mobster is there in the finished *JAWS 2*, but no longer a mobster [The Len Peterson character, played by Joseph Mascolo, who usually plays TV gangsters]."

Hancock feels trouble began for the husband and wife team when "The Sheinbergs had Dorothy and [me] over for dinner and explained why it would be good to have Lorraine go out on the boat [to help rescue the kids from the shark]. I relayed this desire to Zanuck, who said, 'Over my dead body!' Obviously, what I should have done then is get them in the same room and say, 'Okay, you guys should give me direction, because I really don't want to get between you two.'

"Not having the sense to do that, not really being experienced in how to deal in a bureaucracy, I liked Zanuck personally, so I figured 'Zanuck hired me, so I'm gonna go with him — dance with those who brung you.' We turned in the next draft without Lorraine on the boat and Sheinberg stopped meeting my eyes in the commissary. He and Lorraine had been so friendly, I guess they felt betrayed. I was caught between these huge forces like a babe in the woods and paid the price for it. *JAWS 2* is a very bitter, painful experience that took years to recover from.

"I liked Lorraine and never thought she was a bad actress, but she was really floating along on who her husband was. I don't think any producer ever said, 'God, we must get Lorraine Gary!' I asked Zanuck once what he thought about nepotism," Hancock smiles.

"He said, 'I believe in it! Where would I be [without it]?'"

Dorothy Tristan says, "We knew they both wanted their wives in the film.

Female scientist written for Linda Harrison, but played by Collin Wilcox.

What we didn't know was how seriously this would impact upon us in making decisions. Zanuck said to us, 'Don't worry about Sheinberg' and Sheinberg said, 'Don't worry about Zanuck.' Zanuck's wife Linda was beautiful, but not a great actress; Sheinberg's wife was not beautiful, but a mediocre actress. What are you gonna do? Lorraine busted her husband's balls — and everyone else's — to get in that first movie. We were quite close to Zanuck. After the Lorraine 'over my dead body' comment, he said to us, 'Do what you feel is right for the movie.' So we didn't put Lorraine on the boat saving the kids and Sheinberg came down heavy."

Hancock says they "wrote a part for Zanuck's wife Linda as the oceanographic scientist with the dead whale, but she didn't get to play it. Zanuck was trying to hold on to her at that time and asked us, 'Could you write something for Linda?' The beginning of the grief between Zanuck and Sheinberg is they both wanted their wives to play Ellen Brody in the first *JAWS*."

Tristan agrees. "the scientist was for Linda, but Sheinberg wasn't gonna give Zanuck anything for his wife to do. They were playing games with each other.

They stamped out everything we wanted, except the stuff they wanted from the script — they kept that very nicely, including the water skier."

After he "shot for three weeks, maybe a month, everything seemed to be going well, when a Lear jet landed on the island and the next day, I was on my way to Italy! I never saw Sheinberg. He came, talked to Zanuck and Brown, and took off. Zanuck and Brown called me in and said, 'Well, we're letting you go,'" John Hancock says sadly. "That trip to Italy was grim. Are you kidding? I knew what a blow it was. We made a lot of money and we were in Rome, but Holy Shit, what just happened?!"

"It happened so fast and so surreptitiously, we were utterly shocked when they did it to us," Tristan elaborates. "We couldn't put out it of our minds. We were publicly humiliated. When you go to a Hollywood party and everyone turns away from you, it's embarrassing. We were pariahs. That made it very difficult for us. I was damaged by the whole *JAWS 2* experience.

"The thing about *JAWS 2* is it was a sequel, to a big moneymaking movie — the biggest moneymaker of all time at that point. *JAWS* made a humongous amount. We did not know how Hollywood operated and how vicious it truly was. When we landed this big movie, people set their teeth for us, including Verna Fields! She wanted to direct. She actually stepped in the minute they fired us, until the Directors Guild stepped in and said 'No, no, no! No producer will fire a director so they can take over their job and direct.'"

"That's true," says Hancock. "Verna was a great editor, who made huge contributions to the first *JAWS*, but felt she should have been offered the director's chair for the second one. Zanuck said 'No' to that and shot her down. Because of *JAWS'* grosses, she became a Universal executive and still wanted the job. While we were in The Vineyard, she was complaining to Sheinberg."

Verna Fields was about to make her directorial debut. "They ended up offering it to her after they fired me. Sid Sheinberg and Robert Aldrich got into a shoving match at The Polo Lounge over the issue. Aldrich said, 'You cannot do this — it's against the rules! You cannot take an executive on a project and replace a DGA director!' It was a big combustive situation there, so they got Jeannot Szwarc, but Verna tried to direct it through him — Verna was very smart and formidable."

"I felt bad because a lot of kids I cast were fired after I left. I had cast Ricky Schroeder as Sean Brody and he did an amazing job — a really talented kid. He was devastated when he got bumped. They had to bump him because he was my choice. It was a nasty business. They didn't get rid of all the kids, but they HAD to get rid of Ricky, because he was my choice."

As for Dorothy Tristan, "The Writers Guild got me. I didn't know I was supposed to send a letter to The Guild explaining exactly how my script was similar to the one that got made for screen credit. I didn't send that letter. I sent the script, with a note saying, 'When you compare these two scripts, it will be very evident what the story is.'

"They didn't read them. What they did was punish me for being the director's wife. It destroyed my friendship with Sackler; he was there at The Writers Guild. I can't say that I blame him. I was really ignorant. I didn't make a penny off the *JAWS 2* novelization or anything else made from my script. After that, John and I went off and licked our wounds, we wrote *Weeds,* got it made and then our house burned down!"

"It was brutal," John Hancock says of his *JAWS 2* experience. "When people ask what happened, I tell them, 'The Shark ate me!'"

NATIONAL LAMPOON'S "JAWS 3, PEOPLE 0"

Of all of the unmade *JAWS* sequels, this is the one that has the biggest reputation. It's also the one that came closest to being made, in terms of designing a poster and hiring a crew. Now a legend in the history of unmade films, it would have taken the *JAWS* series into a vastly different direction.

After *JAWS 2*, the franchise was considered to be creatively out of gas. Instead of the melodramatic and campy *JAWS 3-D*, the studio almost made the deliberately silly and highly regarded comedy script "JAWS 3, PEOPLE 0." The film was conceived after the success of *Airplane*, a send-up of Universal's *Airport* series.

One reason for the unmade project's cult status is that it was co-written by the legendary John Hughes, the writer/director who started out at National Lampoon, then came to Hollywood and wrote such beloved (and successful) comedies as *Mr. Mom*, *Vacation*, *Sixteen Candles*, *The Breakfast Club* and *Home Alone*. "JAWS 3, PEOPLE 0" was a satire on the making of the original *JAWS*, as a film crew tries to make a movie about a man-eating shark. One scene had Peter Benchley being eaten by a shark in his own swimming pool!

The film may have been made if the studio hadn't been divided in their thinking. One faction felt that a straight *JAWS 3* could be profitable and a satire would be a death blow to the franchise; the other felt using *JAWS* as a parody subject was perfect to surf the *Airplane /Animal House* raucous comedy wave the studio had started.

"I truly feel they didn't make 'JAWS 3, PEOPLE 0' because they couldn't laugh at a franchise they took so seriously and did so well from," surmises Jeffrey Kramer.

Because of the surprise success of his funny/scary *Piranha*, Joe Dante was tapped to direct that *JAWS* parody.

"*Piranha* had gotten me a picture at Dino DeLaurentis' that I didn't make called "Orca 2," about the killer whale — they actually wanted to make a sequel to that! Luckily, it didn't happen, so when it died, I was hired to do 'JAWS 3, PEOPLE 0' instead! *JAWS 3* would have been my very first studio picture. Unfortunately, when I came onto it, there was already a lot of fighting over it at Universal.

"National Lampoon and [*JAWS* producers] Zanuck & Brown disagreed over what kind of movie it should be," Dante continues. "I was more or less stuck in the middle. I honestly don't think it would have been a very good movie had I made it. While they were dickering around over whether to make it or not, the original director on *The Howling* was let go. Mike Finnell, a good friend of mine

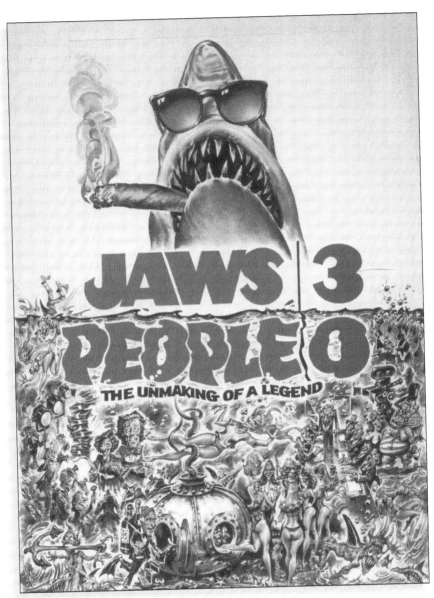

"JAWS 3, PEOPLE 0" poster gives a hint of it's *Animal House*-like irreverence.

who was producing *The Howling*, called me up and asked me if I'd do it. I just said 'Yes' to him, assuming 'JAWS 3, PEOPLE 0' would fall apart and it did!"

In his book, Brown argued against doing a spoof of their most successful film, because "it would be too much like fouling your own nest." *JAWS* production designer Joe Alves says, "I never read the screenplay, but I understand that it made fun of a lot of situations that we went through during the making of that

Joe Dante and friend. PHOTO BY PATRICK JANKIEWICZ.

first *JAWS* and *JAWS 2* — situations that were pretty painful to go through, so I didn't really appreciate that."

Joe Dante says that "'JAWS 3, PEOPLE 0' was a comedy version of a *JAWS* movie — it's about a movie company making a *JAWS* movie and a real shark comes along. It was like those old haunted house comedies where a real ghost or gorilla shows up.

"I liked it … It was written by John Hughes and Tod Carroll, and there was some funny stuff in it, a really funny script, but the corporate take on the movie was pretty restrictive — I went to work and they handed me storyboards that were already drawn!

"They weren't asking me what I wanted to do, they just said, 'Here they are', it was a contract job, so I don't think I would have been able to bring very much to it," Dante asserts. "I had a great cast set for it. The best thing that ever happened to me was not making that movie, because it would have been a big major studio failure and I would have been first noticed on a big failure."

THE FUTURE

Although a cinematic return to Amity seems unlikely, considering the disappointing box-office returns of *JAWS THE REVENGE*, you can't keep a Great White shark down. While there have been rumors of a JAWS 5, or worse, a remake of the original *JAWS,* that seems to be mostly wishful thinking from the online community.

JAWS has been resurrected in non-movie form with *JAWS UNLEASHED*, an Xbox video game. Created by Appaloosa Interactive, who also made the popular game *Ecco the Dolphin*, *JAWS UNLEASHED* is amazing because it allows players to become what the game terms 'Jaws the Shark'.

The storyline has Amity Island making a deal with the corporation Environplus to help the local economy. Their industrial activity and increased population have attracted yet another Great White Shark (or "YOU, the Ocean's most fearsome predator", as the game promisingly puts it.) You are also being hunted by Marine Biologist Michael Brody, in a direct tie-in to *JAWS THE REVENGE*.

You can pilot the Great White man-eater through the waters off Amity Island, devouring swimmers, attacking boats and battling whales and shark-hunters at random. The graphics are excellent and getting to do your own personal *JAWS* sequel, randomly eating and attacking whatever and whoever you like, is immensely satisfying.

Will Bruce be back?

THE
RIP-OFFS

"They caught *a* shark, not *the* shark. Big difference. Not the shark that killed Chrissie Watkins and probably not the shark that killed the little boy."

HOOPER

Like any movie that makes a lot of money, *JAWS* created a shockwave in the low-budget film community when it opened. Since they were all busy doing no-budget rip-offs on *The Godfather*, *Shaft* and *The Exorcist*, they were stunned to see a "monster movie" gross a then-unheard of sum of $250 million.

An adventure at sea with a scary monster! How could it be ripped off?

One solution was to change the locale and the monster. First one out of the gate was *Grizzly*, with a bear as the shark. In essence, Christopher George was Roy Scheider, Richard Jaeckel was Robert Shaw and Andrew Prine was Richard Dreyfuss.

"We started shooting before the script was done," laughs Prine. "The director, William Girdler, was a good guy, but there was no script when I signed on. He told us, 'Don't worry about it — All you guys have to know is that we're making *JAWS* with a bear!'"

The *Grizzly* poster, by comic-book legend Neal Adams, was a horizontal version of *JAWS*. Instead of a woman swimming, with a massive shark coming up under her, it was a woman sitting in front of a campfire, with a massive bear looming over her.

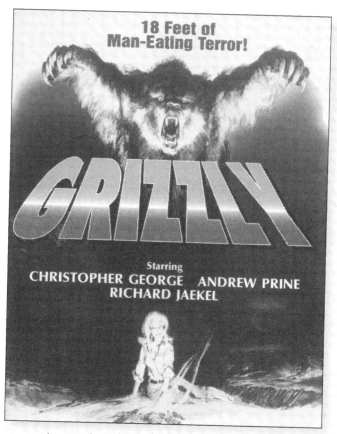

Bear meets girl in *Grizzly*. Art by Neal Adams. ©1976 FILM VENTURES INTERNATIONAL.

"They were looking for that *JAWS*-type image," explains Adams, "so I gave them one."

Besides *Grizzly*, there was *Mako: The Jaws of Death*, *Day of the Animals* (same director and bear as *Grizzly*, with *JAWS*' Susan Backlinie as the first victim), and Universal's own *The Car*, with a killer devil automobile instead of a fish and James Brolin as a Brody-like police chief. Mexico gave us *Tinotera!* with nudity, blood, a shark and appealing actress Fiona Lewis.

Italy joined the *JAWS* sweepstakes with *Tentacles* (1977), substituting an octopus for the shark, Bo Svenson for Robert Shaw and Henry Fonda as the villainous head of the telephone company (!). Ironically, the film featured a boat race very similar to the one a year later in *JAWS 2* and the plot eerily prefigures Benchley's *Beast*.

Most of the rip-offs keep the main details: Monster attacking community, law enforcement hero who wants to protect the public but is not allowed to by greedy Mayor. There's always a holiday festival, because when you copy the *JAWS* plot, you need a big event to rival the July 4th celebration.

Dino DeLaurentis' did the unintentionally funny *Orca*, in which he combined *JAWS* with the plot of his own *Death Wish* and has a killer whale out to avenge the murder of his mate and child. *Orca* even opens with a whale killing a Great White shark! *Orca* featured shapely Charlotte Rampling as Hooper, Richard Harris as Quint and a then-unknown Bo Derek getting one of her well-tanned legs chewed off by the whale!

Ironically, Universal tried to sue the artist of the *Orca* poster for plagiarizing the *JAWS* image. The suit was specious, as *Orca* showed a killer whale crushing a fishing village. The lawsuit was dismissed. Ironically, a brief 1977 re-release of *JAWS* played drive-ins across the country with *Orca* as the second feature.

There have been a plethora of *JAWS* knock-offs made straight for video and basic cable. Most, like *Shark Attack* ("I only made that so I could go to South Africa," laughingly admits star Ernie Hudson) and the fun *Frankenfish*, occasionally wash up on the Sci-Fi Channel.

Renny Harlin, the film director behind *The Adventures of Ford Fairlane* and *Die Hard 2: Die Harder*, has long been known as "The Steven Spielberg of Finland." He put that nickname to the test when he made *Deep Blue Sea*, a film that managed to rip off two Spielberg movies at the same time, *JAWS* and *Jurassic Park*, with genetically smart sharks running loose in a sinking science lab.

"I loved *JAWS* and I had seen real sharks while growing up in Australia," explains *Deep Blue Sea* screenwriter Duncan Kennedy. "Because of this, I always wanted to do a shark movie of my own! I thought our mechanical sharks looked really good. I didn't want to rip *JAWS* off or just blame sharks as evil, so our sharks had their intelligence and behavior altered by scientists. In my script, the main *Deep Blue Sea* shark was eighteen feet long, but it was Renny Harlin's idea for our shark in the movie to be twenty-six feet long ... Just so he would be one-foot bigger than Steven Spielberg's shark in *JAWS*, which I thought was funny and cute!"

While ripping off *JAWS* is common practice in most straight to video/DVD product and cable movies like *Blue Demon*, *Shark Hunter*, *Shark Attack* (1, 2

Deep Blue Sea screenwriter Duncan Kennedy. PHOTO BY PATRICK JANKIEWICZ.

and 3), the most infamous rip-off ever made was 1982's Italian epic by director Enzo G. Castellari, *Great White* (*L'Ultimato Squali*). *Great White* actually played in American theaters beginning on March 5, 1982 (and ran at drive-ins with *Swamp Thing*). With a cool poster showing a beautiful girl floating on a mattress as a massive great white shark rises below her, the *Great White* tagline read: "A quiet, restful summer in the lazy coastal town of Port Harbor is abruptly about to end."

Shark steals dock (and plot) in *Great White!* ©1982 FILM VENTURES INTERNATIONAL.

What makes *Great White* so shocking is that while all of the other films ripped off elements of *JAWS*, they made slight changes to the formula to keep from getting sued, like making it a bear or a car instead of a shark. Not so with *Great White* — which introduces their hero, a Police Chief (James Franciscus), by having him wake up to the radio and talking to his wife in a new house — the exact same way Brody is introduced in *JAWS!*

The rest blatantly stole the *JAWS* plot, with elements of *JAWS 2:* A monster shark is terrorizing a beach community and the Sheriff is not allowed to close the beaches. His name is "Peter Benton," which seems to deliberately parody the name of Peter Benchley.

The film is quite laughable, though it's meant to be utterly serious. Vic Morrow does a very grim impersonation of Robert Shaw, muttering his lines like Popeye. The funniest scene has the remains of a surfboard cruise into the harbor with Morrow noting: "Look — " as we see a very phony rubber hand lying on the board.

As the Sheriff isn't allowed to close the beaches, he has the town build a giant underwater shark cage around the beach, which the shark breaks through. The scene of the shark ramming the cage with his head uses stock footage of over six different sharks — including a hammerhead — although it's meant to be the same Great White! The film also repeatedly uses stock footage of a shark eating meat from a *National Geographic* special.

One hilarious scene has the Murray Hamilton-styled Mayor trying to catch the shark by lowering meat down on a chain (Meat the size of a turkey) from a helicopter. The 35-foot Great White Shark immediately grabs the chain and easily pulls the helicopter into the drink, managing to steal from *JAWS* and *JAWS 2* at the same time. While most foreign rip-offs swam under the radar, Film Ventures pushed *Great White* hard. They arranged promotions (like having sharks in a tank in some theaters) and the movie opened big.

Universal sued for plagiarism and the court ruled in the studio's favor, blocking the film from running in theaters or on television in North America. The film now sits on a shelf in the MCA vaults, with bootlegs of it sold and traded on the Internet and at comic-book conventions. Facing a nasty divorce settlement and the possible bankruptcy of his company, Edward L. Montoro, head of Film Ventures, the proud distributor of *Great White* (and the aforementioned *Grizzly*), absconded with the company profits and has not been seen in almost thirty years.

The rest of the Film Ventures board meets annually to toast Montoro, the D.B. Cooper of schlock, and wonder about his whereabouts. Still, the strong opening of *Great White* is believed to be one of the reasons that Universal finally decided to make *JAWS 3-D*.

Roger Corman produced the awful *Up from the Depths*, a hilarious prehistoric shark bomb where the monster is played by a surfboard and a hand puppet. Corman also did the best of the *JAWS* knock-offs, *Piranha* (1978). A demented send-up of *JAWS* that veers between cheap scares and tongue-in-cheek parody, *Piranha* features a school of genetically altered man-eating fish in a fresh water lake. The film marked the debut of three major talents: director Joe Dante, screenwriter John Sayles (who would make another great rip-off/parody, *Alligator*) and composer James Horner. When *JAWS* brought huge ratings to ABC, NBC paid top dollar to run *Piranha* in primetime.

"Universal felt that *Piranha* was a rip-off on *JAWS*, which it truly was," Dante happily concedes. "Ironically, their *JAWS 2* was the biggest rip-off on *JAWS*! Because *JAWS 2* came out the same summer as *Piranha*, they were gonna enjoin Roger against distributing the picture. Steven saw the movie, saw it was a spoof and he actually liked it, so he told them to leave us alone and said that it was okay."

There's an apocryphal story that the first thing Joe Dante did when he met Steven Spielberg is apologize for ripping off *JAWS*.

"No," Dante laughs. "I would *not* apologize for that, because I meant to rip him off! That's why I can't complain about *The Howling*, numbers 2, 3, 4, 5, 6, 7 and 8! Why should I complain about somebody ripping me off when I got my own start ripping somebody else off?"

None of these films were as effective as Chris Kentis' *Open Water*, which was released in 2004. Made for a paltry $130,000, *Open Water* emulated *JAWS* by keeping the sharks off-camera. This was not just an artistic decision on Kentis' part; he could not afford a mechanical or digital shark. He uses real sharks sparingly to a great scary effect when he shows them (as they circle his wetsuit-clad actors), and like *JAWS*, he keeps the water at the bottom of the frame to create menace. The female character is named "Susan Watkins" as a tribute to Susan Backlinie's Chrissie Watkins, *JAWS*' first victim. The male character's last name is Kintner!

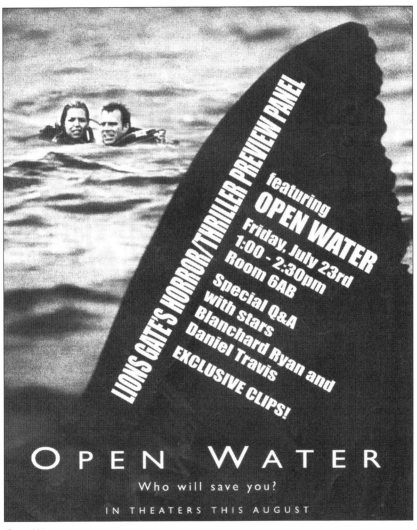

Open Water ©2003 LIONS GATE.

JAWSfest

"...We have, in fact, caught
and killed a large predator
that supposedly injured some
bathers. But, as you can see,
it's a beautiful day, the
beaches are open and people
are having a wonderful time."

MAYOR VAUGHN

Welcome to Amity — and JAWSfest!

As the 30th anniversary of *JAWS* rolled around in 2005, outside of the *JAWS UNLEASHED* videogame and DVD edition of the classic film, there seemed to be nothing going on to commemorate it — no sequel or remake. Little did the world know, the real Amity Island of Edgartown, Massachussets had something up its collective sleeve.

"Our town has always been linked to *JAWS* and this seemed to be the perfect time to celebrate that fact," says Maribeth Priore, a tall, pretty blonde and one of the organizers of JAWSfest. "*JAWS* has always been a part of Edgartown history and it seemed like a fun way to acknowledge its thirtieth anniversary! When we looked into the possibility of doing a JAWSfest, we were happy that Universal and the people involved with the films were eager to participate."

Maribeth Priore notes that "We decided to have JAWSfest here, because if not here, where? Previous generations on Edgartown frowned on having something to commemorate *JAWS*, but there's a whole new generation of people living here, trying to make a living, to make it a viable place for people to come to. Martha's Vineyard is obviously a beautiful place, but we want to make it that much more desirable.

"I work for the Chamber of Commerce and every summer tourists walk in there and ask us, 'Where was this scene in *JAWS* shot?' I said, 'I should get myself a bus and just do a *JAWS* tour!' One day, it just dawned on us — how about doing something to commemorate *JAWS*? That included doing something in Edgartown City Hall (which is where Brody is outvoted by The Mayor and City Council to keep the beaches open). City Hall has the exact same desk and gavel used in the film.

Left: Maribeth Priore. *Right:* Fake Quint Mike Hadgi. PHOTOS BY PATRICK JANKIEWICZ.

"It made sense to do a JAWSfest," Priore reasons, "because a lot of the local people who appeared in the film are still with us, but they're getting older, some are elderly, and we might not have this opportunity to get the fans together with the people who made it happen! The filmmakers are only in their fifties, but people like Bob Carroll and Lee Fierro are delightful and we wanted the fans to meet them. The fans and the locals all had a blast! It worked! We may hold another one in 2010."

During JAWSfest the town is an eclectic mix of tourists, townsfolk, Hollywood filmmakers, film buffs, famed shark fisherman Quint …

Wait a minute, Quint?! Amazingly, yes — as Quint, in full costume, green jacket, fishing cap and sneer, suddenly steps forward in front of Edgartown City Hall.

"You all know me, you know how I earn a livin'," snarls the Irish tourist dressed like Quint (right down to paste-on sideburns) outside of Edgarton City Hall, the tony town on the Island of Martha's Vineyard. Somehow, this set the tone for the 2005 JAWSfest, a veritable "JAWS-a-palooza" that ran from June 3rd to June 5th, celebrating the movie's 30th anniversary with style … An event that the entire town helped Universal Studios pull off.

"I came down from Ireland just to do this," says Mike Hadgi, the Irish Quint impersonator. "*JAWS* is a passion of mine, it meant so much for me to come down here. Being here is like a dream come true! I get very emotional being here, you have to take in so much. Yesterday, doing the speech in front of the towns-people and tourists and documentary people, I had to take deep breaths and just do it the way I know it! They actually had me come into the city hall and do the speech! That was exciting, the very room where Shaw did it.

"To see everybody from the cast and crew mingling with islanders gives it a family feel — it feels really intimate," Hadgi continues. "You speak with them up-close and share stories. Sharing stories is what it's all about; you have recollections of the film, and memories and you made so many friends in one day!"

JAWSfest was a collective family reunion for people who did not know they were family — covering Martha's Vineyard with obsessed fans from as far away as Michigan, Ireland and England. One family's van from Michigan was covered in child-painted images from the *JAWS* movies, of water skiers and leaping sharks.

"We had to come," says the family's ten-year-old daughter. "We love the movie so much, we

Amity Police Department. PHOTO BY PATRICK JANKIEWICZ.

always watch it on cable every time it's on, even the sequels, and it just seemed like the perfect way to celebrate the movie's thirtieth anniversary!"

What's amazing about Martha's Vineyard is that, even if you have never been here before, you get a feeling of *deja vu* — if you have enjoyed *JAWS*, you feel like you've already been here.

Walking through the town, you see highlights from the first film. There's the Amity police station (Actually a private residence, with a 'Please Don't Solicit' sign) and Amity Town Council (Which is actually Martha Vineyard's City Council and the inside is identical — right down to the giant table seen in the 1975 original). Buses whisk people off on *JAWS* tours.

One of the original *Orca* boats sits on an embankment. (People were breaking off pieces of it to keep as souvenirs, a practice that is understandably frowned upon.)

There were bands playing John Williams' *JAWS* theme and his 'Promenade (Tourists on the Menu),' welcoming visitors to town. There was even a collective sing-along of 'Show Me the Way to Go Home,' which Brody, Hooper and Quint drunkenly sing while hunting the shark. Maps were provided showing how to reach various shark attack sights from the film. The house next door to the Brody's home in the original film had a little brass plaque on the corner of the house, reading simply "*JAWS* shot here."

Try the tuna at the Amity Deli. PHOTO BY PATRICK JANKIEWICZ.

Steven Spielberg, who reportedly tried to come to the event, was stuck finishing up his film *War of the Worlds* and prepping his other 2005 film, *Munich*. He did, however, send along a taped greeting that helped set the fun tone for the festival.

> "Well, here we are and thank you for coming. I just want to welcome everybody to the first annual JAWSfest, which leaves me a little bit confused. Does that mean the second annual JAWSfest happens thirty years from now, or are we going to be like celebrating *JAWS* every ten years? Now its fortieth year, fiftieth year, or is this the first of every year? If it is, it will be a blessing for Martha's Vineyard. Martha's Vineyard was certainly a blessing for me.
>
> "It was a great place to make *JAWS*," Spielberg continued. "I lived there as you know for seven months; probably longer than seven months and the people there were amazingly cooperative. I'm sorry we blocked so many of your driveways. I'm sorry about the trucks and all the confluence of extras and I

just want to point out that even though we had a kind of interesting relationship with the Martha's Vineyard community and the production company in 1974, you guys treated us so well until all the summer people came onto Martha's Vineyard and you had all of your business and we began blocking your driveways; all that love was gone. I know that, guys — you stopped loving us for about two months and two weeks

Kelly House, home of the infamous Spielberg Food Fight! PHOTO BY PATRICK JANKIEWICZ.

and then you loved us again when they all went home. But we always loved you and we know that you always really loved us. And it was an amazing time.

"I apologize to The Kelly House for the food fight. I just wanted to work that in; you can talk amongst yourselves about what that is all about. I apologize for the food fight at The Kelly House. Loved The Black Dog; had amazing times there. Got to meet Thornton Wilder and James Cagney and got to sample the wonderful cuisine that James Cagney's personal chef sometimes came over and cooked for [Robert] Shaw, [Roy] Scheider and myself and Rich Dreyfuss. So it was an amazing time. Just an amazing time. I also want to thank all of you for having this festival and for remembering us. I think it's amazing that the shelf life this film has had and that's only because fans like yourselves have kept this film alive and [in] people's consciousness and I only have to thank you for that.

"Have a great festival. Thank you."

The town movie theater, where the world premiere was held back in 1975 (and dailies were screened during filming), yanked a plywood shark head out of storage and put it over the entrance. Karen Marafhio, who runs the theater, explains that, "I wasn't on the island when *JAWS* opened, I have only been here for three years, but I found this wooden *JAWS* doorway in storage. It was actually from when *JAWS* premiered here back in 1975. I was told they used this for the very first screening of cast and crew," Marafhio says proudly.

Island Theater Manager Karen Marafhio, in the Jaws of fear. PHOTO BY PATRICK JANKIEWICZ.

Sold-out screenings ran for the length of JAWSfest. There was also a dinner party highlighted by a radio play restaging of *JAWS*, led by Jeffrey 'Deputy Hendricks' Kramer, who proudly points out "I get to be Brody this time!" A giant smiling shark walked through the crowd, greeting kids and parents alike. The museum had paintings of scenes from the original film. *JAWS* crew shirts were on display.

Visitors to the island included filmmakers shooting *The Shark is Still Working* documentary and "Ain't it Cool News" online film critic "Quint" (a true *JAWS* aficionado, as you can tell by his *nom de plume*).

The documentary's producer Michael Roddy (the man who saved Ben Gardner's head from being nailed to a wall on Universal's Halloween Horror Night) is pleased.

"Roy Scheider is narrating the documentary," he says happily. "He wanted to come to JAWSfest, but he was too sick."

Universal Home Video and the town recreated the beach party from the opening of *JAWS*, complete with bonfire (sadly, the Chrissie look-alike wore clothes) at Vineyard Haven Harbor, where a screening was held as a "Dive In", as some brave souls watched it from the water the shark once sprang from.

There were props on exhibit and a clambake, featuring every *JAWS*-related person on the island. One of the surprise guests was Mike Haydn, the beach guitarist from the opening scene.

"Play that song!" screamed a woman from Ohio, so he did.

"Since I was playing my guitar in the scene, I suggested to the assistant director that I could play Bob Dylan's 'Nashville Skyline Rag' on the beach. Steven Spielberg said to me 'Yes, do it' and it's in the final cut," Hayden explains, as he strums 'Nashville Skyline Rag' for the clambake conclusion of JAWSfest.

"This JAWSfest is just fantastic — a nice reunion, a happy one," says Jay Mello, 'Sean Brody'. "I'm choking up. This was really special, to see all these people that

Where do you get your "Beaches Closed, No Swimming" signs? PHOTO BY PATRICK JANKIEWICZ.

I have not seen in thirty years is really very special — I even met Marc Gilpin, the 'Sean Brody' of *JAWS 2*..."

The townspeople pulled out all the vintage signs used when the film shot there in 1974, like the one for "Amity Hardware," when Brody goes to get paint and wood for the "BEACHES CLOSED, NO SWIMMING BY ORDER OF AMITY PD" warning signs.

Carl Gottlieb, Joe Alves, Jeffrey Kramer, Susan Backlinie, Bill S. Gilmore and Roy Arbogast all flew out from California and the townsfolk who worked on the movies were treated like rock stars.

"Last time we were here, we couldn't wait to get off this island," laughs Alves. "The pressure's off us now," agrees Gottlieb. "A lot of townsfolk didn't want us here originally — they felt we were getting in the way and they really weren't crazy about this big sloppy film crew tying up traffic!"

Gottlieb also feels melancholy at JAWSfest: "This is great ... I was at the log cabin [where he lived with director Spielberg during the duration of the shoot] last night and I cried. I actually cried! I saw my little desk where I rewrote the movie with Steven on a nightly basis — at least it resembled my little desk. It was in the corner of my bedroom, where I sat typing all night. It was an amazing, moving experience to see it again."

"The island is a little more developed than when I first knew it ... There's been an enormous amount of reconstruction and new development. Less than at any other resort, because this is a very expensive and difficult place to build, but those who have money do come here and if they want something ..."

A frail Peter Benchley impressively came out, helped along by his devoted wife Wendy to greet the *JAWS*-lovers, and was given the Key to Amity Island, in what sadly turned out to be his last public appearance.

"If you told me I would be celebrating the thirtieth anniversary of *JAWS* when we were making it, I wouldn't have believed you," the author said laughingly.

The whole downtown became an impromptu JAWS celebration, as people were mobbed, no matter how tenuous their connection to the JAWS franchise. One of these secondary actors was William E. Marks, who played Lenny the Deputy Sheriff in *JAWS THE REVENGE*. Fans took pictures with him and asked for his autograph.

"I could get used to this," he smiled. "People come to Martha's Vineyard and Edgartown looking for something, *anything* from *JAWS* and they get so excited when they see you."

As if on cue, an excited visitor with a disposable camera comes running down the street shouting "OMIGOD — LENNY'S HERE!"

Marks shrugs and smiles. "*See*? What did I tell you?!"

Jonathan Searle appears, noting, "I always say, 'If you're gonna have fifteen minutes of fame, it may as well be in one of the most popular movies of all time where you and your brother have the screen all to yourselves! There was so much drama and excitement coming up to it — the shark fin igniting a panic, and then you find it's just two bratty kids! I have that great line, where I blame my older brother — 'he made me do it!' My brother and I are fond of it, but we forget we're in it. Usually, people find out — friends of mine who knew me for years, and they'll say, 'You never told me you were in *JAWS*!' and I just say, 'I don't really talk about it.' Our names never made the credits, but we do get residuals. Some people when they find out want me to prove it's really me. I really don't need to prove anything."

Now a police detective, Searle notes that "being in *JAWS* is kind of a novelty, a joke — some of the other officers will bring it up at inopportune moments. As I was walking through town during JAWSfest, my Sergeant pointed at me and said to a tourist 'That was the kid with the shark fin from *JAWS*!' Of course, the tourist was thrilled, but it's more embarrassing to me than anything else," he says sheepishly.

The Edgartown assessor, Will Pfluger, now in his early fifties, appeared in the original film. He's the quarreling boater who tells Hooper, 'Yeah, I got a paddle.'

"This is really nice," Pfluger begins, until someone pleads, 'Say it!'

"Okay," Pfluger chuckles, "'Yeah, I got a paddle!'

"I was going to work on *JAWS* as a carpenter," he explains. "I had a choice — I could work on the film as a carpenter, or do this acting bit in the scene that introduces Matt Hooper ... I decided that the chance to be in the movie was a once in a lifetime thing and I'm glad I did it! When Matt Hooper shows up

Just when you thought it was safe to go in the yard! PHOTO BY PATRICK JANKIEWICZ.

in Amity, he sees me and the crowds fighting to get out of the harbor to hunt a shark for the reward, so he asks me, 'Do you have a paddle?' and that's when I did my line."

Susan Backlinie, being the first victim, drew a crowd worthy of Elvis. Touring a museum of *JAWS* memorabilia, Backlinie is delighted to see the buoy she clings to, as the shark pulls her under in the original film.

"Look at this — here it is," she says happily, hugging the prop. "I haven't seen that buoy since I last hung onto it thirty years ago!"

Greg Nicotero, the special FX artist, used Joe Alves' designs to recreate a massive replica head of *JAWS*' Great White shark and brought it to the island.

"*JAWS* meant a lot to me and helped make me want to do what I do now," Nicotero explains. He was in Martha's Vineyard after a long, grueling month of nights spent shooting of George Romero's *Land of the Dead*. "I wanted to help commemorate it [*JAWS*] — I just wish people would stop stealing the damn teeth out of the shark's mouth!"

APPENDIX

WHERE ARE THEY NOW?

The makers of the original *JAWS* and its sequels went on to blaze a path across the entertainment world, among them:

STEVEN SPIELBERG went on to become Hollywood's most successful filmmaker. He directed such acclaimed, diverse epics as *The Color Purple* and *Jurassic Park*, *E.T.*, *Schindler's List* (for which he won the Oscar), *Saving Private Ryan* (another Oscar), *Close Encounters of the Third Kind*, *Munich* and *War of the Worlds*. In 2008, he made *Indiana Jones and the Crystal Skull*, the latest in his *Raiders of the Lost Ark* franchise, nineteen years after the previous installment.

PETER BENCHLEY wrote a string of hits after *JAWS*, including *The Deep*, *The Island*, *White Shark* and his own personal JAWS knockoff, the giant squid epic, *Beast*. He was one of the guests of honor at the first Martha's Vineyard "JAWSfest" in 2005. He died of idiopathic pulmonary fibrosis at the age of 65 in 2006.

CARL GOTTLIEB wrote and directed such films as *Caveman*, *Doctor Detroit* and the sketch comedy, *Amazon Women on the Moon*. A member of the popular improv group The Committee, he has played hilarious characters in movies, including his no-nonsense FBI man in *Into the Night* and "Iron Balls McGinty" in *The Jerk*. As the Vice President of the Writers Guild of America, Gottlieb played a crucial part in negotiating the end of the devastating 2007/2008 WGA strike.

RICHARD ZANUCK & DAVID BROWN ended their long partnership after such films as *JAWS*, *The Sting* and *Patton*, but both men continued making great, successful films. Zanuck and his wife Lily produced such hits as the Oscar-winning *Driving Miss Daisy*, *Charlie and the Chocolate Factory*, *Big Fish*, and the remake of *Planet of the Apes* (in which his ex-wife Linda Harrison has a cameo). Brown, who is married to *Cosmopolitan* editor Helen Gurley Brown, produced the highly acclaimed picture, *The Player* and wrote his great autobiography, *Let Me Entertain You*. Brown and Zanuck reunited with Steven Spielberg to produce *Deep Impact*.

JOHN WILLIAMS not only became the most acclaimed movie composer in history, with such films as *Jurassic Park, E.T., Star Wars, Raiders of the Lost Ark, Superman, Home Alone* and *Schindler's List,* but also served a lengthy stint as the conductor of the Boston Pops. When he won the *Academy Award* for *JAWS* (the first of many), he was actually conducting the music for the televised event.

ROY SCHEIDER (Chief Brody) was Oscar-nominated for his role as the choreographer in Bob Fosse's *All that Jazz*. He also starred in the quirky *Cohen & Tate,* William Friedkin's *Sorcerer, Blue Thunder* and *2010.* He reteamed with Spielberg for the TV series, *Seaquest DSV*. Roy Scheider died in 2008, at age 75, of multiple myeloma. He died the day before his 19th wedding anniversary.

RICHARD DREYFUSS (Matt Hooper) was the youngest actor to win the Oscar (for Neil Simon's *The Goodbye Girl*). Dreyfuss fell out of sight due to a drug problem, recovered and came back stronger than ever, with such hits as *Down and Out in Beverly Hills* and *Stakeout* (the latter has him being teased by co-star Emilio Estevez about the *JAWS* line, "This was *not* a boat accident!"). He reteamed with Spielberg for two films, *Close Encounters of the Third Kind* and *Always*. He played former U.S. Vice President Dick Cheney in Oliver Stone's *W.* Dreyfuss returned to the world of sharks in the summer of '08, when he narrated the Discovery Channel documentary *Ocean of Fear*, which dealt with the sinking of the *U.S.S. Indianapolis*.

ROBERT SHAW (Quint) appeared in numerous films besides *JAWS*, including *The Dam Busters, From Russia with Love, The Sting, The Taking of Pelham One Two Three* and *The Deep*. He died of a heart attack in 1978 at the age of 51.

JOE ALVES is one of Hollywood's great production designers. He not only worked with Spielberg on *JAWS, The Sugarland Express* and *Close Encounters of the Third Kind*, but also with Alfred Hitchcock on *Torn Curtain*, Rod Serling on *Night Gallery*, John Carpenter and James Cameron on *Escape from New York*. Alves directed *JAWS 3-D*, did much of the second unit footage on *JAWS* and *JAWS 2* and produced the action thriller, *Freejack*.

ROY ARBOGAST helped provide the sharks for *JAWS, JAWS 2* and *JAWS 3-D*. Since then, he has worked on many other cult films, including John Carpenter's *The Thing, Innocent Blood,* as well as with George Lucas on *Return of the Jedi* and *Captain EO*. His special effects work includes Harrison Ford's amazing train wreck in *The Fugitive* and the evil car in *Christine*.

BILL BUTLER has been the cinematographer on a number of great films, including Francis Ford Coppola's *The Conversation* (and was uncredited for shooting the hospital scene in *The Godfather*), *One Flew Over the Cuckoo's Nest, Rocky II-IV, Sniper* (for which he devised an amazing speeding bullet POV, an effect that has since been imitated many times), *Grease* and *Child's Play* (the debut of Chucky the killer doll). Butler returned to *JAWS* territory with the thriller, *Anaconda*. He has two daughters, both of whom are actresses.

HOWARD SACKLER did uncredited screenwriting work on *JAWS* (including the very first version of *Indianapolis* speech) and was the original writer on *JAWS 2*. Sackler won the Pulitzer Prize for his play, *The Great White Hope* and scripted the films *Gray Lady Down* and Peter Bogdanovich's *Saint Jack*. Howard Sackler died at the age of 52 in 1982.

VERNA FIELDS was so beloved by the *JAWS* crew that she was dubbed "Mother Cutter." She began her career as an assistant editor on *Belle of the Yukon* 1944) and became a sound editor on the Fritz Lang classic *While the City Sleeps*. In the '70s, she edited Peter Bogdanovich's *Paper Moon* and *What's Up, Doc?* and George Lucas' *American Graffiti*. After being denied the director's chair on *JAWS 2*, Fields became an executive for Universal. She died of cancer in 1982, at age 64.

MURRAY HAMILTON (Mayor Larry Vaughn) is best remembered as the venal Mayor Vaughn in the *JAWS* films, but he also played Elaine's father in *The Graduate* (which had a bit player by the name of Richard Dreyfuss) and "Mr. Death" in a classic episode of *Twilight Zone*. He was approached to reprise his Mayor Vaughn role in *JAWS THE REVENGE*, but died in 1986; he was 63.

LORRAINE GARY (Ellen Brody) will always be remembered for her earthy, sexy performance as Ellen Brody, Sheriff Brody's loyal wife in Steven Spielberg's *JAWS*. In real life she is married to Universal CEO, Sid Sheinberg. "Lorraine" — Lea Thompson's character in *Back to the Future* — is named after her. Since receiving brutal reviews (and a Razzie Award nomination) for her turn in *JAWS THE REVENGE*, Gary abandoned her acting career.

SUSAN BACKLINIE (Chrissie Watkins) reunited with Steven Spielberg to parody her Chrissie character in the World War II comedy, *1941*. The actress/stuntwoman also appeared in the cult B-movies, *Day of the Animals* and *Grizzly*. In the early '90s she went back to school, got her mathematics degree and is now a computer accountant in Ventura, California.

TEDDY GROSSMAN (Estuary Victim) has the distinction of being the shark's goriest victim and was the stunt coordinator on *JAWS* & *JAWS 2*. Grossman worked with Spielberg on *The Sugarland Express, Raiders of the Lost Ark, E.T., The Goonies* and *Indiana Jones and the Temple of Doom*. In the industry, he's known as "Spielberg's favorite stuntman." He also played the ring doctor in the Oscar-winning *Million Dollar Baby*.

ROGER KASTEL painted several illustrated covers for Bantam Books, including the iconic design for the *JAWS* paperback (this later became the film's poster). He also drew the stunning poster for *The Empire Strikes Back*.

CHRIS REBELLO (Mike Brody) never made another film after *JAWS*. Rebello was an assistant coach for the Martha's Vineyard football team. He died of a heart attack while deer hunting in 2000.

JAY MELLO (Sean Brody) did PR work for famed boxer Marvelous Marvin Hagler. He now designs and builds cabinet furniture in Vermont.

JEFFREY VOORHEES (Alex Kinter) still lives on the Island and manages the Wharf Restaurant. (The "Alex Kintner" sandwich is delicious, by the way.)

LEE FIERRO (Mrs. Kintner) still lives on the island and enjoys taking part in reunion events, such as JAWSfest.

BELLE McDONALD (Mrs. Posner) appeared in several films after *JAWS*, all shot in the Boston area, including *Mr. North*, *HouseSitter*, *Night School* and *Celtic Pride*.

JOHN HANCOCK survived his painful *JAWS 2* experience alongside actress/screenwriter wife Dorothy Tristan. They went on to make the critically acclaimed Nick Nolte film *Weeds* and the horror flick, *Suspended Animation* and are currently prepping a new film. John Hancock's cult thriller, *Let's Scare Jessica to Death*, is now on DVD — check it out!

JONATHAN SEARLE (Kid with fake fin) is now a Police Detective in Edgartown, Massachusetts ("I'm like Brody," he jokes).

MARC GILPIN (Sean Brody, *JAWS 2*) had numerous roles in films, including a young Lone Ranger in *Legend of the Lone Ranger* and an alien boy with a pet green monkey in *Earthbound*. He left acting in the early '80s and is now a 3-D animator at Animation Station in Dallas. "I'm on the production side of things now, creating the first interactive educational network for schoolchildren teaching reading." Marc and his wife Kaki recently had a baby boy. His sister is Peri Gilpin, the actress best known for her role as "Roz" on the television show *Frasier*.

JEANNOT SZWARC (Director, *JAWS 2*) made the moving *Somewhere in Time*, the fun *Supergirl*, and the bizarre *Santa Claus: The Movie*. He's now a popular, in demand television director for such series as *Heroes*, *Smallville*, *Bones*, *Without A Trace*, and *Grey's Anatomy*.

JOHN PUTCH (Sean Brody, *JAWS 3-D*) Acted in numerous shows, including *Star Trek: The Next Generation*. Now a director, he helmed a big *Poseidon Adventure* mini-series/remake for Hallmark.

BILLY VAN ZANDT (Bob, *JAWS 2*) produced the successful sitcoms *The Wayans Brothers* and *The Hughleys*. He was also Story Editor for the acclaimed *Newhart* series. Zandt and his wife (actress Adrienne Barbeau) had twins in 1997.

LANCE GUEST (Mike Brody, *JAWS THE REVENGE*) first caught the public's attention in another horror sequel, *Halloween II*. He starred as *The Last Starfighter* (the studio is now considering a sequel — 25 years later!). Guest does solid character actor work on shows such as *House* and *The X-Files*. He and his wife just had a baby.

CARL MAZZOCONE, the *JAWS 3-D* location manager, became a film producer and won an 8.92 million dollar judgment against actress Kim Basinger for backing out of his film, *Boxing Helena*. Mazzocone, now at Twisted Pictures, produced Paris Hilton's *Repo — The Genetic Opera*.

JOE DANTE avoided the crash of "JAWS 3, PEOPLE 0" to attract Spielberg's attention with *Piranha* and *The Howling*. After doing a segment of *Twilight Zone: The Movie*, Dante made the blockbuster *Gremlins*. He teamed with *JAWS* screenwriter Carl Gottlieb on *Amazon Women on the Moon* and made *Gremlins 2: The New Batch*, *Small Soldiers*, *Innerspace* (with Spielberg) and other films and TV shows. His *Piranha* is about to be remade for the second time, in 3-D!

JOHN LANDIS became the director of some of the highest-grossing comedies of all time: *Animal House*, *Coming to America* and *The Blues Brothers*, and made a horror classic of his own, *An American Werewolf in London*. Still doing film and television, Landis also directs documentaries like *Mr. Warmth: The Don Rickles Project*.

ENZO G. CASTELLARI, the Italian director of the derivative *Great White*, now has Quentin Tarantino and Brad Pitt remaking his film, *Inglorious Bastards*.

BRUCE THE SHARK made a series of poor choices after working with Steven Spielberg on the original *JAWS*. He was a Razzie Nominee for Worst Actor in *JAWS THE REVENGE*. Besides the three sequels, he made ill-advised appearances in such forgettable fare as *The Nude Bomb* and *The Harlem Globetrotters on Gilligans's Island*. He still performs 25 times a day, attacking trams at Universal Studios in Southern California, Florida and Osaka, Japan.

APPENDIX

NOTES AND SOURCES

The Book

JAWS, Benchley, Peter. First line.

Publishers Weekly, "JAWS A Monster."

Associated Press, 'Peter Benchley Obituary', 2006.

Empire Magazine, "JAWS: Still Hungry After 20 Years" by Mark Salisbury and Ian Nathan, July, 1995.

"Peter Benchley, JAWS Author" by Bob Greene, *Chicago Sun-Times,* 1974.

The Movie

Brown, David, *Let Me Entertain You, 1992,* New Millineum Books.

New York Times Entertainment section, "Close Encounters With Steven Spielberg," 1977.

In person interview with Carl Gottlieb

In person interview with Joe Alves.

In person interview with Richard Matheson.

In person interview with Bill Butler.

Film Comment, "Spielberg's 1941," 1979.

In person interview with Linda Harrison.

Ebert, Roger, *JAWS* review.

American Cinematographer, Mik Cribben. "Steven Spielberg," 1977

Premiere Magazine, "JAWS AT 20", October 1995, by Nancy Griffin.

In person interview with Richard Dreyfuss.

AMITY ISLAND
In person interview with Jonathan Searle.
In person interview with Belle McDonald.
In person interview with Jeffrey Voorhees.
In person interview with Susan Backlinie.
In person interview with Kevin Pike.

BRUCE THE SHARK
In person interview with Joe Alves.
In person interview with Dick Warlock.
In person interview with Michael Lantieri.
In person interview with Rob Hall.

DA-DUM, DA-DUM
New York Times, "Composing The JAWS Theme," 1975.

Roanoake Times, "JAWS @ 30," 2005.

Hollywood Reporter, "Spotlight On Spielberg," 2002.

MOTHER CUTTER
In person interview with Roy Arbogast.

BLACK LAGOON
Laurent Bozeau, "Interview With Steven Spielberg," *Duel* DVD.

FISH FACTS
In person interview with Roger Corman.
In person interview with June Foray.

THE OPENING
Biskind, Peter, *Easy Riders, Raging Bulls.*

JAWS AND THE CRITICS
Farber, Stephen, *JAWS* review, *Film Comment,* 1975.

Kauffman, Stanley, *JAWS* review, *New Republic,* 1975.

Canby, Vincent, *JAWS* review, *New York Times,* June 20, 1975.

Champlin, Charles, *JAWS* review, *Los Angeles Times,* June 20, 1975.

Crist, Judith, *JAWS* review, *New York,* 1975.

Kael, Pauline, *JAWS* review, 1975.

Cooper, Arthur, *JAWS* review, Newsweek, June, 1975.

Knight, Arthur, *JAWS* Review, *Hollywood Reporter,* June, 1975.

Reed, Rex, *JAWS* review, June, 1975.

A.D. Murphy, *JAWS* review, *Variety,* June, 1975.

National Council of Churches, *JAWS* review, June, 1975.

Time Magazine, "Summer Of The Shark," June, 1975.

In person interview with Bryan Singer

In person interview with Daniel Waters

In person interview with Adam Simon

THE INDIANAPOLIS SPEECH
In person interview with Carl Gottlieb

IGN Film Force, Interview with John Milius, 2008

SHARK ATTACKS/ESTUARY VICTIM
Phone interview with Teddy Grossman.

LEE FIERRO
In person interview with Lee Fierro

JEFFREY KRAMER
In person interview with Jeffrey Kramer

JAY MELLO
In person interview with Jay Mello

JAWS 2

In person interview with Jeannot Szwarc.

New York Times Entertainment section, "Close Encounters With Steven Spielberg," 1977.

Kroll, Jack, *JAWS 2* review, *Newsweek,* June 1978.

In person interview with Marc Gilpin.

Phone interview with Carl Mazzocone.
Phone interview with Jon Putch.
In person interview with John Landis.

JAWS THE REVENGE

In person interview with Lance Guest.

JAWS THE REVENGE REVIEWS
Mooney, Joshua, *JAWS The Revenge* review, *Movieline,* July, 1987.

Kunk, Deborah J., *JAWS The Revenge* review, *Los Angeles Herald Examiner,* July 30, 1987.

JAWS: THE RIP-OFFS

In person interview with Andrew Prine

In person interview with Neal Adams.

In person interview with Ernie Hudson.
In person interview with Duncan Kennedy.
In person interview with Joe Dante.

SUBMERGED SEQUELS

In person interview with Steve DeJarnatt.

JOHN HANCOCK'S JAWS 2
Telephone interview with John Hancock and Dorothy Tristan.

JAWSfest

In person interview with Maribeth Priore
In person interview with Mike Hadgi.
In person interview with Karen Marafhio.
In person interview with William E, Marks.
Quotes from *AICN*'s Quint, Mike Roddy and Mike Haydn.

ABOUT THE AUTHOR

Patrick Jankiewicz has written over 400 articles in the U.S. and England. He's worked as a journalist, publicist, copywriter, teacher and actor. He's written for *Fangoria, Starlog*, Marvel Comics, *Femme Fatales, Wizard, Shivers, Starburst, Film Review* and *Comics Scene*. Jankiewicz has done commercials and on-camera interviews for The Sci-Fi Channel. He would rather eat fish than have fish eat him. He resides in Southern California with wife Lisa and a neurotic Border Collie. He's lost count over how many times he's seen *JAWS*.

Bear Manor Media

JAWS 2: The Making of the Hollywood Sequel
by Louis R. Pisano and Michael A. Smith

Just when film-makers thought it was safe to make a sequel, director John D. Hancock ran into huge difficulties making *Jaws 2* (1978), a thriller film and the first sequel to Steven Spielberg's *Jaws* (1975). Until now, the full story of the sea of troubles during the making of the film has never been told. Authors Louis R. Pisano and Michael A. Smith fished from the original cast and crew the full no-holds-barred story from their behind the scenes experiences, a tale as action packed and occasionally as bloody as the film.

978-1-59393-837-6 $24.95
362 pages

www.bearmanormedia.com

Printed in Great Britain
by Amazon